MUSIC THEORY
THROUGH LITERATURE

MUSIC THEORY THROUGH LITERATURE

VOLUME II

John Baur

Memphis State University

PRENTICE-HALL, INC. *Englewood Cliffs, New Jersey 07632*

Library of Congress Cataloging in Publication Data

BAUR, JOHN, 1947–
  Music theory.

  Includes index.
  1. Music—Theory. I. Title
  MT6.B263M9 1985   781   84-3399
  ISBN 0-13-607847-8

Editorial/production supervision and
  interior design: Dan Mausner
Cover design: 20/20 Services, Inc.
Manufacturing buyer: Raymond Keating
Page layout: Gail Collis

© 1985 by Prentice-Hall, Inc., Englewood Cliffs, New Jersey 07632

All rights reserved. No part of this book may be
reproduced, in any form or by any means,
without permission in writing from the publisher.

Printed in the United States of America

10 9 8 7 6 5 4 3 2 1

ISBN 0-13-607847-8 01

PRENTICE-HALL INTERNATIONAL, INC., *London*
PRENTICE-HALL OF AUSTRALIA PTY. LIMITED, *Sydney*
EDITORA PRENTICE-HALL DO BRASIL, LTDA., *Rio de Janeiro*
PRENTICE-HALL CANADA INC., *Toronto*
PRENTICE-HALL OF INDIA PRIVATE LIMITED, *New Delhi*
PRENTICE-HALL OF JAPAN, INC., *Tokyo*
PRENTICE-HALL OF SOUTHEAST ASIA PTE. LTD., *Singapore*
WHITEHALL BOOKS LIMITED, *Wellington, New Zealand*

Contents

Preface ix
Recordings xi

14 Franz Joseph Haydn 1
Piano Sonata in C major, Hob. XVI/10

early sonata-allegro form, exposition, development, recapitulation, closing section (codetta), Alberti bass, melodic/rhythmic usage, motivic analysis, minuet/trio form, retardation, eighteenth century appoggiatura.

15 Wolfgang Amadeus Mozart 20
String Quartet in Eb major, K. 428

continuation of sonata-allegro principle, transition, re-transition, dissonance use in Mozart, chromaticisn in eighteenth century, transitional development, extended harmonic analysis, extended modulation.

16 Ludwig van Beethoven 33

Sonata No. 10, op. 13 (Pathétique), second movement

binary/ternary forms, small rondo, large rondo, enharmonic modulation, melodic/phrase analysis.

17 Ludwig van Beethoven 58

Sonata No. 21, op. 53 (Waldstein), first movement

motivic usage, expansion/contraction of phrase length and harmonic patterns, expansion of sonata-allegro form, transition usage, coda, extended modulation, sudden shift, ninth chords, chordal mutation, enharmonic modulation, third relation, altered dominant.

18 Franz Schubert 76

Der Doppelgänger

substitute dominants, melodic contour, vocal setting, climactic structure, text setting, use of accompaniment, through-composed.

19 Felix Mendelssohn 100

Symphony No. 5 ("Reformation"), second movement

basics of orchestration, ranges of instruments, transpositions of instruments, score layout, reduction of score.

20 Frederic Chopin 114

Nocturne in Db major, op. 27, no. 2

bi-modality, enharmonic modulation, appoggiatura, dissonance extension, ninth chords, implied thirteenth chords, sectional variation, planing of chords, chordal mutation, rubato.

21 Richard Wagner 147

Prelude to Tristan and Isolde

extension of chordal function, chordal mutation, motivic use, leitmotiv, expanded modulation, expanded dissonance, prolongation of appoggiatura, use of deceptive cadence, bimodal usage, third relation.

22 Johannes Brahms 176
Intermezzo in A major, op. 118, no. 2

use of dissonance, chordal mutation, pedal points, sectional design, hemiola, metric shifts.

23 Claude Debussy 191
La Cathedrale Engloutie from Preludes, Book I

intervallic harmony, motivic usage, planing, expaned tertian harmony, added-tone technique, whole-tone scale, pentatonic scale, modal usage.

24 Igor Stravinsky 220
Symphony in Three Movements, second movement

pandiatonicism, linear construction, bitonality, polytonality, ostinato, motivic use, chordal projection.

25 Béla Bartók 233
Minor Seconds, Major Sevenths, Mikrokosmos, vol. VI

linear voice leaading, synthetic scale, clusters, symmetrical scales, arch form.

26 Arnold Schoenberg 244
Three Piano Pieces, op. 11, no. 1

gesture, intervallic harmony, development of gestural content, motivic development.

27 Anton Webern 260
Three Songs, op. 25, no. 1

row technique, row construction, matrix, motivic design, palindrome.

28 Olivier Messiaen 275
Quartet for the End of Time, movement one

isorhythm, non-retrogradeable rhythm, additive rhythm, birdsong, intervallic construction.

29 Kryzstof Penderecki 305

   Dies Irae, Lamentatio

   linear/harmonic construction, cluster, gesture, proportional notation, extended instrumental techniques.

30 George Crumb 320

   Madrigals, Book IV, no. 1

   motivic organization and expansion, expanded sound resources, gesture, intervallic structure, retrograde of material.

Index 333

Preface

When a college student completes the required theory courses, that student should be able to pick up any piece of Western music, from any period, and understand its basic traits. This is the purpose of this text: to broaden the student's musical perspective, without de-emphasizing the importance of basic skills. Being able to manipulate materials skillfully is important in any profession. In music one must also have musical insight and depth of understanding. This comes partly from theoretical study and partly from an intimate acquaintance with the music itself.

Two ideas in particular rarely embodied in theory textbooks prompted me to initiate and complete this long task: the use of complete musical examples, and the chronological arrangement of theoretical materials. It is vitally important for a theory textbook to utilize complete examples, since this is the only way to demonstrate the actual significance of a musical idea. A two-measure fragment may display a technique in a readily identifiable form, but only the complete piece will give the student (and teacher) the sense of how such a segment relates to the whole. I hope that the student will not only learn the theory of music, but will also take the time to experience the music itself. The most important reason for including complete examples is to enhance the learning of music—not simply to facilitate the teaching of theory.

The chronological arrangement of material has been employed before in theory texts. However, the Middle Ages has previously been discussed only cursorily, and the development of compositional techniques from century to century has never been consistently presented as the basis for a theory text. There are sound pedagogical reasons for presenting the material in this fashion. The most important is that the progression of musical and theoretical ideas from century to century becomes clear and understandable to the student. In addition, by presenting the material in this manner one can avoid any prejudicial emphasis of style or period. One need not explain why a theory course begins with the earliest notated music; in fact, beginning elsewhere ought to require justification.

The second volume is designed for the second of a two-year theory core. The musical examples contain literature from Haydn through Crumb. It is assumed that, depending upon the needs of the individual class, the instructor will begin the course with a brief review of the last chapter of volume I, J. S. Bach. It is always useful to reinforce the theoretical ideas of functional harmony, modulation, chorale harmonization, and figured bass before moving to the principles of the late eighteenth century.

In addition to the harmonic principles employed in the eighteenth and nineteenth centuries, this volume introduces the student to basic approaches to formal analysis and basic orchestration. It is not intended to replace either a form and analysis course or an orchestration course, however.

It is hoped that the inclusion of eight chapters from the twentieth century will create a greater awareness of both the techniques and the styles found in our own century. Since it is impossible to cover all current trends, especially in the last fifteen to twenty years, the instructor is encouraged to supplement the present offering with pieces of his or her own choosing.

A glossary and a summary of style characteristics are included at the end of each chapter to reinforce style concepts and basic theoretical terminology.

The exercises at the end of each chapter are divided into written skills and creative application. While it is necessary to drill on clearly defined skill factors, an important part of every musician's training is the creative handling of musical material. It is hoped that the teacher will include some of the compositional exercises to encourage the student to develop his or her creative abilities.

Several people deserve a great amount of credit for their encouragement, help, and wise counsel, generously given in the course of this project. David Russell Williams has been an inexhaustible source of insight, as well as a particularly kind and helpful editor of the manuscript. Donald Freund has also provided valuable assistance, especially in the twentieth-century portion of the text.

Over the years, my students have patiently shown me the most valuable ways of presenting this material. I only hope that this text will prove as helpful to them as they have been to me.

In addition, four former professors helped to shape my musical perception in ways that will forever influence my thinking: Paul Cooper, Carol MacClintock, James Riley, and Elmer Thomas. Their musical integrity and dedication to humanity should be an inspiration to all.

Finally, I thank my wife, Elizabeth. It is impossible to measure her patience and encouragement throughout this task. I only know it would have been infinitely more difficult without her.

Recordings

Chapter 14: Franz Joseph Haydn, *Sonata in C major: The Complete Keyboard Music;* Orpheus, OR H 101-115 volume 1.
Chapter 15: Wolfgang Amadeus Mozart, *String Quartet in Eb major, K. 428;* Amadeus Quartet; Deutsche Grammophon Gesellschaft, SLPM 139 191.
Chapter 16: Ludwig van Beethoven, *Sonata in c minor, op. 13;* Rudolf Serkin; Columbia, MS 6481
Chapter 17: Ludwig van Beethoven, *Sonata in C major ("Waldstein");* Walter Gieseking; Odyssey 32 16 0314
Chapter 18: Franz Schubert, *Der Doppelgänger* (from *Schwanengasong*); Dietrich Fischer-Dieskau; Angel 36127
Chapter 19: Felix Mendelssohn, *Symphony no. 5 ("Reformation");* Charles Munch, the Boston Symphony; Victrola ALK1-4465
Chapter 20: Frederic Chopin, *Nocturne in Db major, op. 27, no. 2;* Tomas Vasary; Deutsch Grammophon 136 486
Chapter 21: Richard Wagner; *Prelude to Tristan and Isolde,* Chicago Symphony, Georg Solti; London 7078
Chapter 22: Johannes Brahms, *Intermezzo in A major, op. 118;* Walter Klein; Vox SVBX 5430/1
Chapter 23: Claude Debussy, *La Cathédrale engloutie;* Jean Rodolphe Kars, London CSA 2230

Chapter 24: Igor Stravinsky, *Symphony in Three Movements, second movement;* l'Orchestre de la Suisse Romande, Ernest Ansermet; London Records CS 6190

Chapter 25: Béla Bartók, *Minor seconds, major sevenths (*from *Mikrokosmos, Book VI);* Gyorgy Sandor; Columbia SL 229

Chapter 26: Arnold Schoenberg, *Piano Pieces, op. 11* and *op 19;* Glenn Gould; Columbia M2S 736, vol. 4

Chapter 28: Olivier Messiaen; *Quatuor pour la fin du temps;* New York Philomusica Chamber Ensemble; Candide CE 31050

Chapter 29: Krzysztof Penderecki; *Dies Irae;* Cracow Philharmonia; Phillips 839 701 LY

Chapter 39: George Crumb, *Madrigals, Book IV:* Elizabeth Soderlund; Turnabout TV S 34523

Before Reading Chapter 14:

1) Listen to the *Piano Sonata in C major, Hob.XVI/10* by Joseph Haydn.
2) Bracket the phrase structure in the first movement (pages 1 and 2).
3) Note all modulations in the movement, regardless of length.
4) Note the harmonic structure in measures 22–38.
5) Compare the sections beginning at measure 9 and measure 47.

Franz Joseph Haydn

Piano Sonata in C major, Hob. XVI/10

The differences between the late Baroque composers (Bach and Handel especially) and those of the early Classic period are similar to the differences between the late Renaissance and early Baroque. In both cases the texture of the older period is thicker, more contrapuntal, and the style more intellectually oriented. The negative reaction to each of the older styles was strong and sweeping, changing the musical surface drastically. A brief look at the following example will reveal this startling change: gone is the intricate, ever-moving contrapuntal motion, gone are the separate, individual lines. What replaces this contrapuntal fabric is a thinner, more chordally based, and more sectional style. Rhythmically it is characterized by multiple juxtapositions of diverse rhythmic groups and much greater freedom and flexibility.

The early Classic period (ca. 1735–1765) tended to emphasize a relatively thin, light *texture,* with clear-cut melodies supported by the barest of harmonic trappings. In many cases there was only a two-voice texture, used in such a way as to imply more.

ex. 14-1

This example uses only two voices but employs a broken bass line that implies a strong chordal outline. This left-hand part is an example of what will later be called the **Alberti bass,** an accompaniment figure based on triads (and seventh chords) broken so as to be performed as a single line by the left hand. The melody as well is primarily based on triadic motion.

ex. 14-2

Finally, there is a new *rhythmic practice* that expands the Baroque boundaries. Rhythmic use in the Baroque was fairly consistent. Any rhythm was possible, but the juxtapositions within a piece were usually of like nature—duple with duple, triple with triple, and so on. In early Classic music there is a tendency to juxtapose a variety of rhythmic values, including duple and triple divisions. Several completely different rhythmic ideas are used in these fragments, which appear quite extraordinary when compared to the consistency of the previous period.

ex. 14-3

The harmonic material has not changed radically; certainly the basic functional patterns remain the same. If anything, *Classic harmony* is simpler than that of the late Baroque. This new simplicity is also given greater clarity by the openness of texture and slower harmonic rhythm. Although certain outer features have changed considerably, the voice leading has hardly changed at all. The *f♯* leading tone in this example still resolves to *g*, and the *c*, the seventh of the V chord, still resolves correctly to *b*.

ex. 14-4

In addition to changes in the rhythm and texture of the new music, there arose a need for different forms and structures. The old Baroque binary was still a viable form and presented many opportunities for expansion, especially since it had always been associated with music less contrapuntal than that of some other forms, such as the fugue. It will be remembered that there are two important areas in the binary form: the ending of the first section, which almost always modulates to the dominant (or mediant in minor), and the beginning of the second section, which usually continues the modulation process and extends it in a developmental fashion. With these two areas and with the return to the tonic at the end, the embryonic state of **sonata-allegro form** existed.

The preceding movement by Franz Joseph Haydn (1732–1809) is a clear example of an early sonata-form movement. Like the Baroque binary form, it is in two parts, each repeated. The key structure is also the same: ‖:I–V:‖:V–I:‖. But certain other elements distinguish this from the normal binary form. A detailed look at the piece will allow us to identify those elements.

There are four cadences in the first part of the piece: in measures 4, 8, 16, and 21.

ex. 14-5

The first two cadences are in C major, on I and V respectively; although the second ends on G(V), there is no hint of modulation yet. The next two cadences are definitely in G major, however, following a sudden modulation in measure 9. These cadences delineate the sectional design as well. The first section (measures 1–8) has two cadences, each terminating a four-bar phrase; the second section (measures 9–16) has no strong internal cadence, but ends strongly with a descending figure (measure 15); the third section (measures 17–21) is the shortest, and closes the entire first part.

The second major area of the piece is likewise divided into sections by its cadences. It opens in G major, but very quickly moves by *sudden shifts* to other keys. There is virtually no modulation in this case; each new key arrives suddenly, with little or no preparation.

ex. 14-6

The keys explored are those of a minor (measure 26), d minor (measure 33), C major (measure 34), and G major (measures 35–36). Finally, we return to C major and the opening material (measure 39) and proceed much the same as in the first section of the piece. The significant change in this final return is in the key of the second section. Compare measures 39–59 with measures 1–21.

ex. 14-7

Note that both the earlier and later sections have the same number of measures and the same thematic material. The only difference between them is that from measure 45 to the end the music remains in C major, while in the corresponding section at measures 7–21 it shifts to G major. This change in the final section is necessary in order for the piece to end in the same key as it began.

Let us review the sections we have described and put them in order.

	‖: A	:‖ ‖:	B					A			:‖
	a b c		key exploration					a b c			
			a	a–b	b		c				
C:	I V V		V	vi	ii	(I)	V	I	I	I	
m.	1 9 17		24		33	34	35	47			
				26				39		55	

Although this is a somewhat complex scheme, it gives us an accurate picture of the complete design. This design shows a striking resemblance to the older binary form, especially in its modulatory scheme. The differences between them are important, though: a better-defined **sectional design** in both major sections, an expansion of the modulatory section (**B**), and a more clearly articulated return to the original key and opening material. These three sections in the new sonata-allegro form are called the *exposition, development,* and *recapitulation.* The inner sections of the exposition and recapitulation also have specific names: *first theme* (principal theme, primary theme, first theme group), *second theme* (subordinate theme, secondary theme, second theme group), and *closing theme* (codetta, closing theme group).

The most important concept is the structure of the **key relationships.** The form depends on it as a constructional principle and the flow, direction, and shaping of the piece are determined by it. The thematic material is molded, modified, developed, and shaped to flow in the proper harmonic direction, and to achieve a musical balance within the entire structure.

The prominence of the tonic and dominant regions in the exposition of this movement gives way to that of the submediant and supertonic regions in the development section. This is understandable in the total context of the piece, since it creates a standard functional pattern: ‖:I–V–:‖V–vi–ii–(V)–I—:‖. Indeed, most pieces in this period, and later ones as well, seem to show a direct relationship between functional chordal motion and larger key areas within the piece. Chord-to-chord function is thereby extended to broader musical relationships.

The function and use of ***motivic material*** is also of great importance to the shaping of the piece. In this piece, there is surprisingly little motivic material, considering the length of the movement. Five important motives are used, though of these only two or three become truly significant from a developmental standpoint.

The most important is the opening motive in measure 1, which is used to construct both the first and second themes. In addition, the development section uses this motive as its primary material, since the first and second thematic areas are both explored in the development, with only a small bit of new material added for cadential purposes at the end.

In this way Haydn can produce unity and variety at the same time. Along with an exploration of new key areas, the listener is presented with familiar material in various new guises.

This is a typical sonata-allegro movement. Sonata-allegro form is extremely malleable and can be altered, modified, and expanded in all directions. Even when greatly altered and enlarged beyond these Classical models in the next century, the basic structure of exposition-development-recapitulation, with its essential key relationships, remains clear enough to justify the continued use of the term sonata-allegro form. Later modifications change the surface of the form but not the basic structural design. In addition, it comes to be used not only as a first-movement form, but for any, and sometimes all, movements of a piece. It is used extensively in the piano sonata as well as in symphonies, string quartets, and other genres of the period.

Another musical form widely used in the eighteenth century was the **minuet and trio**. Always in ¾ meter, and always in a modified Baroque binary form, it appeared as the second or third movement of the sonata or symphony in the earlier period. Later, it was used almost exclusively as the third movement of the symphony and string quartet.

The following example is the second movement from the same Haydn sonata.

The form is quite straightforward:

| Minuet | Trio | Minuet (repeat)[1] |

‖: a :‖: b a :‖   ‖: c :‖: d c :‖   ‖ a ‖ b a ‖

C: I   V I   c: i   III i

[1] On the return of the minuet, the repeats are not taken.

The choice of the parallel minor key for the trio is typical of Haydn. This is variable, though; in other works, the trio's key may be vi, ii, or IV. What is most important is that the trio is a contrasting section. The original minuet returns at the end, producing a large **ABA** form, each section of which is a binary form.

Especially in the works of Haydn, experiments or further explorations are often found in the minuet-and-trio movement. The trio of this example is unusual in its use of prolonged chains of suspensions and its chromatic inflections, especially in the last six measures.

There are two related dissonances used in the mid-to-late eighteenth century: the *appoggiatura* and the *retardation.* The appoggiatura occurred in two ways, as a dissonance on a strong beat which was approached by leap, or as a dissonance that was used on a strong beat but written as a smaller note (not as an actual part of the rhythm).

ex. 14-11

In the first instance there is a dissonance approached by leap and left by step in the opposite direction. It is rhythmically strong. In the second case there is no dissonance, technically, since it does not sound with any pitch in the left hand. However if harmony were supplied, it would certainly be dissonant. The composer views it as a dissonance, but it can be different ones depending on its context and approach. In addition, the composer views this as being rhythmically part of the piece, and not as a grace-note figure.

ex. 14-12

The eighteenth century appoggiatura is always performed on the beat; the grace note occurs before the beat.

The retardation is simply a suspension that resolves upward. Usually encountered at cadences, it is frequently a 7–8 suspension.

ex. 14-13

In the example, three dissonant notes—*b,f,* and *d*—are "carried over" the bar line. The *d* resolves as a 9–8 suspension, the *f* as a 4–3 suspension, and the *b* as a 7–8 retardation. This is a typical cadential motion in the music of Haydn and Mozart, as well as that of Beethoven and other early-nineteenth-century composers.

STYLE CHARACTERISTICS: PRECLASSIC PERIOD (ca. 1735–1765)
based on Haydn, Piano Sonata in C major

melody	short phrases, usually of regular two-, four-, and eight-measure lengths, though phrases of irregular length also appear • motivic construction • often based on triadic outlines, thus wedded to the harmonic structure
harmony	functional • quick modulations, sudden shifts • generally explores diatonically related keys
rhythm	juxtaposition of various rhythmic elements, such as duple and triple divisions of the pulse • numerous rhythmic motives used for development
dissonance	passing tones, neighboring tones, escape tones, suspensions, appoggiaturas, retardations
forms	sonata-allegro, minuet and trio, rondo, variation
texture	relatively clear texture

Glossary

Alberti bass   an accompanimental figure typical in piano and harpsichord writing in the eighteenth century, consisting of a repeated broken-chord pattern played by the left hand. Named for the eighteenth-century composer Domenico Alberti (c. 1710–40).

Appoggiatura (18th century)   a note written with a smaller notehead, not written as a part of the rhythmic structure; it is *performed* as part of that rhythmic structure, however.

Closing theme   the third area of the exposition and recapitulation in sonata-allegro form; it usually appears in the dominant key (or relative major) in the exposition, and in the tonic key in the recapitulation.

Development   the middle section of sonata-allegro form; the section in which the composer develops, modifies, and extends the motivic material, and explores various key regions.

Exposition   the first major section of sonata-allegro form; usually contains a first and second theme with a closing theme (or codetta).

First theme   the opening thematic material, in the tonic key in sonata-allegro form.

Minuet-trio form   two contrasting dances, each in Baroque binary form. Each is in $\frac{3}{4}$ meter, usually at a moderate tempo; the two sections are often in contrasting keys or modes, but no standard key relation is observed.

Recapitulation   the third major section of sonata-allegro form (after the development section) in which the material of the exposition is repeated entirely in the tonic key.

Retardation   a suspension that resolves upward.

Second theme   the second thematic material of sonata-allegro form; it generally occurs in the dominant key (or relative major) in the exposition, and in the tonic key in the recapitulation.

Sonata-allegro form *(sonata form, first-movement form)*   an expansion of the Baroque binary form into larger and more distinct sections. The repeated exposition uses first, second, and closing themes.

The development and recapitulation are also repeated. The recapitulation is a repeat of the exposition, but entirely in the tonic key.

Sudden shifts a movement to another key center without the benefit of preparation or any other modulatory procedure.

Suggested Exercises

1. With the following motives (derived from a Haydn piano sonata) construct an exposition of a sonata-form movement. Complete the movement if possible, using opening material in the development section.

ex. 14-14

2. Complete the following progressions (extracted from early Haydn piano sonatas).

a. $\frac{2}{4}$ G: I I_6 | V_6 I I_6 | ii_6 V | I | I I_6 | V_6 I I_6 | ii_6 ii | V |

(G): V_6 | vi_6 | V_7/V | V | | | | | |
D: | ii_6 | V_7 | I ii I | V_6 V_7 | I ii I | V_6 V_7 | I | ii_6 V^6_5 |

                G: | | I_6 I | V_6 I I_6 | ii_6 ii V V_7 | I‖
(D): I ii_6 I^6_4 V | I | IV_6 IV |

b.

$\frac{3}{4}$c: i | V_7 | i i_6 | V^6_5 V_7 V^6_5 | $vii°^4_3$/iv $vii°_7$/iv $vii°^4_3$/iv | iv_6 iv |

V^6_5/iv | iv | $♭II_6$ V^6_5/III | III | V^4_2/VI | VI | V^4_3/VI |

VI | $vii°^6_5$/♭VII ♭VII $vii°_7$ V^6_5 | i iv^6_5 | iv_6 | V | V_7 | i ‖

Before Reading Chapter 15

1. Listen to the first movement of Mozart's String Quartet No. 16 in E♭ Major, K.428 (pages 15–19).
2. Locate and identify each section of the piece and its key.
3. Analyze harmonically measures 69 to 100.
4. Listen to the movement again, paying close attention to the melodic motives and their reiteration and development.

Wolfgang Amadeus Mozart

String Quartet No. 16 in E♭ major, K.428

One of the most interesting features of many periods of music is how some particular musical idea is developed, gradually becoming longer and complex. This describes the development of sonata-allegro form in the Classic era. The structure proved capable of multiple expansions and developments, and composers wasted little time developing its potentialities.

The preceding movement by Wolfgang Amadeus Mozart (1756–1791) is the first movement of one of his later quartets, written in 1783. It displays both his penchant for chromatic inflections of lines and his compact but highly expanded use of sonata-allegro form.

One of the basic style features of the Classic period was that thematic ideas were not usually of significant length. In Mozart this was carried almost to an extreme. He often mixes several short motivic ideas together to form one longer phrase, and even this is usually no longer than eight measures. He often uses **_chromatic inflections_** in the individual lines as can be seen immediately in the opening four-measure phrase of his String Quartet in E♭. No change of key occurs here, but $b♭$, c, and f are all briefly tonicized by the use of leading tones to those pitches. It is significant that these harmonies represent a solid tonal progression as well, V–vi–ii, and the ending on $a♭$–g implies V_7–I.

The next four measures are in complete contrast to the first four, perhaps to balance the more extreme opening chromatic gesture. Note the emphasis on the ii chord in measures 5–7, finally resolving in the V–I. This second phrase is repeated, followed by the first. The opening phrase, though, is altered at its return to include a harmonic background that supports the chromatic line. This gives the first fifteen bars an **ABBA** form. It is a strong opening, both thematically and tonally. The key is well established despite (or perhaps because of) the chromatic beginning.

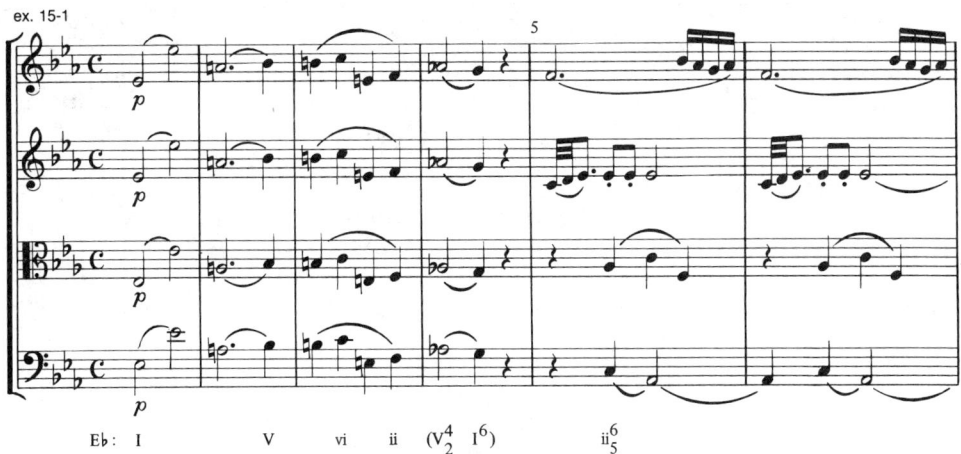

Considering the earlier sonata-form examples, this would seem to constitute the opening idea, perhaps with an added six or eight measures in the home key. The second theme should then appear. However, such is not the case here. In measure 16 there are alterations of all kinds: melodic, motivic, harmonic, tonal, textural, and registral. The first violin shifts up an octave; the second violin's double stops produce a thicker texture; there seems to be a harmonic shift to c minor; and the melodic content is not related to the opening at all. Could this be the second thematic area? If so, we are in the "wrong" key—the second theme is usually the dominant. In addition, by measures 19–22 the key seems to be solidly in E♭, with hints at f minor and A♭ major. Because of the motivic activity, as in the falling eighth-note figure

ex. 15-2

the entire section looks like development of new material. This "development" continues for a considerable period, until measure 40. A strong cadence in measures 39–40 stops the action and signals a close for this section. The cadence is on B♭!

What has happened? We have simply modulated to the dominant level. The process, however, is considerably different from that used in the preceding Haydn example (remember, that sonata was written a full twenty years before this piece). Here, Mozart firmly establishes the key of E♭ major in the first 16 measures, then launches into an involved, 24-measure *transition,* and finally arrives at a convincing B♭-major cadence. The transition to the dominant actually takes longer than the opening theme in the tonic! This seems to represent a considerable shift of emphasis when compared to the Haydn sonata. The development of musical ideas is often the most interesting aspect of a piece, and certainly the most challenging to the composer; thus, it is perhaps understandable that developmental passages sometimes come to dominate movements in sonata form.

The second thematic area is in the dominant, as expected, and begins in measure 40. It has a decidedly different character from the opening theme, but retains some of its chromatic inflection. Its eight-measure theme is repeated, with the melodic emphasis shifted to the viola the second time. What ensues is much like another transition: a pedal $b\flat$ in the cello with chromatic motion above it. The augmented-sixth chord in measure 62 reestablishes the key of B♭ and the strong cadence in measures 63–64 solidifies it. Measures 64–68 constitute the closing section of the exposition, emphasizing the B♭ tonality once again before the return to the beginning of the movement.

As a comparison with the Haydn examples will make clear, the exposition has undergone considerable change, especially in its length. All its sections are longer, but the most significant extension occurs in the transitions. The first transition, linking the first thematic area to the second, is the most expanded. Simple repetition of material contributes somewhat to the overall expansion, but it is the development of ideas, especially in the first transition, that significantly changes the size and structure of the exposition.

The *development section* is *expanded* in proportion to the exposition. After an obligatory treatment of the opening thematic material, the major part of the development deals with motives from the second thematic area, particularly this small fragment:

ex. 15-3

Even the ending of the development employs material from the second thematic area (compare m.41):

ex. 15-4

This reliance on the second theme for developmental material is significant when viewed in terms of a structural balancing of events and musical ideas. The emphasis on the first theme and its transition in the exposition has to be balanced by the remaining thematic material, and Mozart has used the development section to do so.

The procedure of combining old and new material for developmental purposes is most important. The development of the second theme begins in measure 75, as has already been noted. Measures 77–78 contain simply a triplet arpeggio (the harmony will be discussed later). The two come together from measure 85 on. Each instrument (beginning with viola, then first violin, second violin, and finally cello) is given the triplet figure once, while two others add the second-theme motive and the fourth plays a pedal note.

A passage leading to the recapitulation follows. Measures 93–100 constitute the *retransition*, so called because of their function linking the development section to the recapitulation. They represent a concentrated effort to reestablish the tonic, moving us back to the opening material. This is accomplished convincingly by means of a circle-of-fifths progression and a slowing-down of the rhythmic tension and motion.

There are no significant changes in the recapitulation, melodically or harmonically, except that, as expected, the second theme is now in the tonic key instead of the dominant (measure 136). What is most intriguing in this section is the process of getting to the second theme but staying in the tonic key, while giving the impression of a transitional passage. Compare measures 12–40 with measures 113–136 in the recapitulation. The differences, although significant, are not jarring to the ear. The familiarity of the material allows the listener to follow the musical action, and the reordering and transposition allows the composer to effect a "transition" without actually changing key. This is sometimes referred to as a ***circular transition*** because, while it seems to modulate, it actually ends where it began, in the tonic.

The rest of the movement is almost identical to the exposition, but transposed to E♭ major. A few slight changes, such as the moving of the second statement of the second theme from the viola to the second violin and the rhythmic alteration of the final measure, produce variety but hardly change the musical content.

The important changes in sonata form have almost always taken place in developmental areas, either in expanded transitions or in the development section itself. It was in these areas that composers were challenged the most. The areas of tonal stability, the first and second theme areas, offered no comparable incentive to creative ideas and therefore were not expanded in proportion.

The subtleties of ***harmonic usage and invention*** were also open to change and development. The progressions of tonal, functional harmony did not radically change in this period, and voice-leading principles were not altered. However, the use of harmonic rhythm was often novel, and both progressions within the key and modulatory passages were strengthened, clarified, and expanded. Mozart usually used chromaticism for two different purposes: 1) to effect modulations, by means of the creation of new leading tones to solidify new key centers; and 2) to tonicize, but not modulate to, a given tonality, through emphasis on several levels *within* the key, adding both melodic and harmonic interest. This second technique is less structured and freer in its use, usually confined to chromatic passing tones and momentary secondary dominants.

Both the first and second thematic areas have more chromaticism and less actual modulation than the first transition. The harmonic progression in measures 12–15 is instructive in this respect, since it functions well within the key, despite a strong reliance on chromaticism.

ex. 15-5

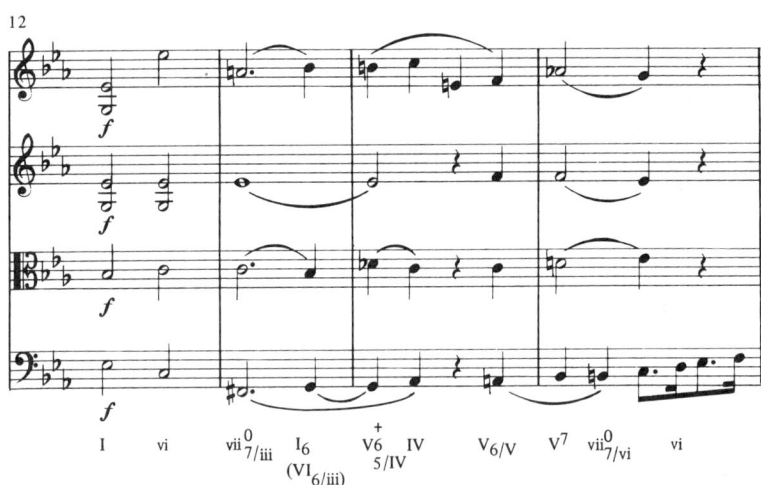

As is usual in most sonata-allegro movements, one of the most challenging areas, especially harmonically, is the development section. After all, a primary intent of such movements is the development of harmonic and modulatory possibilities and the creation of harmonic tension as a result, tension which is released by the recapitulation.

The basic motion of this development section is rooted in two factors, the chromatic lines of the opening motive and the standard root progression by fifths. Measures 69–71 point to the thematic importance of momentary leading tones produced by chromatic inflections.

ex. 15-6

Measures 72–74 show more chordal motion, but this is still derived from chromatic voice leading:

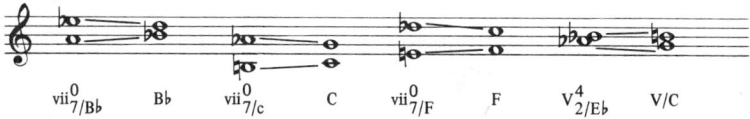

ex. 15-7

This final linear progression shifts us out of the progression by fifths (B♭–F–c) by means of a third relation, B♭$_7$–G$_7$.

ex. 15-8

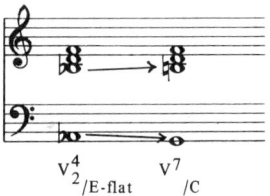

V$^4_2$/E-flat   V^7/C

The impetus here is linear motion and the final goal is c minor. The overall progression is: vii°$_7$/B♭–B♭–vii°$_7$/C–C–vii°$_7$/f–F–V$^4_2$/E♭–V$_7$/c–c.

If we extract the important key centers, the progression becomes clear and logical.

                        Bb---C---F---G---c
FM:IV   V   I

                             cm: IV V i

Measures 75–76 use a pedal *c* and sustain a c minor chord. The pedal *c* persists in the following two measures, with the upper voices moving to vii°$_7$/c, which resolves back to c minor in measures 79–80. In measures 81–82 the pedal *c* still remains, but the upper chord is now vii°$_7$/f. This configuration produces an example of the **dominant ninth chord.** The function of the pedal *c* has shifted from that of the tonic to that of the dominant of f minor.

ex. 15-9

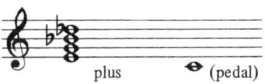

plus   (pedal)

In this case, it is a V$_7$ chord with an added *minor* ninth. Only the first violin has the ninth. The resolution to f minor confirms our analysis.

ex. 15-10

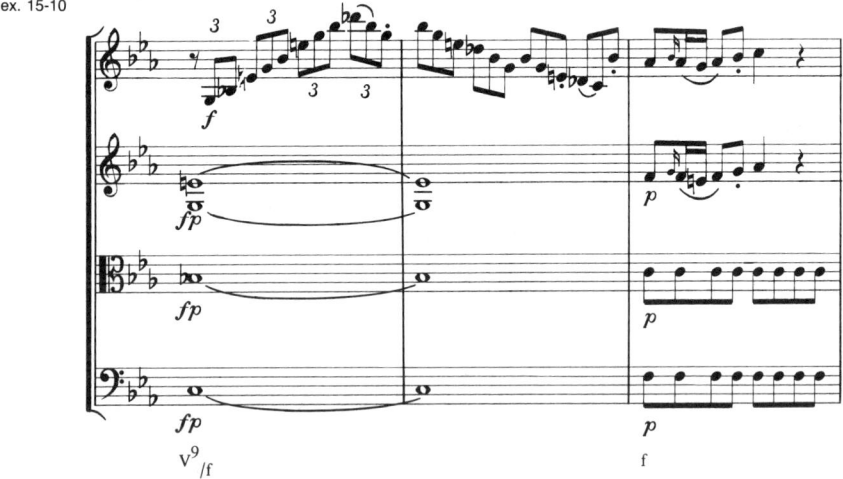

V^9/f   f

The move to the $e\flat$ in the cello in measure 85 produces $V_2^4/B\flat$ which, as happened previously, shifts to V_7/g. The same voice leading that was used in measure 74 is found here. In the first case it moved from $V/E\flat$ to V/c; here, from $V/B\flat$ to V/g. The same third relation of chords is the basis for the motion. The shift to g minor is confirmed in measure 89. From here on, we are on the level of g minor; the progression moves from VI/g (measure 91) to $vii_7^{\varnothing}/V$ (measure 93) to an implied V/g (measure 95) and finally to a convincing $V-i$ in measures 96 and 97. This in turn is used to effect a sudden shift to F, and finally to $E\flat$. This series of V–I cadential figures helps to prepare the recapitulation in measure 101. A basic outline of the development section might help us put it in some kind of harmonic order.

```
  69    70  72    73      73      74     75          83      85         87     89   91
  B♭---F----B♭------C------F------G----c--V₉/f-----f-----V₂⁴/B♭------V₇/g-----g------E♭

       F:  IV    V       I         F:  V₉    i    V²/IV      V₇/ii
              C: IV       V        (i)

                                                  g:   V₇        i      VI

  93         95    96      97  98       99     100    101
  vii⁰₇/D-----D------V₇/g-----g----V₇/F------F------B♭------E♭  (recapitulation)
g: vii⁰₇/V   V     V₇      i
                          E♭    vi   V₇/ii   V/V    V    I
```

There is a constant interplay of keys in the development section in a strong functional arrangement producing a logical progression of individual chords as well as key areas.

STYLE CHARACTERISTICS: CLASSIC PERIOD (ca. 1770–1800)
based on Mozart, String Quartet No. 16 in $E\flat$ major

melody — 4–8 measure phrases, generally fairly regular • motivic construction, with ideas that are expanded and developed

harmony — functional • much use of chromatic inflection, producing secondary dominants, and secondary diminished seventh chords • modulation primarily to dominant, but also to all other diatonic levels • some use of V^9 chords

rhythm — continuation of practices of early Haydn, but with smoother rhythms, few juxtapositions of unrelated elements • emphasis on motivic rhythm and addition of one rhythmic motive to another • persistent forward rhythmic drive

forms — sonata-allegro primary • also minuet and trio, rondo, ternary, binary, variation, occasionally fugue (especially in vocal works)

texture — a slightly thicker texture than in the Preclassic period, with the middle register emphasized more than previously

Glossary

Circular transition   the transition between the first and second themes in the recapitulation, whose function is to transit from the tonic "back to" the tonic and still give the impression of a transition.
Dominant ninth chord   a V7 chord with an added ninth; usually a minor ninth, in the eighteenth and early nineteenth centuries.
Retransition   the transition at the end of the development section in sonata-allegro form, in which the composer transits back to the tonic key for the recapitulation.
Transition   a passage whose purpose is to link two sections together.

Suggested Exercises

1. Harmonically analyze the entire exposition of the Mozart quartet movement discussed in this chapter. Be especially aware of the use of secondary-dominant motion and of augmented-sixth chords and their resolutions.
2. Provide a complete motivic analysis of the whole movement. Compare the use of each motive in all sections, and indicate any changes, however slight.
3. Notate the following progression (derived from the String Quartet No. 14, K. 387, by Mozart).

C: $\frac{3}{4}$ I | I | I_6^4 V I | IV_7 I | V_7 I | V_6^5/V | V | I | V_4^3/V V_7/V |

g: V_4^3 V_7 |

I | VI | $ii_6^{\varnothing 5}$ V_7 | i | V_6^5 i | V | V_7 | V_6^5/V V_7 | i_6 V_6^5/iv | IV |

G: IV | IV ii |

V V_4^2 | I_6 V_4^3 I | V_6^5 | I V_4^3 I_6 | I IV I_6 | V_7/V $vii_7^\varnothing/vi$ vi | ii_6^5 I_6^4 V_7 |

c: I | $vii_4^{\circ3}/IV$ $vii_4^{\circ3}$ | i_6 | $ii_7^\varnothing$ V_7 | I |

C: | I | I_6^4 V I | IV_7 I | I_6^4 V_7 | I ‖

Before Reading Chapter 16

1. Listen to Beethoven's Piano Sonata in c minor, Op. 13.
2. Bracket the phrase structure in the second movement (pages 29–32).

3. Label the key structure throughout the movement.
4. Identify the various sections.

Ludwig van Beethoven

Piano Sonata in c minor, Op. 13 (*Pathétique*), second movement

Sonata-allegro form is not the only principle of construction used in the eighteenth and early nineteenth centuries. Other basic formal designs are the simple binary—**A B**—and ternary—**A B A.** Although many pieces employ binary form of various kinds, the ternary design was probably more often used, possibly because of the concept of return and reiteration. There are several forms that are closely related to ternary which extend the principle of sectional repetition.

rondeau: **a b a c a d . . .** a
small rondo: **A B A C A**
large rondo: **A B A C A B A** (also referred to as sonata-rondo)

The rondeau was used primarily by French composers in the late seventeenth century and early eighteenth century (Chambonnières, Louis Couperin, Rameau, and others). This principle of repetition was altered by limiting the number of episodes and became the ***sonata-rondo.*** The ***small rondo*** was in actuality an expansion of the ternary design[1].

[1]Check the *Harvard Dictionary of Music,* second edition, for further information on this development.

The key structures of small and large rondo are usually as follows:

```
small rondo:    A    B    A    C           A
     major:     I    V    I    optional    I
     minor:     i    III  i    optional    i

large (or sonata) rondo:  A    B    A         C                      A    B    A
               major:     I    V    I    varies: functions as a      I    I    I
               minor:     i    III  i    development section         i    i    i
```

The musical example (pages 37–39) by Ludwig van Beethoven (1770–1827) is a small rondo, but there are several structural ideas contained in it that show a different overall balance. Discovering the sectional form of a piece is only a beginning step in any analysis. The real shape of the piece is sometimes considerably different from its abstract, sectional form.

In the present example, the **A** section is strongly stated in A♭ major, followed immediately by a repetition. Notice that this is a literal repetition in terms of melody and harmony, but the texture and registration has expanded, making the original presentation sound almost like an introduction to the second presentation.

The **B** section (measures 17–28) does not begin in E♭ major as would be expected, but rather in f minor. The modulations are rapid, and the tonal fluctuation is constant until measure 23, where E♭ is solidified as a dominant and leads back to the **A** section in measure 29. There is only one presentation of **A** this time. The **C** section (measures 37–50) begins in a♭ minor, the parallel minor of the tonic key. The other change that occurs at this point is the rhythmic shift from duple to triple subdivision in the accompaniment. Its significance will be discussed later.

The key of a♭ minor gives way to E major (!) and finally to E♭ major (V of A♭ major), with a transition back to A♭ major and the **A** section. This first section is again repeated, and is followed by a closing section or small coda (*codetta*), which functions as a **cadential extension.** The entire plan can be diagrammed as follows:

```
no. of measures:     8m   8m   7m    5m      8m   14m     8m   8m   7m
thematic materials:  A    A    B     trans.  A    C       A    A    codetta
tonal area:          A♭   A♭   f+d   E♭      A♭   a♭–E–E♭ A♭   A♭   A♭
```

The bulk of the movement is devoted to two thematic areas, **A** and **C,** since **B** is very short and contains no highly significant material. The outer repetitions of **A** give it an increased dominance not found in the abstract diagram of a small rondo.

However, the real division of the piece is not as it seems. In terms both of aural effect and actual duration, the movement divides approximately in half: 35 measures for the first half (**A A B A**) and 37 measures for the second half (**C A A** codetta). This is reinforced by the use of duple and triple divisions of the beat: the first half employs exclusively duple subdivision and the second half exclusively triple.

On the other hand, the dramatic division of the piece is approximately 2/3–1/3. The motion moves toward the transition which moves back to the **A** section, from measure 45–51. This is the most complex section harmonically and it moves through a variety of changes proceeding back to the tonic key and the original theme. It is in this section that the greatest amount of harmonic tension exists.

The entire **C** section, with its closing transition, is the most intriguing from a harmonic standpoint. The a♭ minor key with which it begins is somewhat of a shock. It can be referred to as a ***change of mode.*** The progressions within this key (measures 37–41) are straightforward and strongly functional.

ex. 16-1

From measure 42 onward there is an interesting development, more obvious on the page than to the ear. The shift from a♭ minor (six flats) to V_7 of E major (four sharps) seems to take us far from the original key, and its appearance on the page is rather startling. But the theoretical implication is less astounding. V_7 of E is in actuality an enharmonic spelling of V_7 of F♭ (c♭-e♭-g♭-b♭♭) and therefore is nothing more than V_7/VI in the key of a♭ minor, spelled enharmonically. This demonstrates the essence of **enharmonic modulation.** The reason for it is the obvious, practical one of the unwieldy nature of F♭ major, with its eight flats. E major is simply easier to write and to read, and the spelling does not affect the sound and function of F♭.

This sojourn into E major is countered by motion leading away, which takes place in measure 48. The purpose is to move to E♭—the dominant of A♭—in order to get back to the home key. The theoretical motion of the whole section, then, becomes clear. The overall harmonic motion of the **C** section is i–VI–V–I. The transition back to the **A** section can be harmonically analyzed without difficulty.

STYLE CHARACTERISTICS: EARLY NINETEENTH CENTURY
based on Beethoven, Piano Sonata in c minor, Op. 13, and Piano Sonata in C major, Op. 53

melody   usually fragmentary, except in slow movements • primary emphasis on motivic use and development • terse melodic lines constructed from motives • strong harmonic basis for melodic content

harmony   strongly functional • use of V9 chords • modulation to more distantly related keys, sometimes by third relation, including use of altered dominants (early usage, not highly developed) • enharmonic, chromatic, and diatonic modulation

rhythm   motivic in nature • expansion and contraction of rhythmic motives

forms   sonata-allegro, more highly developed than before, with extended transitions, developments, codas • rondo (small and large), variation, minuet and trio (becomes scherzo and trio in Beethoven)

Glossary

Binary form   a two-part form with distinct sections: **A B**.
Cadential extension   the lengthening of the final phrase before the cadence.
Enharmonic modulation   a modulation through the use of enharmonically related pitches, usually to a key that is enharmonically related to the old key (for example, a♭ minor to E major).
Rondeau   a typically French form of the seventeenth and early eighteenth centuries; it uses a refrain that returns after contrasting sections: **a b a c a d a e . . . a**.
Small rondo   an expansion of the ternary idea of repetition: **A B A C A**.
Sonata-rondo   also called **large rondo,** in which the **C** section functions as a development section. The final three sections are in the tonic key, producing a resemblance to sonata-allegro form.
Ternary form   a three-part sectional form: **A B A**.

Suggested Exercises

Analyze harmonically the Bagatelle, Op. 119, No. 1, by Beethoven.

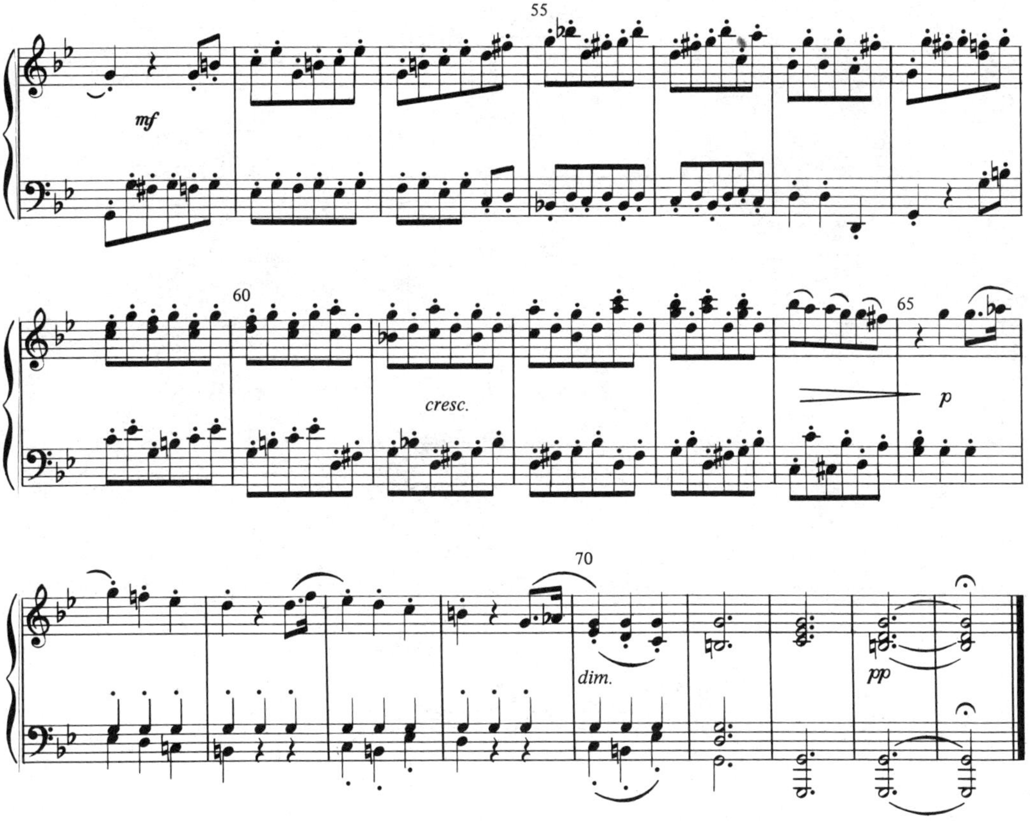

Before Reading Chapter 17

1. Listen to Beethoven's Piano Sonata in C Major, op. 53 (*Waldstein*).
2. Analyze the form of the first movement (pages 39–57).
3. Harmonically analyze the end of the exposition and the beginning of the development, measures 70–111.

SONATA, Op. 53 **L. VAN BEETHOVEN**

Allegro con brio

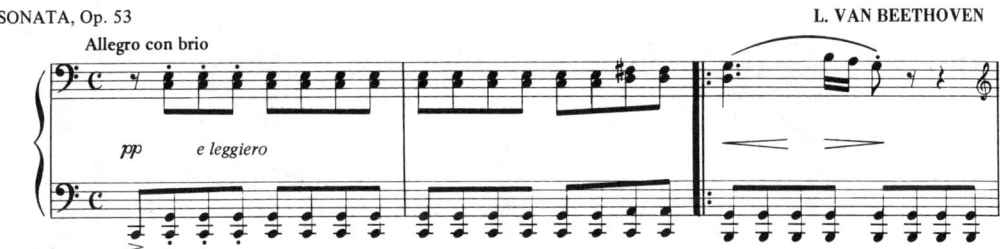

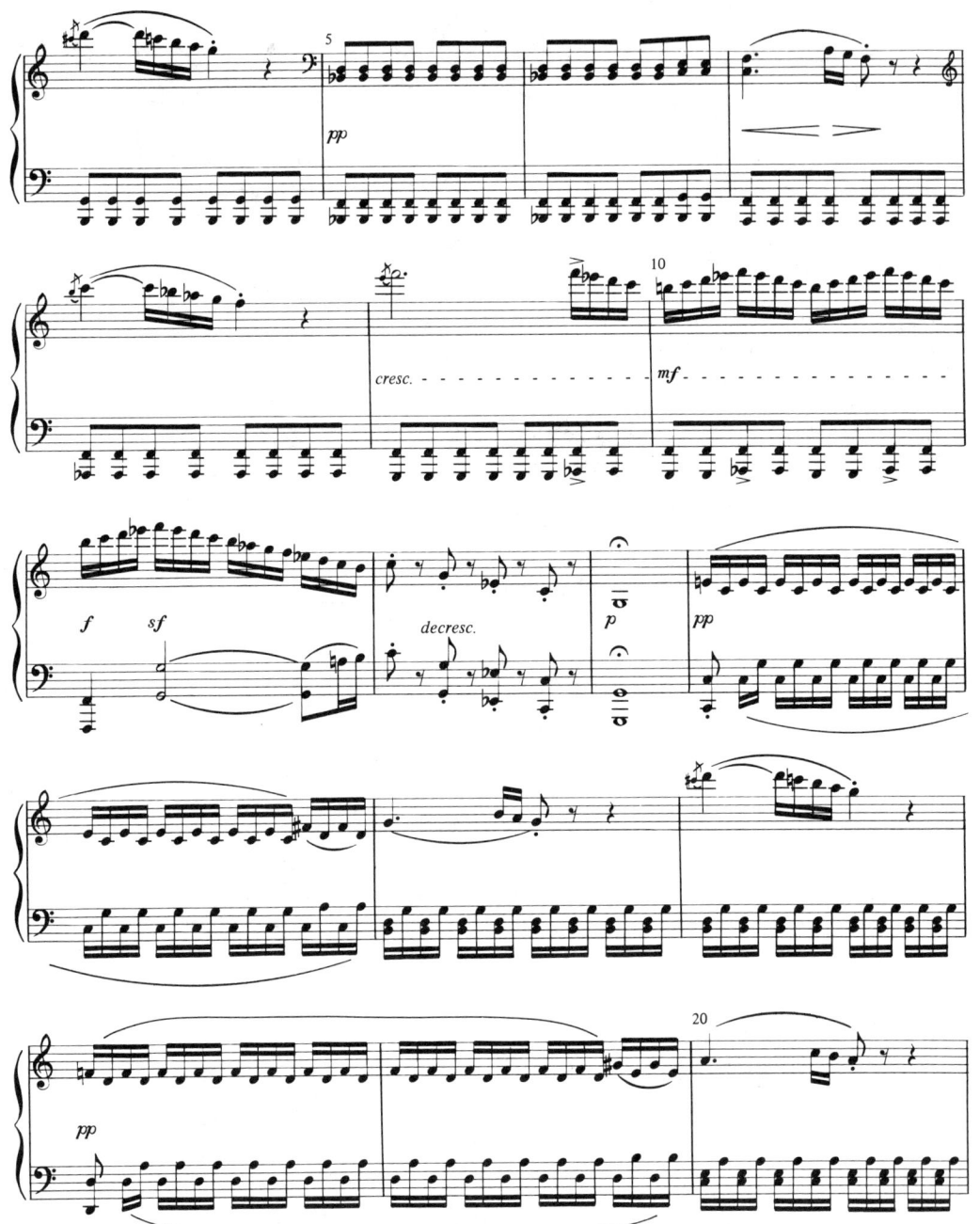

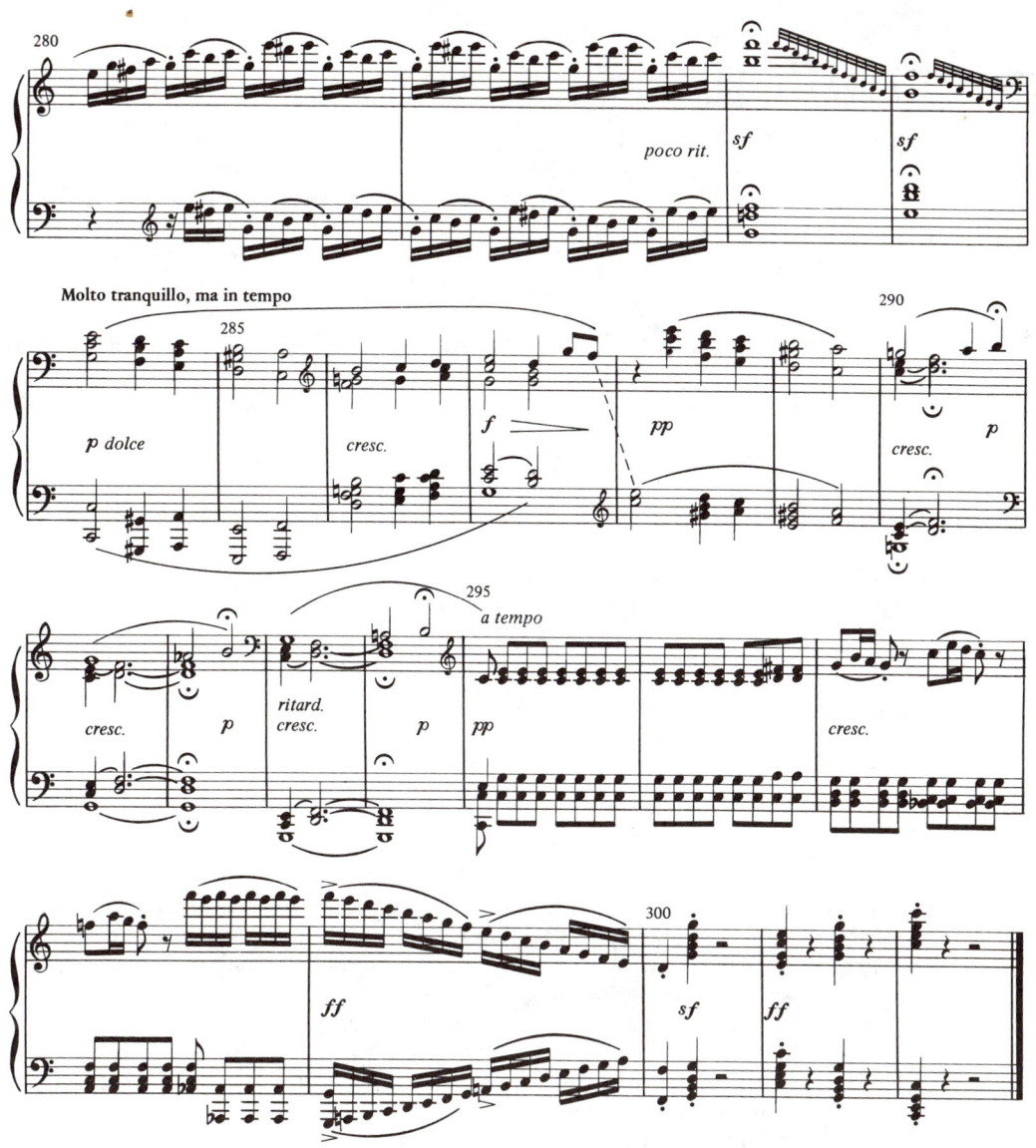

17

Beethoven

Piano Sonata in C major, Op. 53 (*Waldstein*), first movement

In relation to the other works in this book, the most immediately apparent feature of this Beethoven example is its length. Although compact in its motivic use and its exploration of musical ideas, it nonetheless overwhelms us with its fecundity of expression and sheer size.

The compositional process of a composer is perhaps the most important feature for any theoretical study. Beethoven's unique processes must be discovered in order to understand how a piece can approach such large proportions. The most logical place to begin is the broad perspective.

Where are the large divisions in the piece? This movement divides at the double bar in measure 87, the whole first section being repeated. Therefore, it is in a large binary form.

The next step is to break down the two large sections. The first seems to divide thematically at measure 35 and then at measure 74. The second section seems to have three large divisions—measures 87 to 156, 156 to 249, and 249 to the end. The first two of these are approximately the same length, the third being somewhat shorter. Within each section further divisions occur.

The thematic material and the succession of keys in each section contribute to a basic proportion and design. The first three thematic divisions, in measures

1 to 86, are essentially repeated in measures 156 to 249. These areas are fairly harmonically stable, although some modulation does occur. Measures 87 to 156, on the other hand, are quite volatile in their key relations, as is the final section.

With its repeated large first section, its developmental section, and the altered repeat of the first section, the movement is obviously in a large sonata-allegro form. The only new area is the addition at the end. This is called the *coda* and was common in the Classic and Romantic periods. Its general purpose will be discussed later in the chapter.

Therefore, the whole design is:

Exposition (mm. 1–86)

1st thematic area	transition	2nd thematic area	transition	codetta
m. 1–13	14–34	35–49	50–73	74–86
C	C—E	E	E	E—(C)

Development (mm. 87–155)

m. 94   100   104   120   130   132   136
   g—   c—   f—   B♭—   G—   c—   G——

Recapitulation (mm. 156–249)

1st thematic area	transition	2nd thematic area	transition	codetta
m. 156–173	174–197	198–210	211–234	235–249
C	C—A	A—C	C	C

Coda (mm. 249–302)

D♭—G—C

Note the choice of key for each of the main sections. C major is the tonic, and one would therefore expect G major as the key of the second area. Instead, Beethoven moves to E major! By opening this **unexpected key area** in the exposition, Beethoven almost promises an expansion of key usage and modulation in the remainder of the movement. The germinal idea is at least present in this first modulation.

Next, note the length of each major section and its relationship to the length of the transitions. The importance of the transition in the process of expanding the sonata form cannot be overemphasized. This is where the true weight of this movement lies; the transitions, with the development section, account for a large proportion of the entire movement. As in Mozart, the sections based on development of motives and keys are apparently more interesting to the composer than those solidly in a single key.

Two other areas of development especially important to Beethoven are those of **motivic use** and the **expansion and contraction of phrase lengths.** The motives that open the piece are quite distinctive. The repeated chords, which are used to open the important sections of the piece (the exposition, the development, the recapitulation, and the coda), constitute the most characteristic and memorable motive of the movement. The other motives are subjected to greater manipulation, possibly because of their more malleable melodic and rhythmic basis.

An interesting feature of Beethoven's style is his penchant for building his movements from short motives. The first twelve measures contain four motives that are used later, especially in the development section.

ex. 17-1

The use of these should be noted in the first major section of the development section as well as in the coda. The coda is especially fascinating in this regard because of the expansion of these motives which occurs there.

The obvious purpose of a ***transition*** is motion, usually harmonic, from one area to another. The process is slightly different for each composition, and in every case reveals the true structural perception of the composer. In the first transition here (measures 14–34), we feel a strong sense of direction, truly compelling the listener from one stage to another. Through careful linear and harmonic control Beethoven weaves his way from measure 18 to 20, finally adding an A♯ in measure 22 to shift to V/E, and finally V7/E. The modulation is firmly established by strong reiteration of this dominant harmony.

We have arrived on the level of *e* by measure 23. At this point, however, it is e minor rather than E major. Beethoven needs more time to reiterate the tonal level; only at the end of the transition does he shift from minor to major mode. A reduction of these few measures shows the process.

ex. 17-2

[E major!]

Note that the harmonic motion accelerates in measure 27 and then settles on the dominant in measure 29, delaying its resolution until measure 35, where the second thematic area begins.

A further, and even stronger illustration of harmonic acceleration, occurs in the transition between the second area and the codetta, measures 50 to 59. It is given below with a harmonic analysis.

ex. 17-3

The impact of this passage is remarkable. The first measures (50–53) present three ideas: a *b* pedal, a repeating V–I alternation (changing every half measure), and triplet arpeggio figuration. This figuration is then contracted to sixteenth notes and the harmonic alternation to every beat instead of every two. Finally the harmonic changes occur on every eighth note.

The tension produced by this contraction of the harmonic/linear/rhythmic complex is overwhelming. The release, by means of arrival at the internal cadence, begins a new phase of the transition (measures 61–73), where the same basic progress begins anew.

To understand Beethoven's achievement of musical momentum, it is vital to grasp the nature of his directional control at all levels. The motivic, melodic, harmonic, rhythmic, and phrasing aspects of the piece all unite in a dramatic and logical procession of events. This is a major reason for the strength of the forward motion in Beethoven's works.

The development section contains a wealth of new and expanded ideas that must be understood.

The opening section modulates to three, or possibly four, levels almost immediately. The process is through chromatic motion in various parts, and is a fascinating study of modulation through linear means.

This process is usually referred to as ***chromatic modulation*** because of the use of chromaticism to produce the result. The characteristic of chromatic modulation is that the pivot chord is chromatically altered, that is, it is not diatonically present in the original key. However, the pivot chord does appear in the key which is the goal of the modulation. Thus, a chromatic modulation usually moves to a key which does not have any chord in common with the original key.

In this case the F major chord moves logically to G_2^4 (measures 90–91), allowing the *f* in the bass to move to *e* in the resolution to C major. This moves chromatically down to $e\flat$, creating a c minor chord. The final motion is from $e\flat$ to *d*, and from *g* to *a* in an inner voice; *f♯* is then added in the right hand. Beethoven's purpose in this progression is clear: he is moving logically and carefully, to g minor, via a D major chord, V of g. The process is linear, chromatic, and ultimately functional.

ex. 17-4

ex. 17-5

The second area of the development section is related to the first by motivic similarity. The important technique found in measures 104–111 is harmonic and melodic sequence. For modulatory purposes there can hardly be a better device, as can be seen in these few measures.

ex. 17-6

The harmonic root movement within each measure is by descending fifth; in most cases, the first chord is a dominant seventh chord, resolving to its proper tonic, thus creating the strongest possible function. The melodic sequence can also be seen in groups of two (four-chord units).

In addition, the whole passage is organized above a stepwise bass line: f-$e\flat$-$d\flat$-c-$b\flat$-$a\flat$-g-f-e-$e\flat$-d-$d\flat$-c. The cumulative effect makes the momentum of the forward motion strong indeed.

A significant area of the development section begins in measure 112, where the texture changes, the rhythmic ideas are altered, and the harmony takes on added significance and strength. The harmonic rhythm is slower than in the measure directly preceding, but there is a new harmonic complication. The basic harmony in measure 114 can be shown as follows:

ex. 17-7

The sound is unmistakably that of a ***V_9 chord.*** This section is based on that sound throughout. The modulations, from f to $b\flat$ to $e\flat$ (measures 114–125), all employ the V_9 harmony; in each case the ninth is minor.

ex. 17-8

Once having arrived at e♭ minor, Beethoven begins the process of getting back to C. This motion is primarily by ***third relation of keys*** (including an enharmonic third), followed by a V–i motion: e♭–b–G–c

ex. 17-9

The final section of the development is crucial to the whole movement, since it must emphasize the dominant of *C* in such a way as to prepare the recapitulation of C major. A close study of measures 142 to 156 shows a subtle rhythmic structuring designed to create heightened tension and motion toward the C major goal. The phrases are contracted until reaching the recapitulation.

The ***recapitulation,*** unlike those in our previous examples of sonata-allegro form, produces some surprises. The first occurs in measure 168, where the cadential note is $a^\flat$ rather than the expected *g*. This gives the impression of moving away from the tonic; the subsequent harmonic motion of measures 171–173 cleverly moves back to C.

ex. 17-10

A highly significant change occurs in measure 181, by comparison with the corresponding measures in the exposition.

ex. 17-11

In the first instance the harmonic progression moved toward e minor, using the Italian sixth (measure 22) to strengthen the motion. In the recapitulation a similar progression occurs, again using the Italian sixth, but this time in the key of a minor. This is an important shift: the second tonal area in the exposition is a third *above* the tonic (E major), while in the recapitulation it is a third *below* the tonic (A major).

However, as might be expected in the recapitulation, Beethoven does modulate away from A and, by measures 199–200, has established the tonic key, where he remains for a considerable time.

The closing theme, beginning at measure 234, moves immediately to F major/minor. The reason? The **coda** begins in measure 249, with deceptive motion to D♭ major:

Since the D♭ major triad occurs naturally in f minor (VI), Beethoven employs f minor in order to shift to D♭. The deceptive cadence in measures 248–249 begins the new section. In larger terms, the progression is C–F/f–D♭–G–C. The implication of the Neapolitan to C major is strong.

The whole section almost sounds like another recapitulation, or perhaps a new development section, because of the use of the opening motive. There are indications that development will be important in this section. Initially only the familiar motives are seen, used in much the same way as before. In measure 261, however, a new syncopated theme is introduced in the right hand, coupled with the repeated eighth notes and other motives.

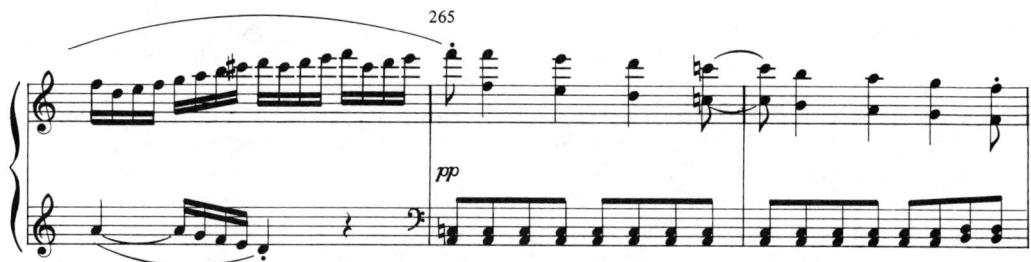

The idea of rhythmic contraction is present throughout the coda. Especially from measure 267 on, it can be seen to lead directly to a cadence in measures 275–276.

Harmonically, the cadence itself is unusual.

ex. 17-14

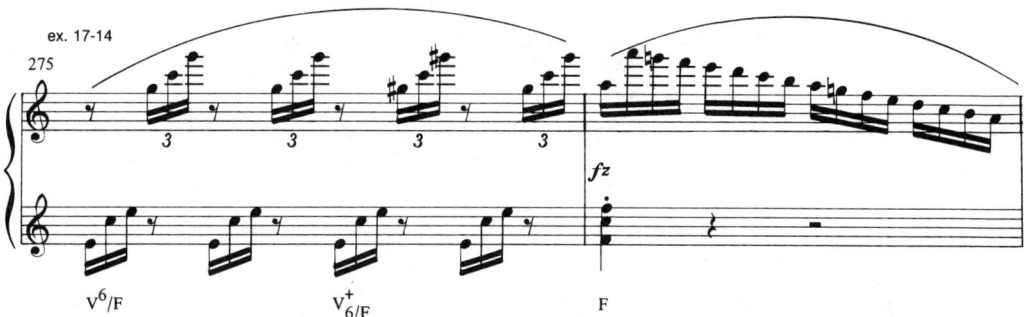

The augmented harmony in measure 275 is understandable in a linear sense. From measure 275 to measure 276 we can analyze the root motion as V–I, C–F. But perhaps the stronger motion is through the tones *e* and *g♯*. The leading tone *e* moves to the *f;* however, there is also a "leading tone" to the third of the F chord. As a result, the V chord is now an augmented instead of a major chord. This is an example of an **altered dominant**—that is, a chord that acts like the dominant but is constructed somewhat differently.

ex. 17-15

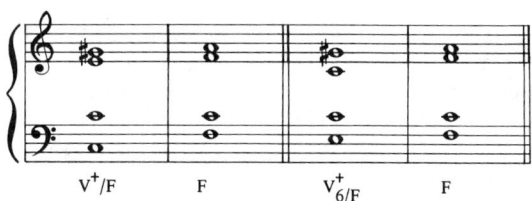

Finally, the close of the piece is unique. The quoting of the second theme in a slow, cadenza-like passage creates an anticipatory feeling, which is resolved by the strong reiteration of the opening chords. In this way Beethoven takes us full circle, ending with the same material with which he began.

In his shaping of musical ideas, his development of both concepts and musical motives, and his control of large and small aspects of balance, Beethoven creates a uniquely compelling design and flow. As stated earlier, the areas that employ development—the transition, development section, and coda—constitute the bulk of the movement, and seem to have stimulated the composer most strongly.

It is as if the compelling harmonic motion used in previous centuries has been extended to the motivic, rhythmic and phrase levels. This projection of musical ideas, with an ever-present and strong forward motion, is a most insistent musical premise. It is a legacy left to the nineteenth century, to be molded and shaped for the remainder of the century and into our own. As such, it is a powerful addition to musical thought and process.

STYLE CHARACTERISTICS: EARLY NINETEENTH CENTURY
based on Beethoven, Piano Sonata in c minor, Op. 13, and Piano Sonata in C major, Op. 53

melody	usually fragmentary, except in slow movements • primary emphasis on motivic use and development • terse melodic lines constructed from motives • strong harmonic basis or melodic content
harmony	strongly functional • use of V9 chords • modulation to more distantly related keys, sometimes by third relation, including enharmonic, chromatic, and diatonic modulation • use of altered dominants (early usage, not highly developed)
rhythm	motivic in nature • expansion and contraction of rhythmic motives
forms	sonata-allegro, more highly developed than before, with extended transitions, developments, and codas • rondo (small and large), variation, minuet and trio (becomes scherzo and trio in Beethoven)

Glossary

Altered dominant   a dominant chord which has been chromatically changed but retains its dominant function. Usually the change enhances the functional pull.

Chordal mutation   the nonfunctional use of chords, usually in a linearly-directed fashion.

Chromatic modulation   modulation to a key which does not have a common chord with the original key.

Coda   an extended section in the tonic at the end of a movement; found particularly in late Classic and early Romantic pieces, especially those in sonata-allegro form.

Codetta   the closing section of the exposition in sonata-allegro form. Also called the closing theme. In the exposition it appears in the dominant; in the recapitulation, in the tonic.

Dominant ninth chord   the dominant seventh chord with an added ninth above the bass (usually a minor ninth, but sometimes major).

Sonata-allegro form   an expansion of the Baroque binary form into larger, more distinct sections. The repeated Exposition used first and second and closing themes. The Development and Recapitulation are also repeated. The Recapitulation is a repeat of the Exposition, except entirely in the tonic key.

Third relation of keys   modulation from one key center to another a third away; the new key does not fit within the old, as in CM–am, but is a more distant relation, such as CM–AM.

Third relation of chords a relation of roots by thirds, so that the second chord does not belong to that of the key of the first, for example, CM–am = I–vi (root movement by third, but *not* third relation), and CM–AM = third relation.

Suggested Exercises

1. Analyze the first movement of the *Pathétique* Sonata, Op. 13, for keys and form. Discuss the use of the recurring slow introduction.
2. Harmonically analyze the following two short pieces by Beethoven.

Bagatelle Op. 119, No. 8

Bagatelle Op. 119, No. 9

Before Reading Chapter 18

1. Listen to *Der Doppelgänger* (The Phantom Double) (pages 72–74).
2. Read the text carefully and relate it to the music.
3. Analyze harmonically the first fifteen measures and the final thirteen measures.

Der Doppelgänger
H. HEINE

FRANZ SCHUBERT

The Phantom Double

The night is calm, the streets are silent,
This is the house where my dear one dwelt;
She has left the city long since,
But the house still stands, in the same square.

A man, too, stands there, staring up aloft,
And wringing his hands in overwhelming grief;
I shudder when I see his features,
The moonlight shows me my very own form.

You phantom double, you pale-faced fellow there!
Why do you ape the pangs of love
That tortured me here in this very place,
So many a night, in times gone by?

18

Franz Schubert

Der Doppelgänger

As we have seen previously, solo song has been an important musical genre since the earliest times. In the eighteenth and nineteenth centuries it gained a remarkably wide and varied public. Schubert is perhaps the best known of the nineteenth-century "tunesmiths" and his reputation is well deserved, as the example in this chapter will show.

The first consideration in any vocal work is the text: What is it, how is it constructed, and what kinds of ideas are contained therein? The composer's answers to these questions usually provide the beginnings of his creative process.

The most important musical premise of a song is certainly the **melody,** which, with its accompaniment, makes up the fabric of solo song. In both these elements Schubert excelled all other song composers in the early nineteenth century. His melodies are clear, beautifully shaped, and free of excessive embellishment, while the accompaniments are both simple and subtly suggestive at the same time.

The text of *Der Doppelgänger* (*The Phantom Double*) is in three stanzas; the song likewise divides into sections according to these stanzas. Since there is no exact repetition of musical material, its structure is referred to as **through-composed.** Each stanza is clearly defined and is developed in a different way. The first is sombre ("The night is calm") and the melody revolves around a b minor triad, with $f\sharp^1$ as the primary "reciting" note for the singer.

ex. 18-1

The second stanza is the most dramatic, with a large sweeping line (measures 25–41) still based on the arpeggiated b minor triad.

ex. 18-2

The third stanza (measure 43–end) moves to a climax followed by a descent and moving away at the end, and a balancing gesture is heard in the piano after the final vocal phrase.

ex. 18-3

The accompaniment adds a chordal foundation for the vocal line, but does not intrude. The stillness of the first stanza and the drama of the second are conveyed not through rhythmic changes but through subtle alterations of texture and dynamics. A more detailed study of the text would give greater insight into the composer's musical conception, and possibly explain why certain of his musical ideas are shaped the way they are.

Harmonically, the piece exhibits an apparent simplicity, but there are several intriguing features which may not be immediately noticed. The opening four measures are like a passacaglia/chaconne in their repetition; the measures 10–14 present new material, changing the premise. The alternation of these two harmonic areas provides the accompaniment for most of the piece.

The two important ideas of the opening are the *f♯* **pedal** in both hands and the intriguing chord in measure 3. The *f♯* pedal is a constant force until the climax in measure 41; it returns to haunt the ending as well, providing many harmonic possibilities along the way. The third chord of the piece is somewhat more difficult. On the surface it seems to be simply a III chord in b minor, but that has nothing to do with its real function. In broader terms it is a i chord, being a resolution of the preceding V chord. Obviously one can raise objections to this analysis on the grounds that there is no tonic pitch present in the chord. The ear, though, forms some fascinating perceptions in certain cases and, because of the first two chords, one might assume that the b is present in measure 3. The V chord, then, is resolved in measure 3.

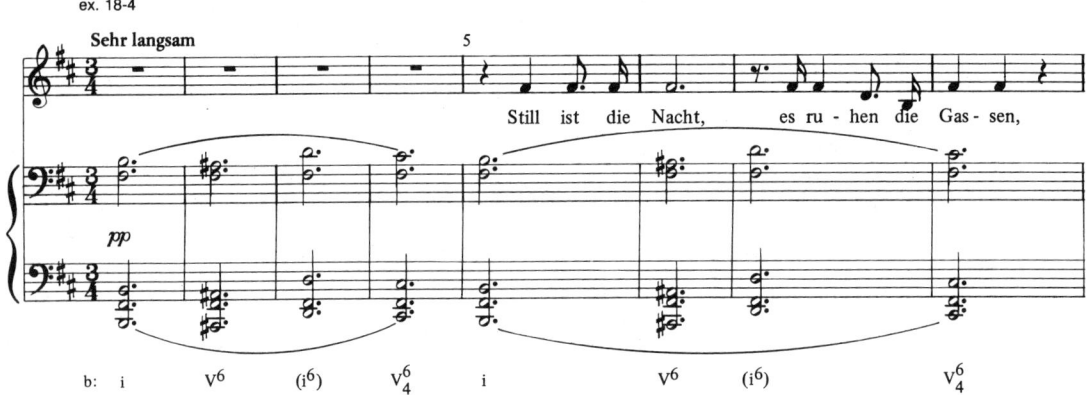

ex. 18-4

Three other areas of harmonic ambiguity occur in the piece, at measures 10–12, and measures 32, and 41. In the first instance a minor v chord moves by third relation to III and then proceeds by stepwise motion to V. All of this is accomplished not by functional motion but through linear means, very much like the **chordal mutation** found in the Beethoven example.

The second idea is similar, but functionally different. Note the harmony in measure 32:

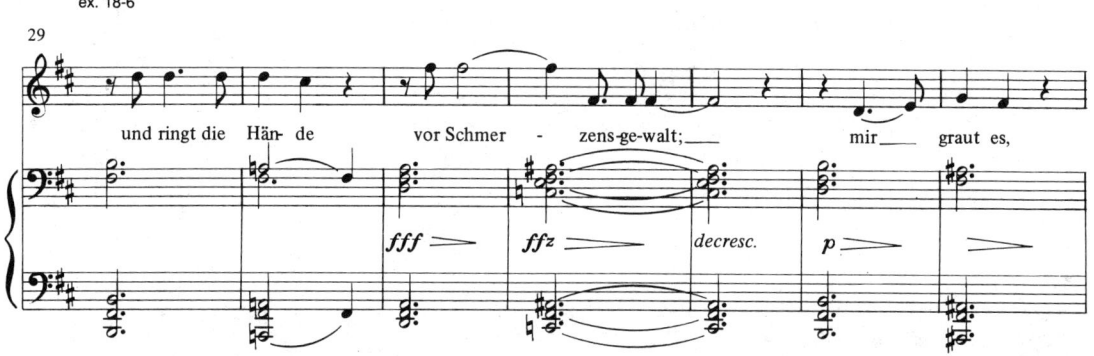

The construction is that of a French sixth chord. As we have seen, the French sixth is normally a ii$^6_{4\atop 3}$ chord that moves to V. Here, however, the French sixth moves to the tonic; its function in this case, then, is as a dominant. We call this type of chord a ***substitute dominant.***

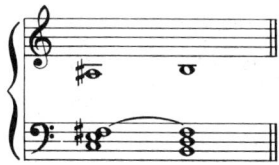

Like the Beethoven example, it has the function of a dominant chord but is differently constructed.

The same progression is displayed in measure 41, except that in this case the first chord is constructed like a German sixth chord. It should be noted, though, that the g acts as an extended upper neighbor and moves back down to the f♯, thereby creating a French sixth on the final beat of measure 42.

ex. 18-8

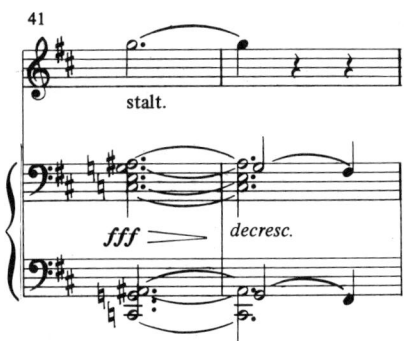

After the climax in measures 41–42, the harmony moves to a different key level for the only time in the piece, by means of a strong V–i cadence in d♯ minor. This chordal mutation is accomplished in a surprisingly smooth but dramatic way. The return to b minor is then brought about by the "proper" use of the German sixth chord in measures 51–52.

ex. 18-9

The ending phrase, for piano only, contains two harmonic ideas worth exploring. The C major chord in measure 59 has two possible functions: as a Neapolitan chord in b minor, or as a VI chord in e minor (a possibility that exists because of the motion to the level of e minor for a brief moment). If viewed as a Neapolitan, then it is in root position and does not move to V or i_4^6 in the normal way. If viewed as VI/e, then it makes functional sense in that it moves to V7/e and then to e ($_4^6$!). The retention of b minor is important to note, though. We have briefly tonicized the level of iv and not actually modulated to it.

There is the additional implication of the "double" image at the end. The *sub*dominant is emphasized here, as the dominant has been emphasized throughout the piece. This is Schubert's opportunity to point out musically the double image of the dominant as being the subdominant—the first being the chord a fifth above the tonic, the second the chord a fifth below the tonic. The other double image implied at the end is seen in the final B major harmony. A simple Picardy third gains in significance in view of the text, since it represents the other mode, the alternate image of the key.

ex. 18-10

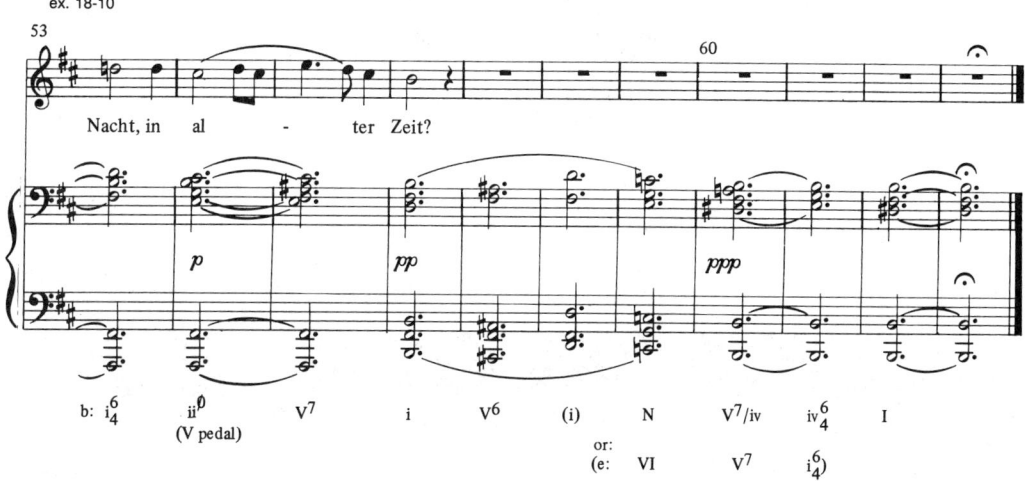

STYLE CHARACTERISTICS: EARLY NINETEENTH CENTURY
based on Schubert's songs

melody	relatively smooth and fluid, with few skips of more than a fifth • frequent melodic arpeggiation of triads • goal-oriented, moving toward and away from specific climactic points
harmony	functional • modulations to diatonic keys predominantly, though some further modulatory motion does occur • substitute dominants and passages of chordal mutation
rhythm	(vocal writing) primarily follows the rhythm of the text, but a rhythmic motive is usually developed • (instrumental accompaniment) fairly simple and repetitive, but subtly suggestive of ideas expressed in the text
texture	varies from very thin to quite thick • use of piano in mid-to-low range
form	(for songs) through-composed, strophic, ternary, binary (influenced primarily by the text)

Glossary

Pedal (pedal point) the sustaining or repetition of a single pitch, especially in the bass, while the harmony changes.

Strophic design use of the same melody and accompaniment for several stanzas of text.

Substitute dominant a chord that is not constructed as a dominant (V or V7) but functions as a dominant by moving to the tonic.

Through-composed without repetition of musical sections; particularly, with new music for each stanza of text.

Suggested Exercises

1. Compose a short strophic song in the style of Schubert. Include some use of substitute dominants as well as a short section of chordal mutation.
2. Discuss the use of text, melody, and accompaniment in the following song. Be prepared to discuss the reasons for its phrasing, sectional design, accompanimental textures, and basic harmonic features.

The Atlas

An ill-fated Atlas I!
The whole world of sorrows must I bear.

I bear the unbearable,
And my heart is fain to break within me.

Proud heart, you have indeed willed it so!
You wanted to be happy, infinitely happy,
Or infinitely wretched, proud heart,
And now you are wretched.

Before Reading Chapter 19

Listen to the second movement of Felix Mendelssohn's Symphony No. 5 (*Reformation*) (pages 86–99).

Symphony No. 5 in d minor ("Reformation")

MENDELSSOHN

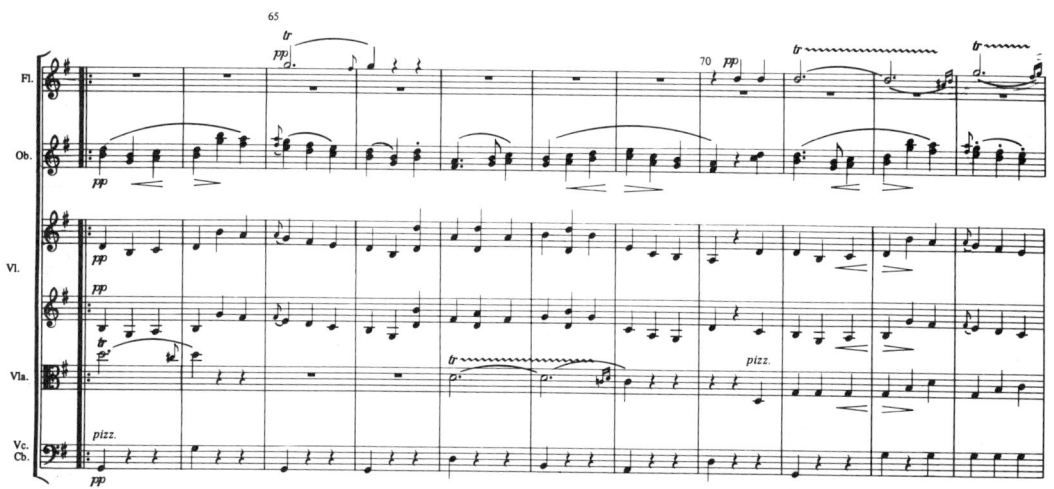

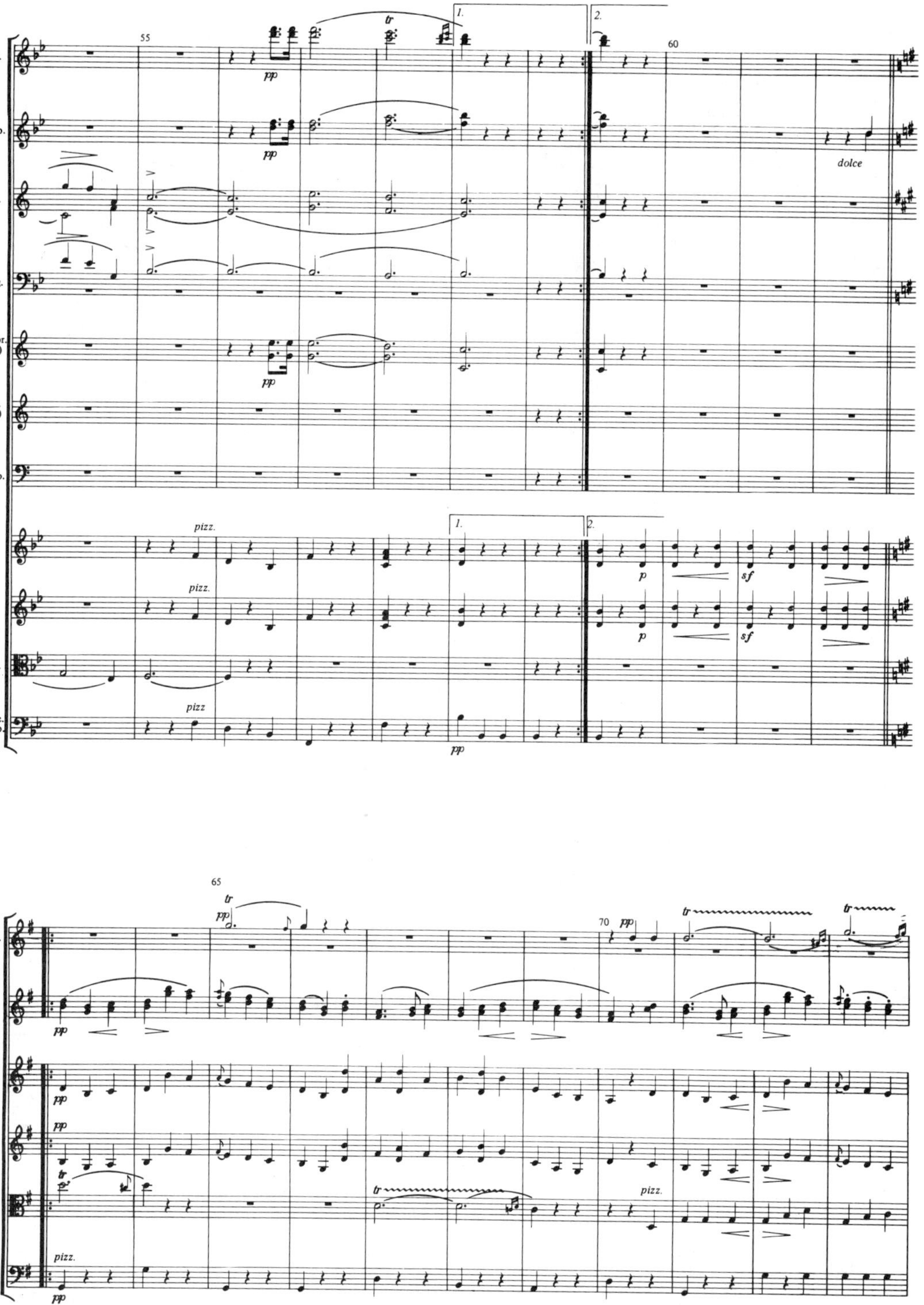
Fl.
Ob.
Cl.
Fg.
Cor. (B)
Tr. (Es)
Timp.
Vl.
Vla.
Vc. Cb.
55
60
65
70
1.
2.
tr
pp
p
sf
pizz.
pizz
dolce

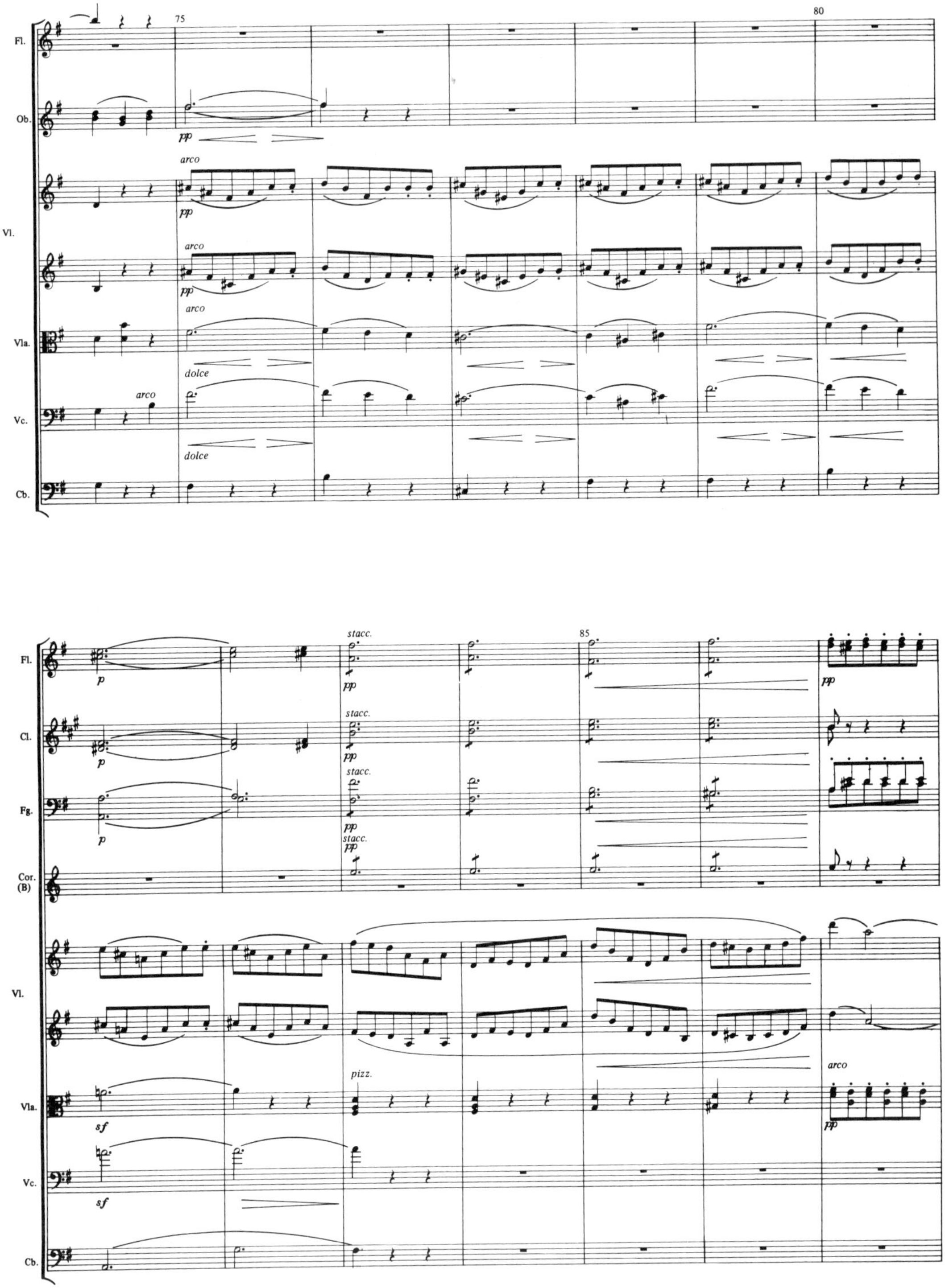
Fl.
Ob.
Vl.
Vla.
Vc.
Cb.
75
80
arco
pp
dolce
Cl.
Fg.
Cor. (B)
stacc.
pizz.
85
p
sf

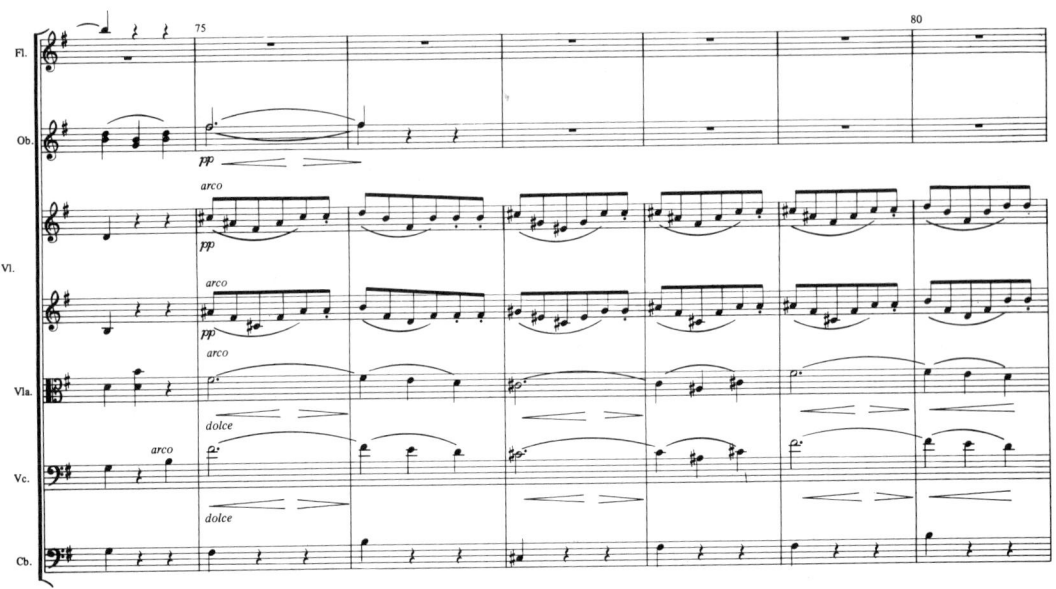

93

99

Felix Mendelssohn

Symphony No. 5 (Reformation), second movement

With the advent of the Classic era, the modern orchestra began to evolve. Before this time, ensembles consisted of small chamber groups or mixed large ensembles with no standard instrumentation. These ensembles gradually became centered around a core of strings in five parts: two violin parts, viola, cello, and double bass. In the earlier years of this development, the double bass part was usually only an octave doubling of the cello part. Winds were added when needed, but rather sparingly. The early orchestras usually had two oboes and two horns, with an occasional flute or bassoon.

In the course of the eighteenth century the orchestra took on a larger and more definite form. The standard score was arranged, from top to bottom, by four main instrumental "families": woodwinds, brass, percussion (usually only timpani), and strings. In the score, the highest-pitched instrument of each group appears at the top of each family, the lowest at the bottom. Partly for the sake of balance, partly because of convention, the winds are usually grouped in pairs. If a solo instrument is used, as in a concerto, it is placed below the percussion and above the strings.

Below is given the specific disposition of the instruments as found in the score of a late Classical symphony.

woodwinds { 2 flutes
2 oboes
2 clarinets
2 bassoons

brass { 2 or 4 horns
2 trumpets
(2 or 3 trombones, from early nineteenth century)
(tuba, from mid-nineteenth century)

percussion soloist   timpani (other percussion introduced in nineteenth century)

strings { 1st violins
2nd violins
violas
violoncellos
double basses

Here is a list of the instruments in English, Italian, French, and German, along with their abbreviations. You should be familiar with these in all forms.

English	Italian	French	German
flute (fl.)	flauto (fl. gr.)	flûte (gde. fl.)	Flöte (Fl.)
oboe (ob.)	oboe (ob.)	hautbois (htb.)	Oboe (Ob.)
clarinet (cl.)	clarinetto (clar.)	clarinette (cl.)	Klarinette (Kl.)
bassoon (bsn.)	fagotto (fag.)	basson (bon.)	Fagott (Fg.)
horn (hn.)	corno (cor.)	cor (cor)	Horn (Hr.)
trumpet (trp.)	tromba (tr.)	trompette (tromp.)	Trompete (Trp.)
trombone (trb.)	trombone (trb.)	trombone (tromb.)	Posaune (Pos.)
tuba (tuba)	tuba (tuba)	tuba (tuba)	Tuba (Tuba)
timpani (timp.)	timpani (timp.)	timbales (timb.)	Pauken (Pk.)
violin (vl.)	violino (viol.)	violon (von.)	Violine (Vln.)
viola (vla.)	viola (vla.)	alto (alto)	Bratsche (Br.)
violonello (vlc.)	violoncello (vlc.)	violoncelle (velle.)	Violoncell (Vcll.)
double bass (d.b.)	contrabasso (bassi)	contre basse (c.b.)	Kontrabass (K.b.)

As indicated above, the orchestra was enlarged during the nineteenth century. The winds were frequently augmented from pairs to threes with the addition of instruments such as piccolo, English horn and contra-bassoon; four horns became standard; harp was added on occasion. Although it is not apparent in the scores, the string section was increased to match these forces in the winds.

Because of basic limitations in the technical development of certain wind instruments, there is a need to use various instruments in different keys. Brass instruments, for example, because of the lack of valves at this time, could only produce the overtone series based on the key of the instrument. The C trumpet, for example, could play only the following notes reasonably well in tune:

ex. 19-1

Because of these acoustical handicaps, composers frequently requested instruments tuned in different keys; hence the numerous examples of ***transposing instruments.*** Even after the advent of valves, many composers continued to write parts in a variety of keys for natural horn and trumpet. Since most nineteenth-century scores do this, we must be able to transpose these parts efficiently. The following is a guide to figuring out how a given instrument sounds in relation to what is actually on the page.

clarinet: B♭ clarinet
            A clarinet

ex. 19-2

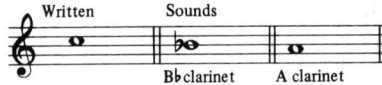

The B♭ clarinet sounds a major second lower than written; the A clarinet sounds a minor third lower than written. When *c* is written, it sounds its name.

horn: F horn
        E♭ horn
        E horn
        D horn
        C horn

When *c* is written, it sounds its name. Horns will *always* sound *below* the written pitch.

ex. 19-3

trumpet: A trumpet
           B♭ trumpet
           C trumpet
           D trumpet
           E♭ trumpet
           E trumpet
           F trumpet

When *c* is written, it sounds its name. Trumpets always sound in the register closest to the written pitch.

ex. 19-4

Two other instruments sound the written pitch, but displaced by one octave. The piccolo sounds an octave higher, the double bass an octave lower.

ex. 19-5

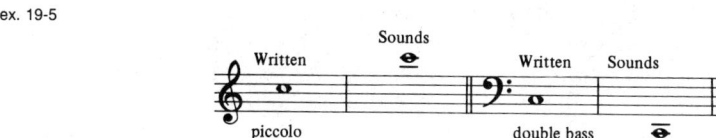

In the string section, the first and second violins frequently move together (in unison, parallel octaves, or in thirds or sixths) with the cello and double bass doubled on the supporting bass line and the viola providing the inner harmonic voices. A good example of this texture is at measure 17.

ex. 19-6

The sound is sometimes that of a four-part texture. Indeed, voice leading in the strings is often as careful as in a four-voice chorale, although the ranges are extended due to the greater capacities of the instruments.

In addition to chordal writing for the string section, there are numerous occasions for contrapuntal writing. In the passage beginning at measure 95 there is three-voice counterpoint, with the cello doubling the first violin at the octave. Before this, at 91, the strings alternate the melodic content and the winds provide the harmonic underpinning.

ex. 19-7

There are two instruments that sound the pitch given, but displaced by one octave: the piccolo part is written one octave lower than it actually sounds, and the double-bass part is written one octave higher.

In the second movement of the Symphony No. 5 by Felix Mendelssohn (1809–1847) we find a standard Classical orchestra.

The winds are used either in this way, as a harmonic support to a more melodic string passage, or to carry the melody themselves.

ex. 19-8

In some cases the winds double the string lines for power and support.

ex. 19-9

The timpani and brass, as seen in the previous example, are usually reserved for a few supporting notes only. In both the pitches available are severely limited—only two in the case of timpani and relatively few more in the trumpet. (Remember that we are discussing the situation in the late eighteenth and early nineteenth centuries only.) Both the horn and the trombone are more versatile, the trombone because of its slide, and the horn because of the expanded number of partials available in its upper register.

Note that the trumpet is used in this example only on three notes—*g, c,* and *e,* or, at concert pitch, *b♭, e♭,* and *g.* The horns are somewhat more flexible. The two timpani here have a fixed tuning on *d* and *a.* This is because the first movement is in D major, thereby emphasizing the tonic and dominant. Since the second movement is in B♭, the timpani uses the *d* as the third in a tonic chord and the *a* as the third in the dominant chord.

The overall sectional balance of the orchestra is admirably demonstrated by the *tutti* sections. The cellos and double basses are in the lower register along with the bassoons; the flutes and violins are in the upper register; the oboes, clarinets, trumpets, violas and horns fill in the middle register.

Suggested Exercises

1. Analyze the second movement of Symphony No. 5 for form and key structure.
2. Make a piano reduction of measures 160–172.
3. Provide a harmonic analysis of measures 63–90.

Before Reading Chapter 20

1. Listen to the Nocturne in D♭ Major by Frederic Chopin (pages 107–113).
2. Determine the basic sectional design of the piece, noting any repetitions.
3. Analyze harmonically measures 1–9 and 26–37.

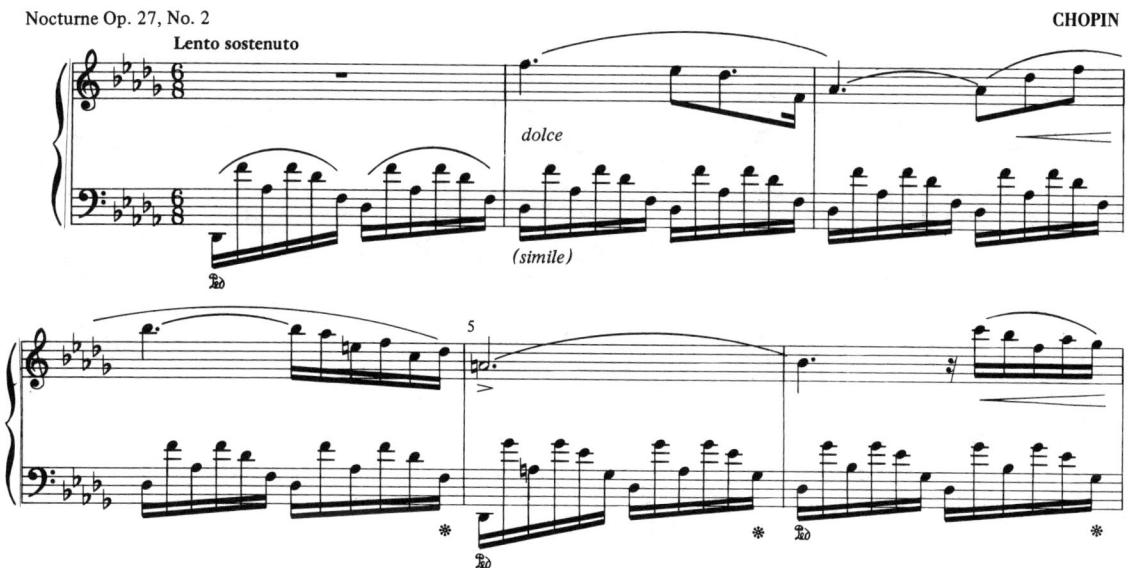

20

Frederic Chopin

Nocturne in D♭ major

The nineteenth century expanded the germinal ideas of Haydn, Mozart, and Beethoven. These were extended, modified, and developed in a myriad of ways. Chordal function, use of dissonance, and melodic-harmonic formations were extended and changed, producing a wholly different sound, but without destroying the underlying foundations laid in the previous century. Nineteenth-century music rests on harmonic and linear principles that had existed for perhaps 200 years; its special character lies in the use that is made of these developments.

Frederic Chopin (1810–1849) is the most important piano composer of the mid-nineteenth century. His enormous output helped to shape piano composition for the rest of the century. Both his technical use of the piano and his harmonic-melodic constructions are highly innovative. Among his eighteen Nocturnes, the one in D♭ major is a striking example of the exploration of piano timbre, technique, and harmonic and expressive range. Although simple on the surface, the work demands great subtlety of the pianist. The harmonic and melodic usage is at once simple and complex, requiring considerable analytical flexibility.

A notable feature of this piece is mode flexibility. ***Interchangeability of***

mode—the use of chords from both the major and minor modes within the same key—is a basic principle of the piece.

It is always necessary to keep in mind the chordal possibilities from the major as well as the minor mode when studying this piece, (and indeed a great many pieces in the mid-to-late nineteenth century).

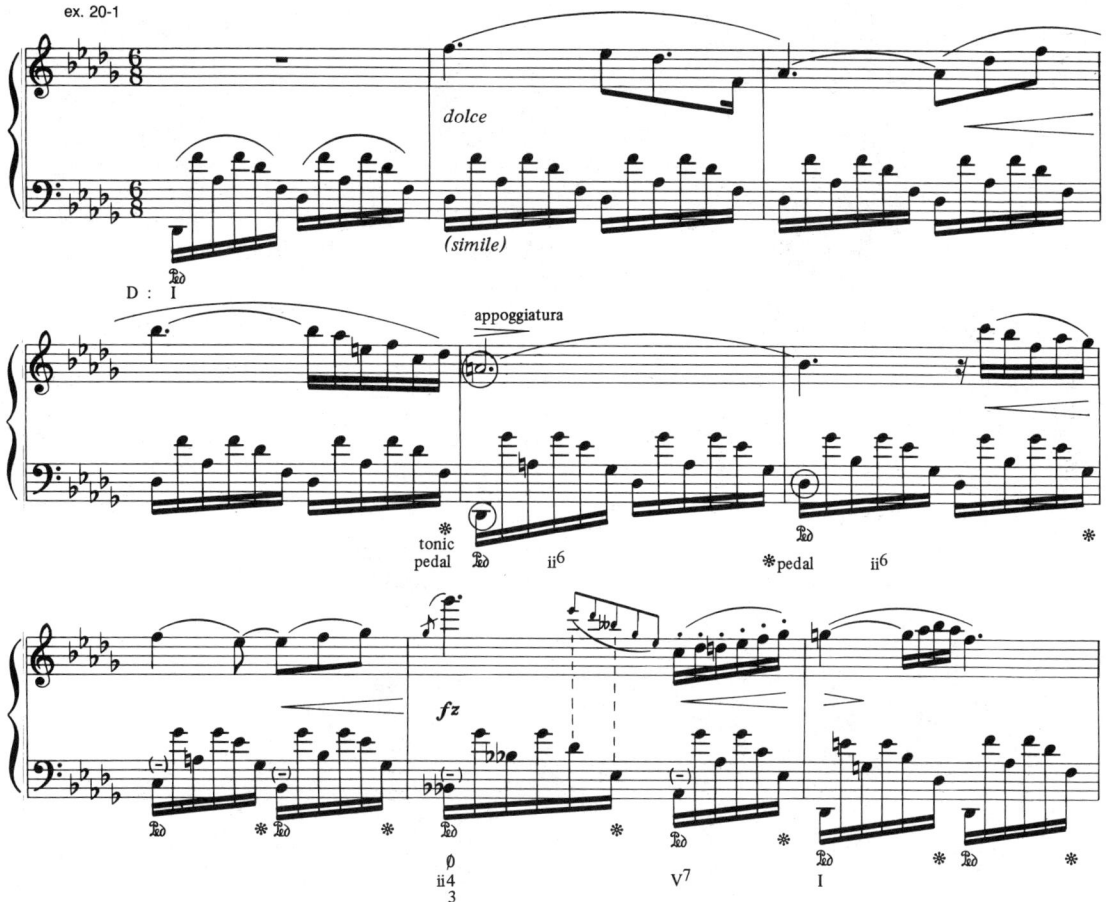

The fact that the key here is D♭ major in no way deters Chopin from using chords that normally would appear in d♭ minor. This ***bimodality*** is seen clearly in the opening measures.

ex. 20-2

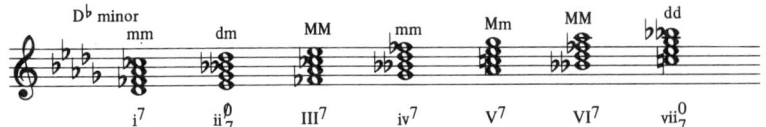

Notice that the first chord in measure 8 is ii$^{\varnothing}_{4\atop 3}$, a chord which would normally occur in the minor mode. The function of the ii chord has not changed, since it still resolves to V. However, the color of the chord is unusual in the major mode, and it is this subtle sound difference that is probably so important to Chopin.

In highly embellished piano works such as this, the extraction of harmony is often a problem. In this piece, it is eased by the broken chordal presentation in the left hand, an extension of the Alberti bass of the previous century. But one must be particularly careful of pedals—*inner pedals* as well as **bass pedals**—and passing notes when analyzing these works. The linear aspect of the harmony is in some cases as difficult as it is fascinating.

ex. 20-3

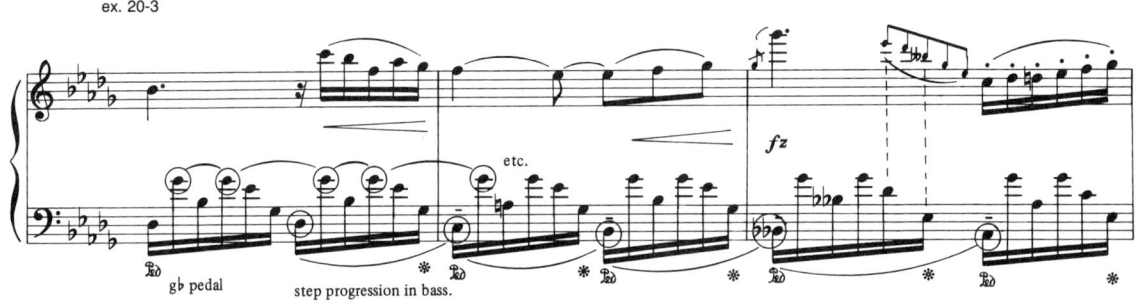

In the following passage, enharmonicism is a significant aspect of Chopin's thought.

ex. 20-4

It should be noted that the harmony of this passage is quite functional. The C♭ major chord (measure 22) is a secondary dominant, V_7/III in d♭ minor (F♭ being the third scale degree of d♭ minor). However, when the resolution occurs, in measure 23, it is spelled as an E chord rather than an F♭ chord. This chord of resolution is a dominant itself, because of the presence of the *d*, and it resolves properly to A major. In relation to d♭ minor, the A major chord is a VI chord—that is, it is enharmonic to B♭♭ major, the true VI in d♭ minor. The *a* in the bass becomes *b♭♭* and the chord likewise changes, to ii^6_5. This leads us back to V, and finally to the tonic. The purpose of all of this enharmonic activity is practicality, to avoid the constant use of double flats and notationally unwieldy chords. Below, the progression is given in both forms.

ex. 20-5

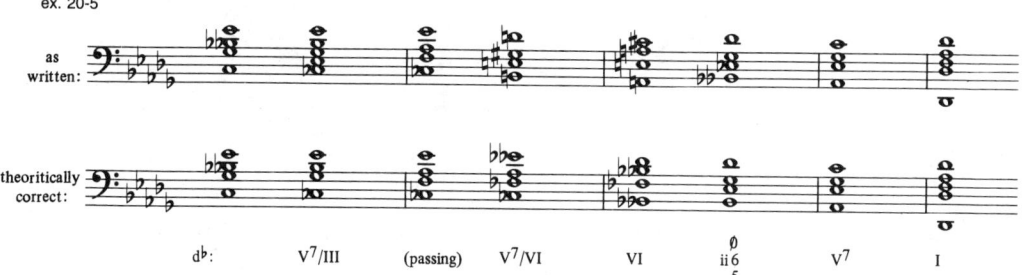

Another difficulty in analyzing nineteenth-century music is in the isolation of dissonances in the harmonic fabric. The dissonant notes are often emphasized by their duration; this rhythmic extension of dissonance may create an increased anticipation of the resolution, a marvelous feature of much nineteenth-century music. An important dissonance often used in this manner is the ***appoggiatura.*** Unlike the eighteenth-century appoggiatura, the nineteenth-century appoggiatura is a dissonance that is approached by leap and left by step, usually in the opposite direction. Note that it is rhythmically strong, usually appearing on the downbeat of a measure to produce an even greater dissonance.

ex. 20-6

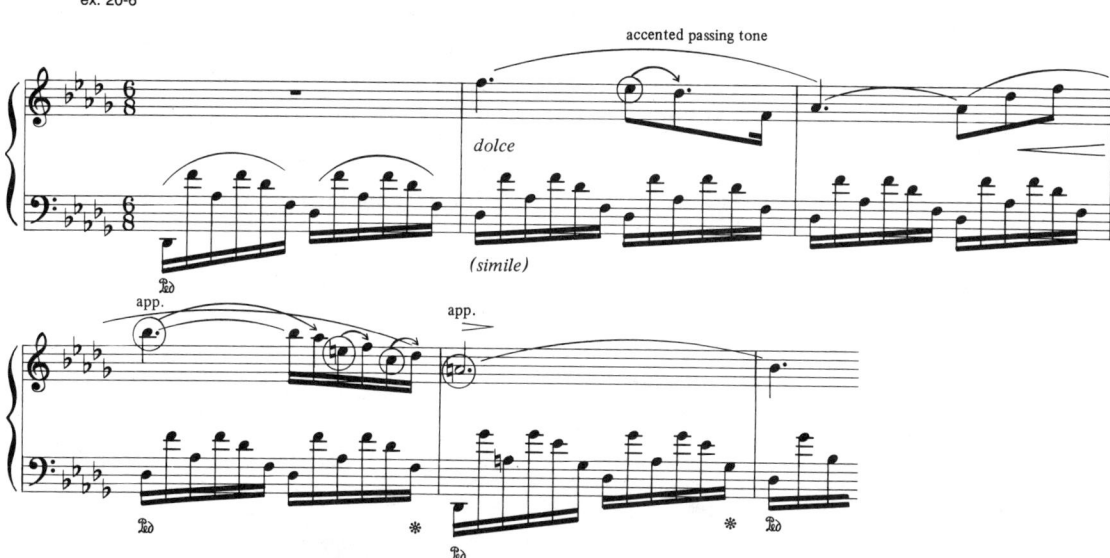

In this example there are two very short appoggiaturas as well as two that are rhythmically extended. The tension produced by these appoggiaturas, both long and short, is striking, and they form an important element in the characteristic sound of the piece.

In some instances the dissonances become the primary focus. In measures 8–9, for example, the harmonic content can be shown in the following manner:

ex. 20-7

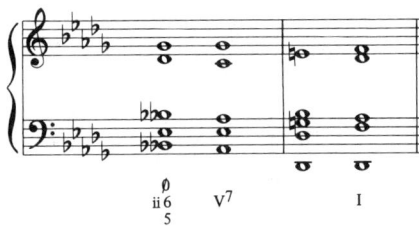

The first chord in measure 9 could be viewed in a variety of ways. It is almost totally dissonant, and its sound suggests multiple appoggiaturas. If one looks closely, however, certain details emerge that explain each pitch. There is one appoggiatura, a lower neighbor, and an escape tone.

ex. 20-8

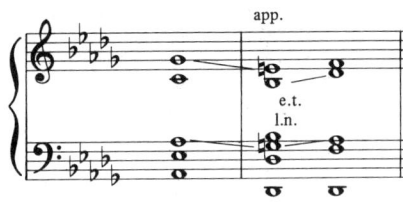

Is all of this detail heard as linear motion? Probably not on a conscious level. The overall effect is of a delayed resolution to the tonic chord. The resolution implied by the bass note $d^\flat$ is delayed in the other voices, with an effect of great poignancy. Both the strength and the duration of this kind of dissonance are hallmarks of nineteenth-century style.

Another use of dissonance must be discussed, if only briefly. The use of *fast, passing dissonance* in the right hand is most important in this type of piano writing. Above a solid harmonic basis in the left hand, Chopin adds an array of arabesques in the embellished melodic line. In much of the piece, the right hand moves rapidly, with runs and chromatic motion, including frequent dissonance. These surface dissonances, a very important component of the style and overall sound of the piece, do not interrupt the flow of the basic harmony.

ex. 20-9

A few extraordinary passages in this Nocturne indicate not only a change in harmonic procedures, but also a future development that will extend those procedures into the twentieth century. The tonal progression in measures 33–34 sounds quite logical to the ear, though it appears rather unusual on the page. This is an **enharmonic modulation,** similar to that seen in the second movement of Beethoven's *Pathétique* Sonata. Here, D♭ major becomes c♯ minor (=d♭ minor). The purpose for this is twofold: to simplify the notation and to ease the modulation to the level of VI, in this case A major rather than the enharmonic equivalent of B♭♭ major (with a key signature of nine flats!). The primary purpose is simplicity of notation. The actual sound remains quite conventional. It might be wise to compare this section with the transition back to D♭ major in measures 43–46. The procedure is smooth and technically facile, the work of a careful and skilled composer.

ex. 20-10

chordal mutation

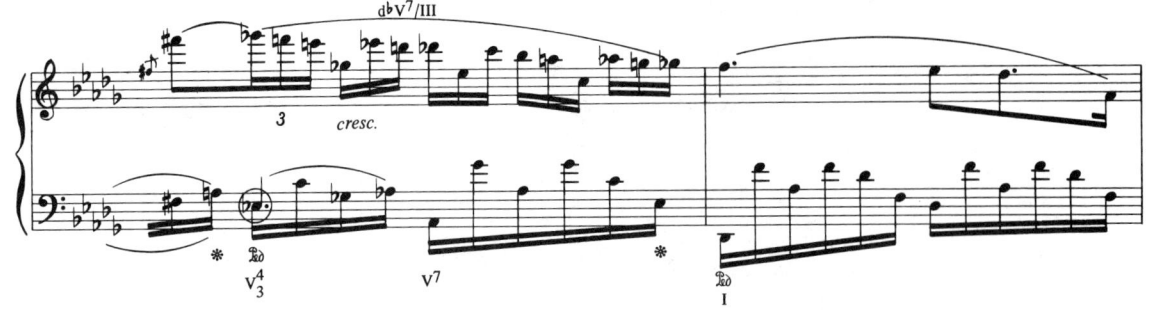

Another area of harmonic ambiguity occurs in measures 62–65 (and its embellished repeat in measures 66–69).

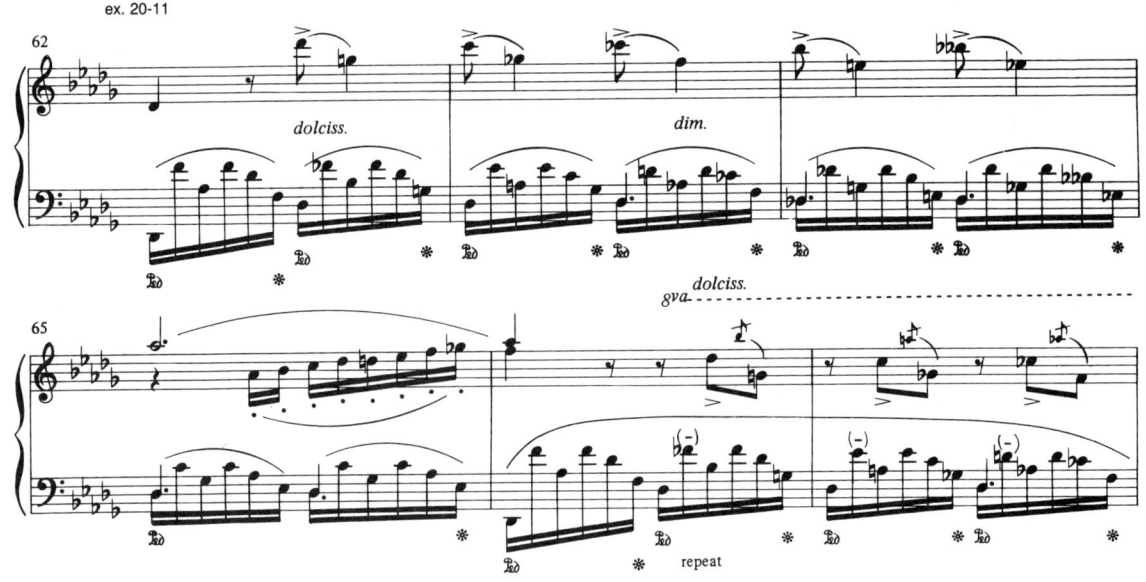

As can be seen, this section employs sequence, both melodic and harmonic, over a constant pedal $d\flat$. The chordal outline can be extracted as follows:

The general harmonic motion is from tonic to dominant and back to the tonic. The harmonies in between are passing chords which move gradually to the V chord in a linear fashion. **Chordal mutation,** or the nonfunctional use of chords, is a procedure seen before as early as Haydn, Mozart, and Beethoven. In this case we have a series of nonfunctional diminished-seventh chords (nonfunctional because they do not resolve properly). This particular technique, which will appear in later works as well, is sometimes referred to as ***planing.*** This refers to motion by a parallel sequence of chords which move as though on a plane from one point to another. Obviously, if this principle is carried to an extreme it can result in a very tenuous sense of tonality. Indeed, this is what tends to happen toward the end of the nineteenth century as the consequence of various factors. In this Nocturne, however, the bounds of the tonal framework of D♭ major are carefully observed.

The extension of the tonic in the final five measures (measure 73 contains V7 harmony over a tonic pedal; measures 74–77 remain firmly in the tonic) is followed by a cadence in the final two chords. Although theoretically a III$_6$–I progression, the aural impression of the penultimate chord is similar to a dominant. Play the last few measures and decide for yourself.

If this chord is analyzed as a V, then the notes need to be accounted for. By stacking thirds above the dominant, the chord can be derived:

ex. 20-14

This analysis is obviously open to question, especially because of the number of important tones left out (such as the third and seventh, both critical to the sound of a V chord). However, the progression does seem to imply this kind of analysis. The ultimate analysis is left to you, based on your own aural perception of the ending.

The Nocturne has an obvious rondo-like quality, with the theme of the first section being repeated almost unchanged at measures 26 and 46, and in a more variegated version at measure 58. The other sections, though, are not so easily accounted for.

Thematic variation tends to cloud the ***sectional repetition.*** If we remain flexible, however, it is possible to determine certain repetitions of basic material even when they are considerably changed. The second section comprises measures 10–22, with a transition in measures 22–25. This basic material is used again in measures 34–45 after the repetition of the opening theme. The treatment of the material here resembles a development of the material found in measures 10–22. Similar material can be found, in a shortened version, in measures 53–57, followed by a truncated repetition of the opening section. The final section (measures 62–end), an extension of the musical material with an extended cadence, functions as a coda.

The entire sectional design is as follows:

A	**B**	**A**	**C**	**A**	**B**	**A**	Coda
1–9	10–25	26–33	34–45	46–52	53–57	58–61	62–77
			(quasi-development)		(shortened)	(shortened)	

The basic form, then, is perhaps a large rondo. Variation is a strong underlying principle, while the rondo outline helps to hold the entire structure together.

Chopin's rhythmic technique shows several interesting features. The expansion of the "inside of the pulse" is evident throughout this piece, but especially in the **B** and **C** sections. The left hand controls the actual pulse, while the right hand is considerably freer.

There is a strong suggestion of improvisation in certain passages. The important theoretical principle here is the expansion of rhythmic exactitude and interest as well as the overall solidity of actual pulse.

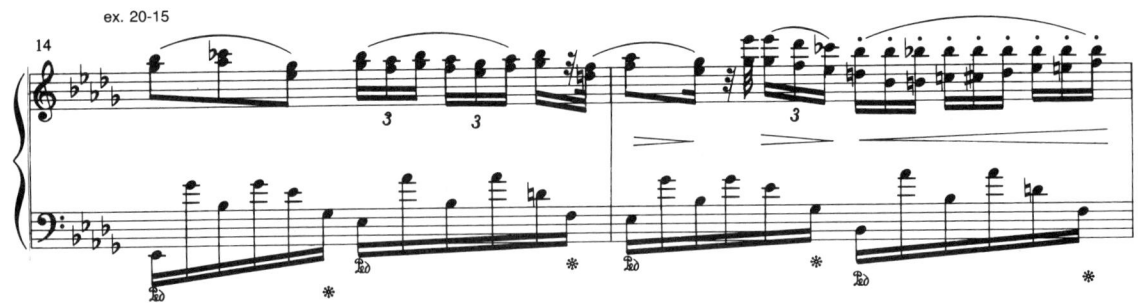

ex. 20-15

Chopin uses another rhythmic premise, **rubato.** Although many composers imply this kind of principle, Chopin brought it to a more important position in his works. It is difficult to describe fully, since it has much to do with traditional interpretative features. The basic concept is one of speeding up the tempo and slowing it down, or as Chopin described it, the expressive fluctuation of tempo in the right hand with a steady left hand. This rhythmic freedom of the right hand, with a more steady and controlled left hand, is an important style feature of Chopin.

STYLE CHARACTERISTICS: MID-NINETEENTH CENTURY
based on Chopin's Nocturne in D♭ major

> **melody**   can be either circumscribed within a relatively small range (usually when the rhythm is predominant) or broad, with large, sweeping motion and many leaps • strongly based on and generated by the harmonic content, with much use of triadic arpeggiation • extensive embellishment of fairly simple lines, by means of grace notes, passing and neighboring tones, etc.

harmony	basically functional • experimentation in bimodality, chordal mutation, and extended chords (ninth, eleventh, and thirteenth chords) • enharmonic, chromatic, and diatonic modulation • use of planing as a harmonic device
rhythm	(melodic) fluid, with long "improvisational" interpolations, embellishment, and use of rubato • (harmonic) fairly strict patterns, often with unvarying rhythm • overall, quite fluid and free, almost producing a cessation of pulse at times
texture	ranging over the entire keyboard • chords often spaced thickly in the middle range (from small c to e^2) and more sparsely at either extreme

Glossary

Appoggiatura (nineteenth century)   a dissonance which is rhythmically strong, and which is approached by leap and resolved by step, usually in the opposite direction.
Bimodality   the use of both the major and minor modes within the same tonality.
Chordal mutation   the non-functional use of chords, usually in a linearly directed fashion.
Pedals
   inner pedals   a held note within the chord.
   bass pedals   a held note in the lowest voice.
Planing   the succession of a series of chords of the same structure, all voices moving in parallel motion.

Suggested Exercises

Analyze the two following Preludes by Chopin. Deal with the harmonic aspect as well as other compositional procedures.

Prelude, Op. 28, No. 20

Prelude Op. 28, No. 6

CHOPIN

Before Reading Chapter 21

1. Listen to Richard Wagner's Prelude to *Tristan and Isolde* (pages 127–46).
2. Provide a piano transcription of the first 17 measures.
3. Write out all the significant motives.

TRISTAN AND ISOLDE, Prelude to Act I RICHARD WAGNER

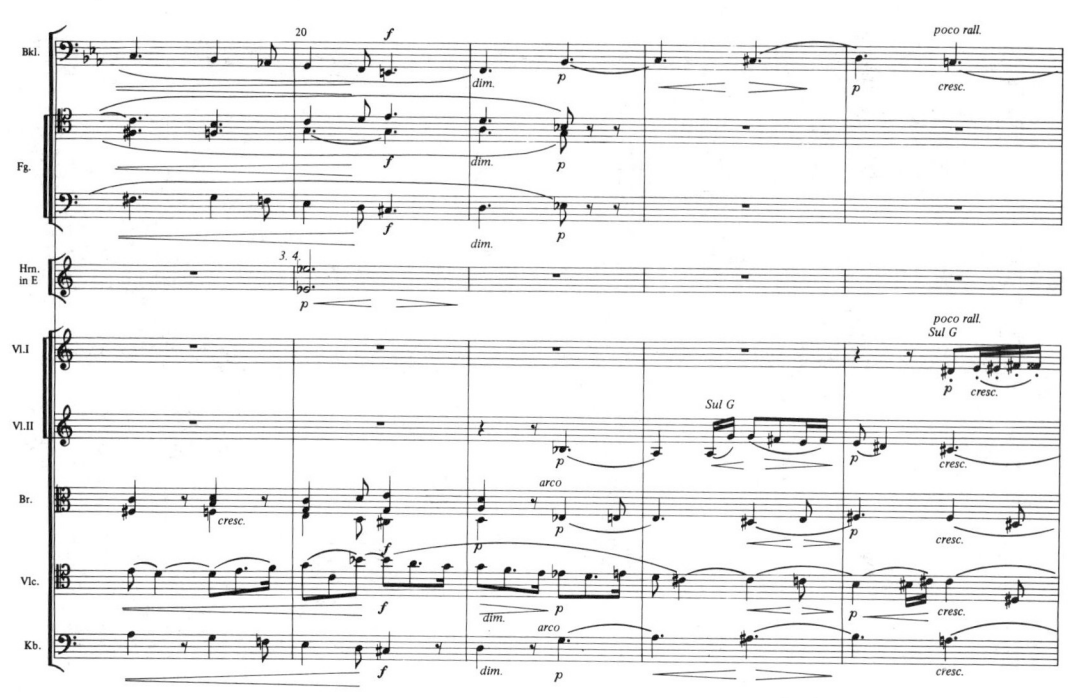

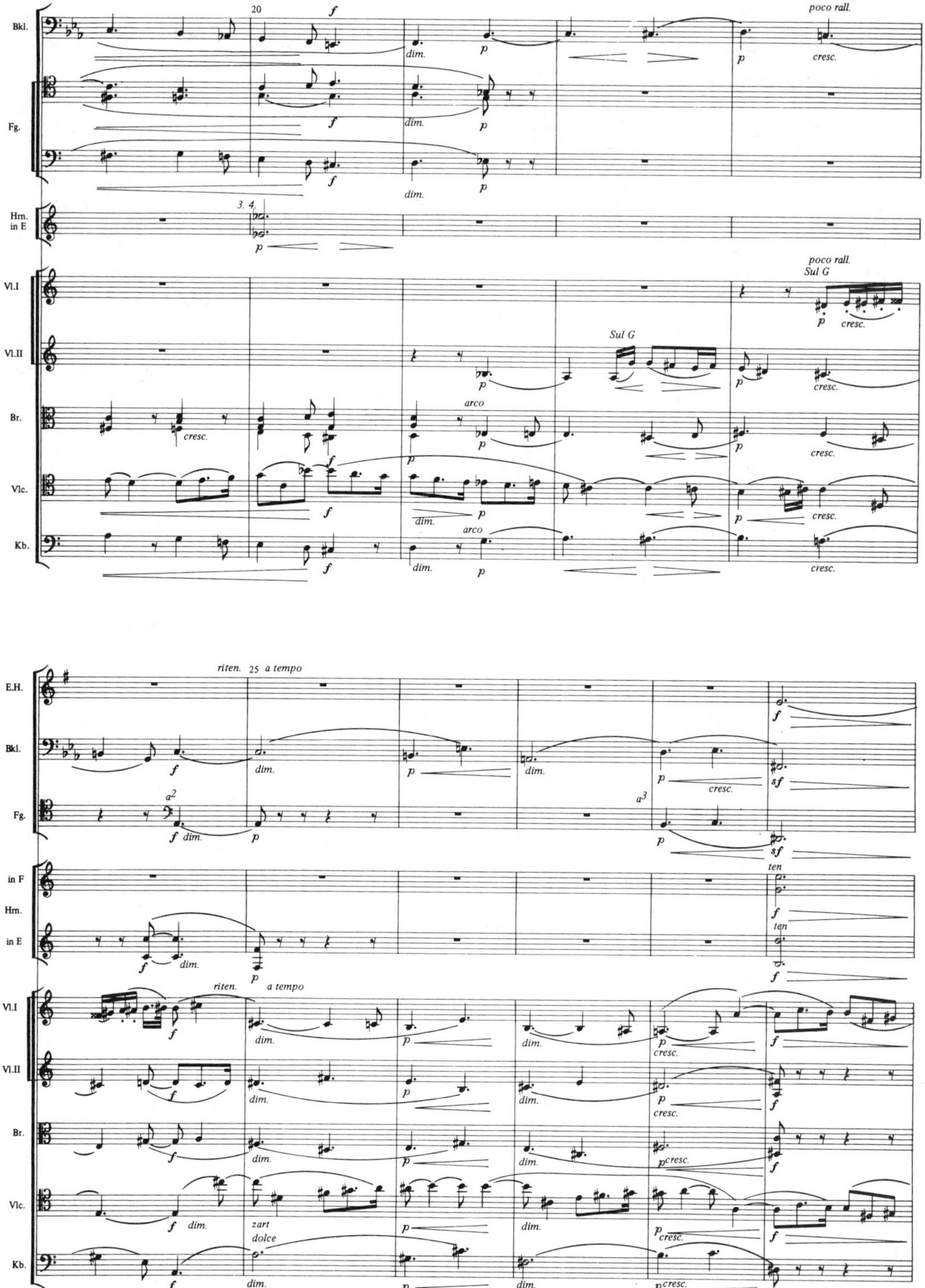
Bkl.
Fg.
Hrn. in E
Vl.I
Vl.II
Br.
Vlc.
Kb.
20
poco rall.
3. 4.
Sul G
arco
dim.
cresc.
E.H.
in F
Hrn.
in E
riten.
25
a tempo
a2
a3
ten
zart
dolce

133

141

21
Richard Wagner

Prelude to *Tristan and Isolde*

In the second half of the nineteenth century numerous changes took place in all parameters of music. There were two significant directions in which harmonic use moved both involving the use and development of chromaticism. First, there was an increased use of chromaticism, primarily in strong functional relations, often modulating frequently, obscuring the sense of key. In some cases this kind of highly chromatic writing utilized strong, prolonged dissonances that further obscured the harmony and its ultimate functional goal. A second type was a direct offshoot of the concept of chordal mutation. In this case there is a broader functional direction, without the chord-by-chord functional usage. This type of harmony could also occur in highly chromatic settings or in almost totally diatonic ones. Each type of harmonic expansion helped to redefine harmony, and shape areas of development in the early part of the twentieth century.

Richard Wagner (1813–1883) was an extraordinary force in the music of his time and one of the most important figures in the redefinition of harmonic principles. Throughout his work one can find an expansion of the basic functional system of earlier composers. At the same time, it can be observed that in most cases the harmonic motion follows the overall tenets of that older system.

In Wagner's music the functional attributes of chords are stretched, expanded, obscured, and embellished, but rarely destroyed.

One of the most discussed and analyzed pieces from the late nineteenth century repertory is the Prelude to the opera *Tristan and Isolde*. The amount of interest in this piece is justified by its extraordinary expansion of harmonic and melodic technique. When analyzed carefully, it can be seen to be almost totally functional in its chordal usage. Still, the large array of obscuring dissonance, the constant chromatic modulation, and the frequent deceptive cadences produce a perfect touchstone for the period.

At first glance even the opening of the piece is harmonically obscure. However, by recognizing the elongation of the appoggiaturas and the use of chromatic passing tones, the opening predicts the sound of the entire opera.

ex. 21-1

From this point onward, Wagner shifts key centers rapidly and without warning. Certain keys seem to be favored (especially am, CM, EM, and AM—all related by third) but the ***modulatory motion*** is both fast and surprising. With this in mind, let us look at the first thirteen measures.

ex. 21-2

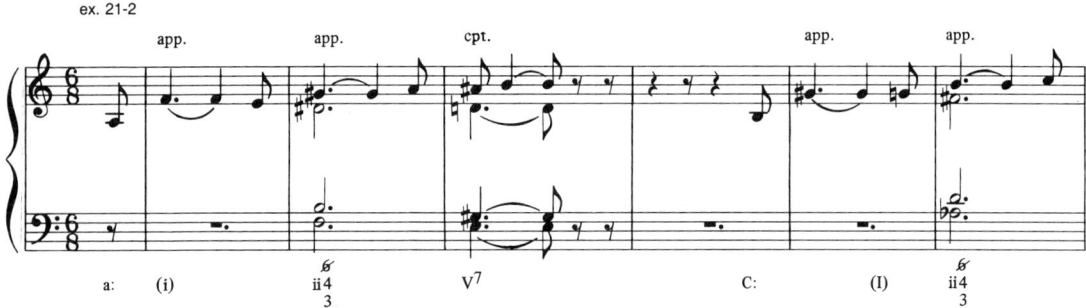

The opening three measures are simply extended and repeated in three key areas, a, C, and E.

The *length of the dissonance* as well as the amount in these few measures is substantial. Dissonance is, without a doubt, the backbone of Wagner's style. Without it the impetus and flow of the harmony would be greatly impaired.

Two harmonic techniques are particularly important to Wagner's style: the deceptive cadence, especially those in which he employs harmonies from both modes, and the progression by third relation.

We can see the deceptive cadence employed here so as to effect a modulation by third—A major (implied) to C major. This is accomplished by the progression from V of A major to F major, or VI of a minor (measures 16–17). This F major acts as a pivot chord to C major; what follows is motion to d minor and finally back to A major for the only strong cadence in the section (measure 24).

ex. 21-3

In this example the tonal motion is not obscure, but the speed of that motion—the harmonic rhythm—is quite rapid. In addition, the number of chromatic passing tones, appoggiaturas, and other dissonances is remarkable. The general feeling evoked is one of constant evolution, with no solid key center on which to depend. This feeling is produced not only by the fast harmonic rhythm but also by the avoidance of strong cadences as a result of deceptive motion or quick modulation to a new key center. The only rhythmically strong cadence in the entire section is in measure 24, from which point Wagner moves rapidly to a new key.

ex. 21-4

As can be seen in these measures, the emphasis is initially on E, the dominant of A and the third above C. Beginning in measure 31 the motion is to d minor, with an unusual passage of nonfunctional chromatic motion in measures 32–33. The shift to the flat side is accomplished by motion through C major, F major, (with hints of d minor, f minor) and g minor; the progression continues to an A/E axis before moving (measures 43–44) to c♯ minor, avoiding a cadence on that harmony by means of a deceptive cadence.

This is one of the most complicated sections in the entire Prelude. The concentrated dissonances, the rapid shifts of key, and the frequent unresolved V chords all help to produce the fluid motion of which Wagner is so fond. Because of the linear chromaticism one is tempted to say that the entire piece is melodically derived and leave it at that. Indeed, melody probably provided the initial impetus for this music. But the harmonic shape and flow is equally convincing in its functional use, as can be seen by the above analysis.

Measures 45–62 can be seen as a repetition of the preceding section, followed by a passage of sequence and a short area of chordal mutation. The student is encouraged to discover the harmonic content of measures 63–72 on his own.

The following harmonic reduction might be a useful guide to the difficult passage in measures 73–83.

ex. 21-5

This whole section is an elaborate transition, designed to bring us back to the opening material (which is essentially repeated from measure 84 to the end of the Prelude) and to develop in various ways the material previously introduced. Although complicated on the surface, the harmonic progression from measure 76 is mostly ii or V function. The g minor chord in measure 76 (approached via vii$^{\varnothing}_7$/d, which resolves to d, leaving the *g* and *b♭* in place) becomes the pivot chord which helps to establish *b♭* as the tonic:

$$\begin{array}{llll} & \text{gm} \!-\!\!-\! & \text{cm} \!-\!\!-\! & \text{a}^{\varnothing}_7 \\ \text{B♭:} & \text{vi} & \text{ii} & \text{vii}^{\varnothing}_7 \end{array}$$

This is repeated, using harmonies from the minor mode (measure 78):

$$\begin{array}{llll} & \text{c}^{\varnothing}_7 \!-\!\!-\! & \text{a}^{\varnothing}_7 \!-\!\!-\! & \text{F}_9 \\ \text{B♭:} & \text{ii}^{\varnothing}_7 & \text{vii}^{\varnothing}_7 & \text{V}_9 \end{array}$$

When we actually arrive on B♭ in measure 79, via the French sixth *c♭-e♭-f-a*, the addition of *a♭* to the B♭ major chord establishes it as the dominant of E♭.

Why did Wagner move to the V7/e♭ in this manner, and what was the reason for the choice of E♭ major? We may assume that Wagner was fully aware of his goal in measure 84, the V7/a, and we may also assume he had an idea as to how to reach that goal. To bring back the motive from the Prelude's opening required reaching the French sixth *f-a-b-d♯* in measure 83. This could be accomplished in the same manner as in the opening of the piece, by using a *g♯* appoggiatura. If one compares the first and last chords in measure 83, the clue can be found:

ex. 21-6

They are enharmonically equivalent. In addition, the first chord can function with little difficulty as ii$^{\varnothing}_7$ in the key of E♭. (This is precisely the same formula followed in measures 77–78 on the level of B♭.) The addition of *a♭* to the B♭ major chord in measure 79 is required to create the chord progression ii$^{\varnothing}_7$—V$_7$ in E♭ major. The ii$^{\varnothing}_7$ provides the *a♭* needed for the eventual enharmonic change to *g♯*, which then becomes an appoggiatura and resolves to *a*.

ex. 21-7

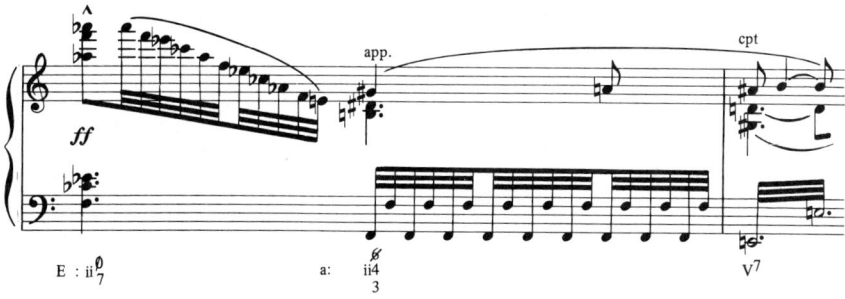

From the preceding we get a glimpse of the basic harmonic thought process of Wagner, and essentially of all tonal composers, that of projecting harmonic goals over a large time span. Bach, Mozart, and Beethoven all project their tonal thought process over large spans, and this concept is still used in the twentieth century, albeit in a slightly different guise.

The ending of the Prelude is very much like the beginning. The same motives are used, and the texture is much thinner than in the dramatic middle section. Harmonically, much the same material is used, with great emphasis on the French sixth chord and much use of appoggiaturas. The Prelude ends, however, not in a minor but in c minor. The ending is a simple line, but it implies much harmonic content.

ex. 21-8

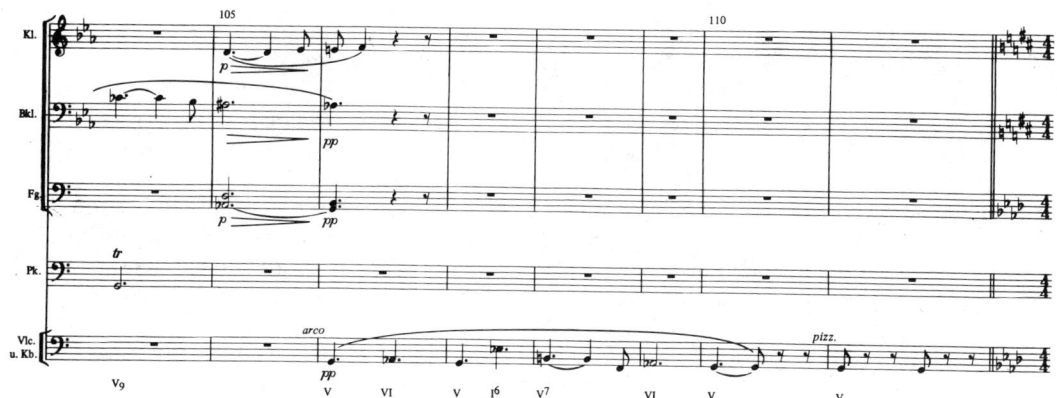

Two other aspects of the piece should be mentioned. The use of the orchestra and the system of *leitmotiv* structures are both of primary importance to Wagner's thought.

Especially in his later operas, Wagner uses a highly organized system of motives, many of which have a specific reference to a person, idea, or object. In the present example at least three such ***leitmotives*** are used (there are various opinions on the actual number, as well as their meaning).

ex. 21-9

Love potion motive

a.

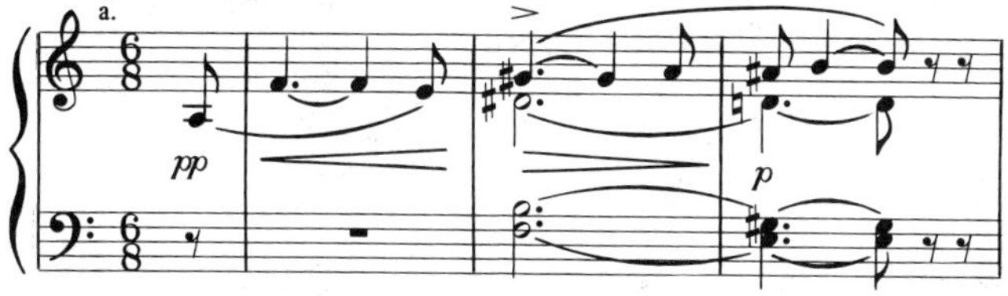

Longing motive I

b.

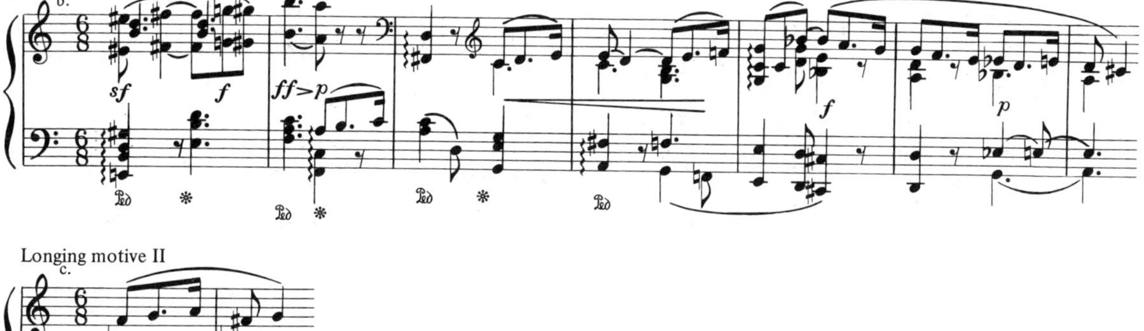

Longing motive II

c.

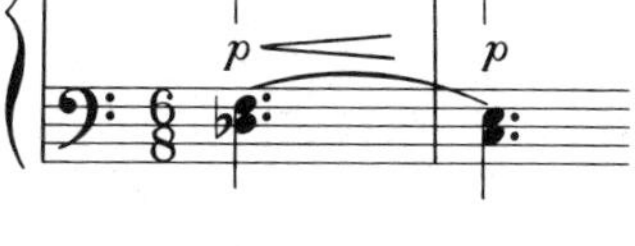

These motives, and many others which are used in the opera, influence the melodic and contrapuntal flow, permeating every stratum of the music. They exercise a decided influence on the harmonic structures as well. Though it is always difficult to determine whether a composer's original conception is rooted in harmony or melody, the important use of the leitmotiv strongly suggests that Wagner was initially concerned with melody. His strong harmonic instincts, however, are evidenced by those motivic ideas which seem essentially harmonic in formation. This essential interplay of harmonic and melodic ideas is the heart of Wagner's compositional process. The melodic ideas, through the extension of the leitmotives, are merged with the everchanging and modulating harmonic structures.

The three basic motives are marked in the extended excerpt following. They are used both individually and contrapuntally. The combination, juxtaposition, and constantly evolving use of the motives creates a great intensity of sound at the climax of the Prelude.

By the late nineteenth century there are many **changes in the use of the orchestra.** The concepts of orchestration expanded to include numerous new sound combinations, created both by new combinations of instruments and by the addition of new instruments to the orchestra. It is now common for an orchestra to use three flutes, two oboes plus English horn, two clarinets plus bass clarinet, three bassoons (with one often alternating with contrabassoon), four horns, three trumpets, three trombones, and tuba, as well as an enlarged percussion section, and a harp. Although it is not apparent in the score, the string section was also considerably enlarged to balance this increase in the wind section. This is precisely the orchestra used in the *Tristan* Prelude.

ex. 21-10

A few transposing instruments which appear in this score were not discussed in Chapter 18.

ex. 21-11

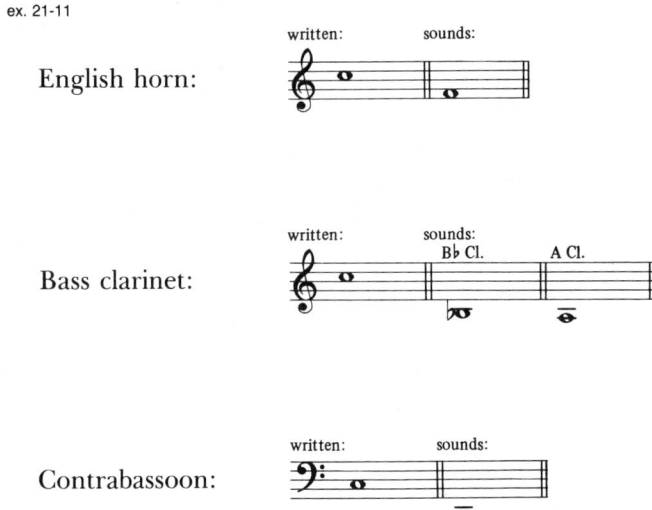

The additional instruments provide the composer with expanded resources and spark the imagination, not only with possibilities of larger sound, but with the fascinating sound combinations now possible. A beautiful example of the use of color by doubling of unlike instruments can be seen in the oboe, clarinet and horn in measure 32.

Another use of orchestration, one of considerably more power, is found in measures 73–83. Note the various usages of instruments:

—very solid bass line (in double bass, bassoon and trombone), to outline firmly the important harmonies
—the extended range of the violin
—the expanded linear function of the brass from earlier scores, especially in horns and trumpets
—the viola tremolo
—doublings in strings and winds, both at unison and octave

STYLE CHARACTERISTICS: LATE NINETEENTH CENTURY
based on Wagner's Prelude to *Tristan and Isolde*

    melody   chromatic, sweeping, usually conjunct, but employing larger intervals for dramatic passages • wide range, sometimes covering as much as three to four octaves (for instruments) • highly motivic, especially in the later operas • motives developed through extension and manipulation

harmony	primarily functional, but extended radically through quick modulations, use of secondary function, chordal mutation, and altered chords • speed of harmonic rhythm dramatically increased along with an increase of chromaticism • linear considerations important to the harmonic flow
texture	a much fuller texture than those of previous composers; range extended, partially as a result of the extended orchestra • thickest texture in mid-range (c to e^2), but outer limits also used frequently, especially by the strings

Glossary

Leitmotiv   a musical motive which depicts a specific idea or character, usually within an opera; used extensively by Wagner.

Suggested Exercises

Analyze the following passage from the ending ("Liebestod") of *Tristan and Isolde*.

Richard Wagner 169

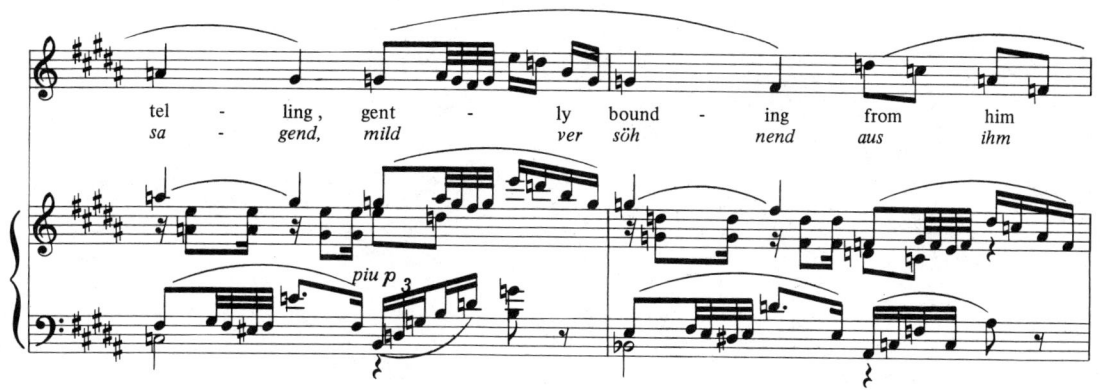

Before Reading Chapter 22

1. Listen to the Intermezzo in A major by Brahms (pages 171–75).
2. Bracket the phrases throughout.
3. Analyze the key structure.
4. Listen again, giving special attention to phrase lengths and rhythm.

INTERMEZZO (Op. 118, No. 2) **BRAHMS**

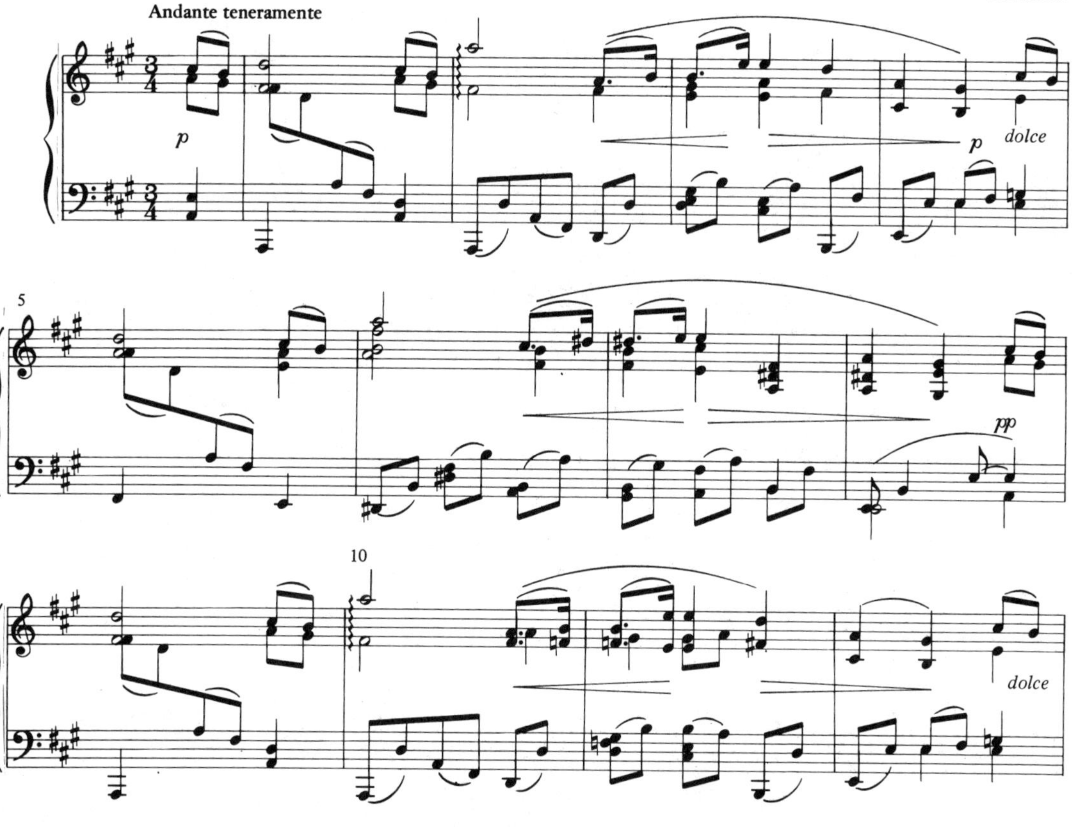

Johannes Brahms

Intermezzo in A major, Op. 118, No. 2

As though to counter the radical Romantic thrust of Wagner, there arose another trend in the late nineteenth century, a renewal of certain principles of classicism. Johannes Brahms (1833–97) is often described as a classicist because of his clear harmonies (at least by comparison with Wagner) and his distinct formal designs. But although these both are essential to his musical language, Brahms remains a Romantic composer, even while his temperament moves him in different directions than many of his contemporaries.

The present Intermezzo is one of many character pieces for piano in which Brahms explored the world of the diminutive. The musical gestures are not large, but the shaping and control of the harmonic and rhythmic language creates an intensity of expression rarely encountered elsewhere.

The opening conveys the impression of clear, straightforward **harmonic content** and stable phrase structure. The harmonic progression in the opening two phrases is clearly functional, with a moderate harmonic rhythm, and noticeably lacks the intense chromaticism of Wagner.

ex. 22-1

Beginning in measure 15 the harmonic motion is logical to the ear, but the individual chords do not seem to move in the expected functional manner. Two new factors come into play in this section. One is the use of bimodality, with frequent borrowings from the minor mode, even including an implied cadence on the minor tonic in measure 24. The other, equally important factor, is the emphasis on linear motion in favor of strict harmonic function. This is a form of chordal mutation in some cases and extended passing tones or chords in others.

ex. 22-2

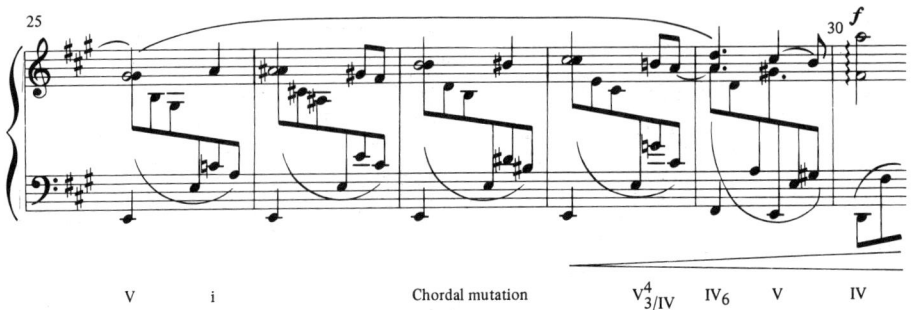

V   i   Chordal mutation $V^4_{3/IV}$ IV_6 V   IV

As the example demonstrates, the overall directional goals of the piece are always implicit. The use of **pedals** and linear chromaticism is a reflection of that directional consideration, using means other than strict chordal function. Measures 25–29 are an extension of this principle. They employ both features prominently—the dominant pedal in the bass indicates the projected direction (toward the tonic), while the **chromatic step progression** of the top voice adds the linear impetus.

ex. 22-3

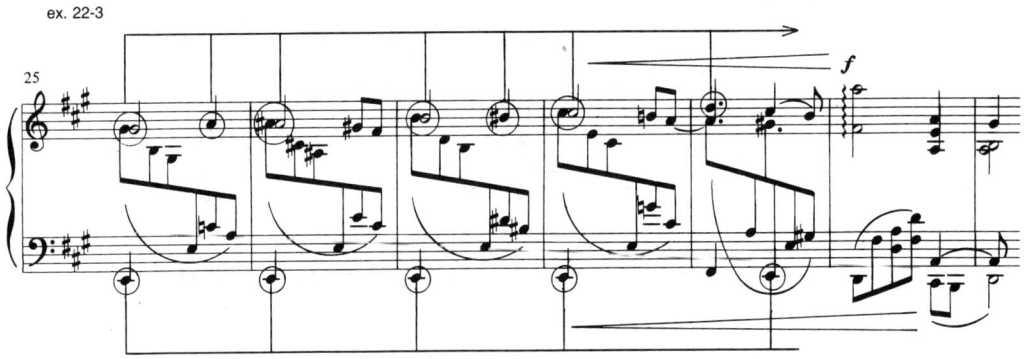

Thus, although the beginning of the piece is fairly straightforward harmonically, the further into the piece we progress, the more chromatic and complicated the harmony becomes. In fact, strict chordal function is all but lost in the passage before the repeat of the first section in measures 29–30.

The middle section of the piece (measures 49–76) presents several similarities to the first section. The first phrase, measures 49–56, contains few difficulties.

ex. 22-4

The second phrase, measures 57–64, introduces harmonic difficulties that stem from a focusing on linear motion. An $a\sharp$ inner pedal is retained for several measures against the soprano and bass lines (both of which are doubled at the octave). This emphasis on the melodic aspect maintains musical motion forward, but undermines the chord-to-chord function of the piece.

ex. 22-5

The momentary *enharmonic change* in measure 59 should be mentioned briefly. The shift from sharps to flats, not noticeable to the ear, is primarily for notational reasons. The progression c $\emptyset\atop{6\atop 5}$–F–a♯ is in fact a cadence on a♯ (b♭): ii$\emptyset\atop{6\atop 5}$–V–i. The complexities of notating this totally in a♯ (b♯ $\emptyset\atop{6\atop 5}$–E♯–a♯) led Brahms to this enharmonic solution.

Brahms's overall use of harmony, in this piece as in many others, is a fascinating combination of strong functional relationships mixed with functional ambiguity. In addition, the phrases are usually marked off by strong cadences, often ii$6\atop 5$–V–I.

An important, though peripheral, study relates to the actual spacing of the notes within the chords. In many cases Brahms uses spacing as part of the musical projection of the phrase. In the first section, for example, the chords increase in their thickness, within each phrase, defining the cadence in each case. There is finally a textural change in measure 16–17. This "thin-to-thick" concept helps define the stress content of each phrase. Notice also that the notes added thicken both the top and bottom register. Indeed, there are many closely spaced chords in the left hand in the lower part of the piano, creating a warm, dark quality.

One of the most remarkable aspects of the music of Brahms, and that of late-nineteenth-century composers in general, is his *use of rhythm.* Both on the phrase level and on the level of the individual pulse, the rhythm is constantly in a state of flux. Many phrases are regular, with lengths of four or eight measures.

ex. 22-6

Others change size and shape freely, producing irregular time spans and *shifting the metrical units.*

ex. 22-7

On a lower level, it is informative to examine the combinations of pulse arrangements. A fascinating spot occurs in the middle section (measures 49–56).

ex. 22-8

The pulse grouping of the left hand tends to weaken the notated meter, while the right hand reinforces it strongly.

right hand pulse groupings: 3   3   3   3   3   3   3   3
left hand pulse groupings: 1+2   2+1   2+1   2+1   1+2   2+1   1+2   3

The slurring tends to reinforce this rhythmic/metric counterpoint between the two strata.

An additional metric complexity occurs in measures 57–64. There is a strong sensation of **hemiola** throughout this section. The metric shaping of $\frac{4}{4}$ can easily be heard within the $\frac{3}{4}$ context.

ex. 22-9

The overall structuring of the piece demonstrates formal logic at each level. As noted before, the first two sections—measures 1–48 and 49–76—are structured in very similar ways. Each consists of three subsections arranged in an **A B A** design. The first subsection of each (two phrases long) strongly establishes the key (A major and f♯ minor respectively). The second subsection (also two phrases) explores new tonal realms, with much linear/chordal mutation. The third subsection is a repeat of the first with some minor changes (especially at the cadences).

Perhaps the most striking formal feature of the Intermezzo is that its overall form is the same as that of each of its sections: **A B A**. The **A** section explores the realm of A major while the **B** section moves to different tonal areas (f♯ and a♯), only to return to the familiar **A** material, which is repeated with minor modifications.

STYLE CHARACTERISTICS: LATE NINETEENTH CENTURY
based on Brahms' Intermezzo in A major

melody	primarily diatonic and smooth lines, with stepwise and third motion • occasional use of larger, dramatic leaps
harmony	emphasis on diatonic harmony, with modulation to diatonic areas • chromatic harmony and chordal mutation used in transitions • enharmonic and chromatic modulations
rhythm	expansion and contraction of phrases • primary emphasis on four-measure phrases • use of hemiola and shifting meters
forms	binary, ternary (in small piano pieces) • sonata-allegro, rondo, variation, scherzo (in larger, symphonic works)

Suggested Exercises

Provide a complete analysis of the following Intermezzo by Brahms. Indicate the following:

a. harmonic use
b. rhythmic use
c. phrase structure
d. sectional design

INTERMEZZO (Op. 76, No. 7)
Moderato semplice

Johannes Brahms **185**

Before Reading Chapter 23

1. Listen to *La Cathedrale Engloutie* (*The Sunken Cathedral*) by Claude Debussy (pages 185–90).
2. Bracket the sections throughout.
3. Identify the primary motivic/melodic material.
4. Determine basic "key" centers throughout.

La Cathedrale engloutie

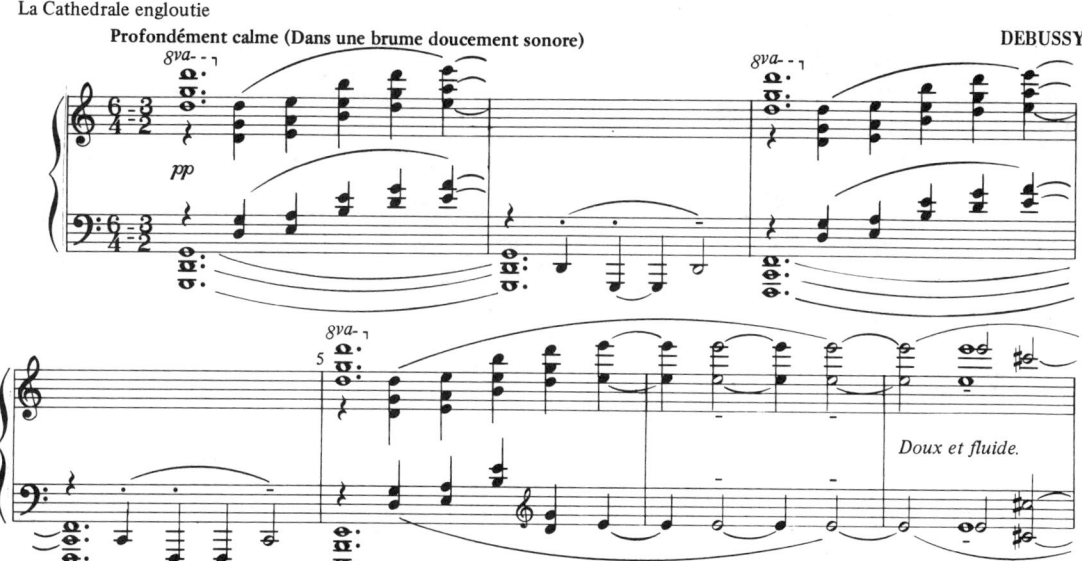

23
Claude Debussy

La Cathedrale Engloutie (Preludes, Book I, No. 10)

    The late nineteenth century and early twentieth century saw profound changes in the conception and use of musical space. The extension of some of these musical concepts led to a redefinition of musical sound.
    Two essential concepts which had formed the foundations of music for more than three hundred years were called into question and consequently redefined: tonality and chord function. The entire hierarchical arrangement inherent in the use of key centers and chord-to-chord functionality was altered in drastic ways. As has been noted, tonality was in a state of flux for much of the late nineteenth century. Wagner's use of tonality, in particular, became so flexible and tenuous that one key would hardly be suggested before another had usurped it. This tendency pushed tonality to its extreme. It developed in two distinct directions, sometimes even within the same composer's works: 1) adherence to a firm tonal center (or scale) with little or no modulation, and 2) absence of a specific, single tonal center, employing instead a succession of tonal centers throughout, with ample chromaticism. Both can be found in the works of Claude Debussy (1862–1918) as well as in those of Stravinsky, Ravel, and Bartók.
    The change in specific chordal function is perhaps more crucial to the sound and progression of the piece. As we have found in earlier music, both the

specific construction of chords and the manner in which these chords are used largely determine the overall sound of a piece. Two general types of chordal formation are widely evident in the music of the early part of the twentieth century, and in Debussy's music in particular: those derived from a particular melody or motive, and those based on superimposed thirds, with or without added tones.

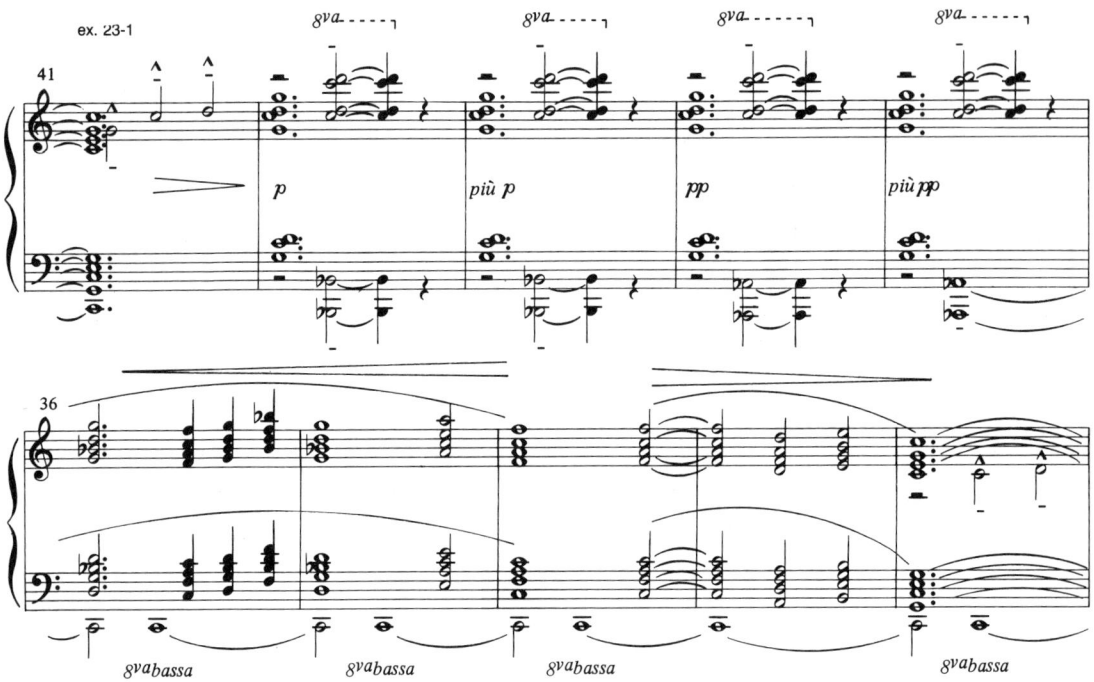

The use of either type is determined by the musical requirements of a piece. In the abstract, these are only sound sources, with no specific musical purpose; thus, they are always flexible.

Debussy's chords can usually be derived from thirds or from melodic intervals, and are used functionally or nonfunctionally depending on his purpose within a given work. This can be observed in *The Sunken Cathedral*.

The piece begins with an open fifth, followed by the intervals of the opening melodic ascent (second, fifth, third, and second).

Claude Debussy **193**

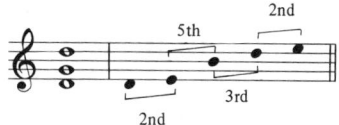

This ***intervallic premise*** will become important later in the piece for both harmonic and melodic motivic development. It can be seen in measures 16–17.

Note that the melodic line is virtually intact (though transposed to the level of B) and the harmonies reflect that melodic premise.

Beginning in measure 28 there is a shift into tertian harmonies. Although all of the harmonies are triadic, the melodic idea is derived from the opening second/fifth combination, sometimes substituting a fourth for the fifth.

The harmonic premise shifts back to the second/fifth combination in measure 42 (the transition to the next section) and is used in this melodic/harmonic combination throughout the section from measures 47–71.

Triadic harmony is again exploited in measures 72–83—over a multiple pedal in the left hand all of whose pitches derive from the opening motive.

ex. 23-7

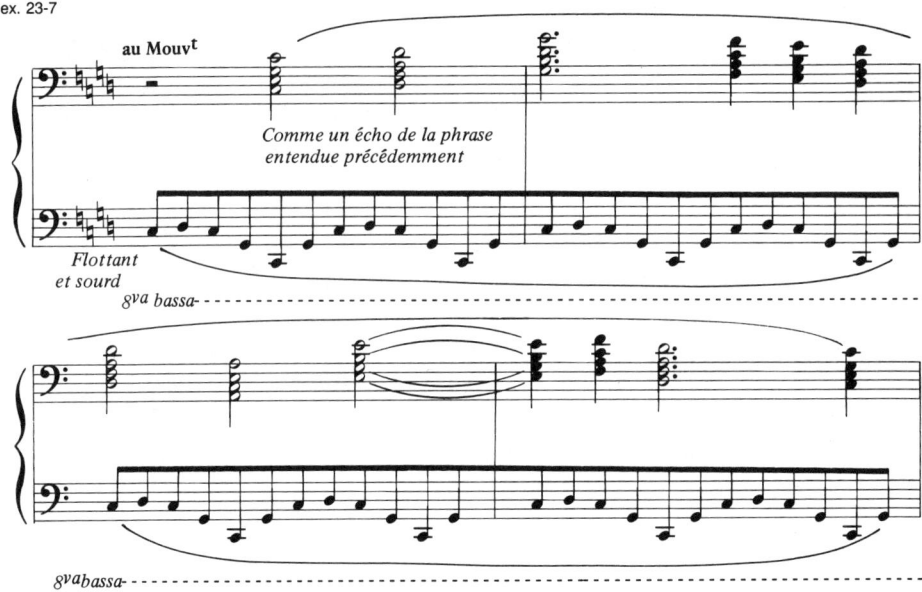

The ending brings us back to the material from the beginning of the piece.

ex. 23-8

The piece, therefore, is divided into sections based on two distinct harmonic constructions, tertian-derived or melodically-derived. Each produces a characteristic sound. There is no attempt at functional progression in the traditional sense. The primary chordal motion, regardless of the basic harmonic construction, is that of *planing,* or parallel chord motion. Measures 28–30 provide a clear example of this principle.

ex. 23-9

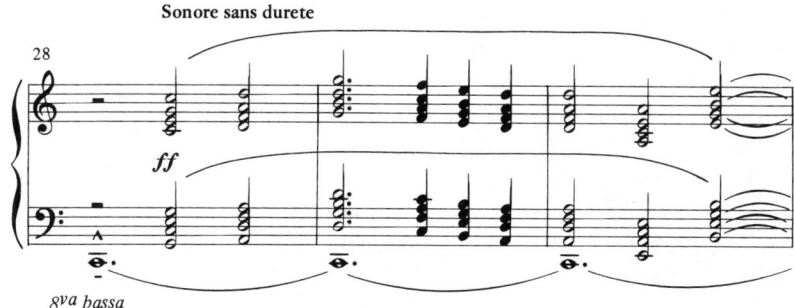

Although planing produces a strong sense of motion from one point to another, the root movement is not derived from or related to functional chord motion. Sonority and line, rather than specific tonal function, are the important ideas.

There are several different types of planing, depending on the kind of scale used. Diatonic planing is given above. Notice that although all these chords are triads, their quality changes depending on their position in the diatonic scale. Planing based on the pentatonic scale produces varying constructions because of the gap in the scale. If a construction of 1-3-4-5 is chosen, then the extension of this would be 2-4-5-1, 3-5-1-2, and so on. Notice how the harmonic structure changes in each case.

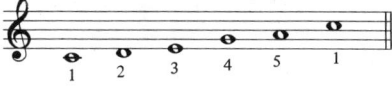

Real planing preserves the original intervals precisely throughout.

The combination of planing and the consistency of the melodic/harmonic constructions produces a strong sense of harmonic logic throughout the piece. Intervallic consistency is one of the hallmarks of the twentieth century, seen here in one of its earlier manifestations.

The opening motive can be traced throughout almost every measure of the piece. In some manner, either melodic or harmonic, that fragment permeates the entire piece. In addition, the shape of the completed phrase (measures 14–15) is the general shape of most succeeding phrases and sections.

ex. 23-10

The multiple permutations of the interval structure of the first measure in the intricate and facile compositional technique of Debussy.

Another facet of Debussy's technique is his **use of pedal points.** Pedals have been used for centuries, but they gain a new significance in Debussy's works. The opening of this Prelude uses a pedal that gradually moves from *g* to *f* and then to *e*.

ex. 23-11

This *e* is held for a considerable time in several registers, with a melodic idea moving around it, before continuing downward to *d* and finally to *c*.

ex. 23-12

This descant establishes the important tonal levels of the piece: G, E, and C.

ex. 23-13

The later sections of the piece are constructed from two ideas found in the beginning.

ex. 23-14

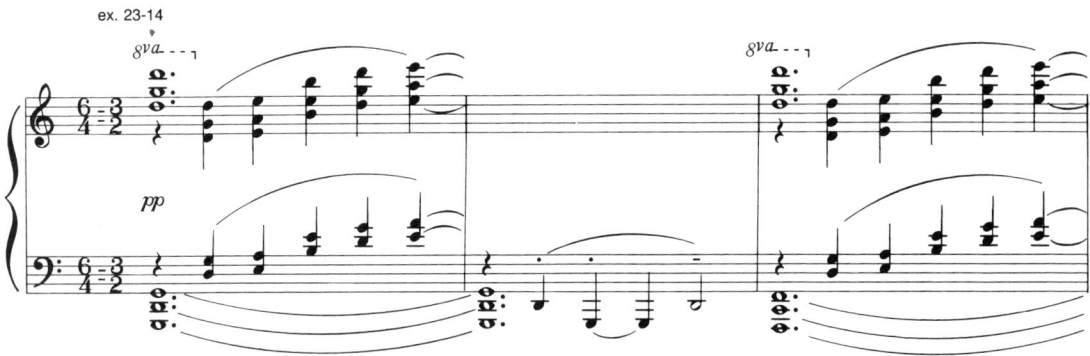

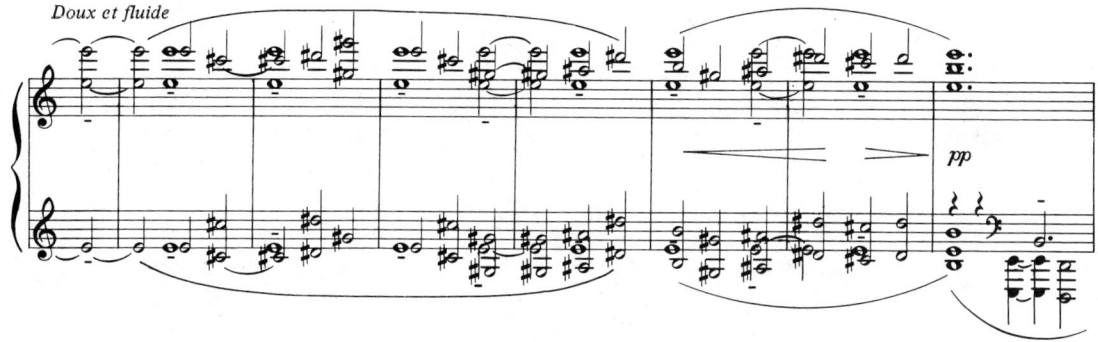

A third idea is presented much later, in measure 28, and is freely derived from the opening melodic idea.

ex. 23-15

Measures 14–22 are essentially based on developments of the opening harmonic motive. The melodic idea in measures 7–13 returns in measures 47–72, somewhat extended and developed. The third idea (measures 28–41) is repeated from measure 73 to the end, above a bass arpeggiation.

The entire structure can be outlined as follows:

A	transition	B	A'	A''	transition	C	transition	B	transition	C	A'''
1–4	5–6	7–13	14–15	16–22	22–27	28–41	42–46	47–67	68–72	72–83	84–89

Although this is not a traditional formal plan, there is a certain resemblance to the earlier rondo forms. Certainly, the principle of repetition is extremely important. More than anything else, it is the differing uses of harmony that establish and differentiate the individual sections.

The piece has an obvious *programmatic intent.* The story goes that at certain times of day the ancient, submerged cathedral at Ys rises out of the water, amid the singing of the monks and the sounding of the bells. Musically, Debussy has captured many of these sounds, or at least impressions of them. The opening, with its spacious setting, depicts the vast cathedral, and its bells are heard in the bell motive, *D-E-B*. The shape of the bell–motive is used throughout the piece, as well as this bell-like sound itself. From the bell fifths at the beginning to the bass arpeggiation in measure 72, the cathedral-like arch is evident throughout.

ex. 23-16

Perhaps the most important programmatic technique is the modal usage, especially prominent in the middle section of the piece. In apparent imitation of singing of the monks, the melody soars in a chantlike manner. This melody is in the Mixolydian mode, transposed to the level of C.

ex. 23-17

Although this particular modal reference probably has programmatic purposes, Debussy frequently explores various kinds of scales, those of the church modes being prominent among them. The numerous examples of modal usage seen throughout Debussy's works represent one way of extending and exploring tonality without completely abandoning it.

An additional aspect of Debussy's harmonic style is that of **added tones.** In some pieces the "color" of the chord is determined not so much by a melodically derived construction but by a tertian basis with added notes, i.e. added seconds, fourths, sixths, sevenths or ninths.

ex. 23-18

In this case the spacing of the chord is often crucial to both perception and analysis. The technical basis could sometimes be a seventh or ninth or eleventh chord in an inversion, but the spacing precludes that analysis because of the strength of the root in the bass.

ex. 23-19

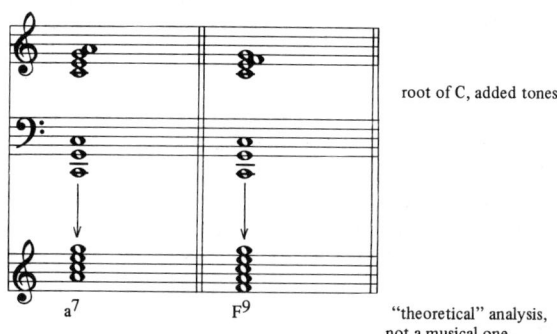

root of C, added tones

"theoretical" analysis, not a musical one.

In addition, multiple added tones also can create interesting colors.

Debussy frequently uses scales other than those of the church modes and the major and minor modes. His other scale patterns include the pentatonic and whole-tone scales.

ex. 23-20

The pentatonic scale shown here is the traditional one found in numerous of Debussy's works. Since the term merely means "five-tone," however, various other pentatonic constructions are obviously possible.

Although Debussy rarely used either of these scales in a straightforward manner, they are often employed fleetingly or used as the substructure of a passage. A good example of the use of these scales is the famous piece for solo flute, *Syrinx*.

STYLE CHARACTERISTICS: LATE NINETEENTH AND EARLY TWENTIETH CENTURY
based on Debussy's *La Cathedrale Engloutie*, and *Syrinx*

melody	tends to be fragmentary, constructed motivically • often based on scales other than major and minor, particularly modal, pentatonic, and whole-tone scales
harmony	two basic types: harmony derived from a melodic line, often emphasizing one or two intervals, and expanded tertian harmony, with the use of added tones • some references to tonal function, particularly at strong V–I cadences • extensive use of nonfunctional planing
rhythm	frequently regular • in orchestral scores, mixture of regularity and overlapping rhythms in accompanimental figures • a wide range of subtle rhythms, in motivic arrangements, seen in slow pieces, often approaching a nonmetric, almost arhythmic sound
texture	extended ranges of instruments • two basic textures: fairly thick, with expanded harmonies, and extremely thin, usually emphasizing extreme ranges, with large spaces between pitches or chords

Glossary

Added-tone harmony   tertian harmony to which notes have been added, such as a second, fourth, sixth, or seventh.

Arpeggiated pedal   a multiple pedal which is sustained through the repetition given each note by arpeggiating; usually found in piano writing.

Pedals
  inner pedals   a held note within the chord.
  bass pedals   a held note in the lowest voice.

Pentatonic scale   a five-note scale; usually equivalent intervallically to the scale $d^\flat - e^\flat - g^\flat - a^\flat - b^\flat$.

Planing
  diatonic   planing that employs only the tones of the diatonic scale.
  real   planing that is intervallically strict.
  pentatonic   planing that employs only the tones of the pentatonic scale.

Tertian harmony   harmony constructed by superimposing thirds above a given pitch.

Whole-tone scale   a scale using only whole tones. There are only two whole-tone scales, one including the notes $c-d-e-f\sharp-g\sharp-a\sharp$, the other including the notes $d^\flat-e^\flat-f-g-a-b$. All others are duplications of these, beginning on different pitches.

Suggested Exercises

1. Write a piece for piano in the style of Debussy, using the technique of planing, with added tones and modal or whole-tone usage. It should be approximately 25–30 measures long, in two or three distinct sections. Special consideration should be given to tonal orientation in each section.

Le fille aux cheveux de lin

© 1910 from PRELUDES, BOOK I
Durand S.A. Used by permission of the publisher,
Theodore Presser Company, Sole Representative U.S.A. and Canada.

2. Write a short piece for solo flute, solo violin, or solo clarinet, using as a basis the whole-tone scale, pentatonic scale, or a combination of modal scales.

Before Reading Chapter 24

1. Listen to the second movement of the *Symphony in Three Movements* by Igor Stravinsky (205–19). (Review the transpositions for A clarinet and French horn.)
2. Note the use of scale patterns throughout.
3. Identify the major phrase endings and consider the harmonic content of each cadence.

206

Claude Debussy

Claude Debussy 211

Claude Debussy

Claude Debussy **219**

Igor Stravinsky

Symphony in Three Movements, movement two.

    In the early twentieth century, composers experimented with various tonal and expanded tonal ideas. Pieces were written which radically extended the chromaticism of the late nineteenth century; others sought to further explore diatonicism, but with no less radical an approach. There were pieces which followed the concept of harmony derived from melodic/intervallic premises, as well as works which were more linear/scalar in orientation.

    Igor Stravinsky (1882–1971) experimented throughout his life. Always ready for a radical change in his style, he led the musical world more than once in establishing the "new." One of his several stylistic changes occurred in the early 1920s, with the composition of the *Octet for Wind Instruments.* This important style, to which Stravinsky was to return on numerous occasions, entailed the extension of diatonicism. In addition, his formal designs were usually clear and seemed to have strong roots in earlier musical periods. Hence, the music written in this style is described as **neoclassic.** Generally, the textures were thinner than in previous pieces, the melodic lines and harmonic motion were clearly and cleanly wrought, and the sectional design and phrase structures were outlined with classical clarity.

    One of the most important factors determining the sound of this music is its predominant use of the major and minor scales. The emphasis on the diatonic scale is not functional in the nineteenth-century sense; in fact, it is sometimes difficult to determine whether the major or the natural minor scale is being used. When the diatonic scale is used in a free, nonfunctional way, the term ***pandiatonicism*** is used to describe the tonal style. This free diatonic use opened a whole new sound-world. The diatonic scale is heard and there is always a sense of tonality, but the sound is fresh and does not relate directly to the world of the late nineteenth century. However, as we saw in certain pieces of the late nineteenth century there was a definite movement toward this freely diatonic style.

The opening of the second movement of the *Symphony in Three Movements* (1945) demonstrates this free use of the diatonic scale. The accompanying violins express D major, and the flute's melodic line also uses the D-major scale and emphasizes the tonality of D. Note, however, the use of the harp, with its emphasis on *g* and *d*, and the counterforce of the basses and cellos, with their emphasis on *f♮* reflecting the parallel-minor side of the D tonality.

ex. 24-1

Throughout the first section of the movement we notice examples of pandiatonic melodies and harmonies. The harmonic activity seems to employ a rather free combination of pitches, with a strong emphasis on the basic tonal center of D. The basses and cellos always function as a disruptive element, however. Their insistence on other key centers and scalar structures eventually leads to a change in design.

At measure 25 the melodic and harmonic framework shifts from D to C. At this point, all the instruments seem to share the basic scale. A few measures later, Stravinsky introduces a few notes outside of C major, but it appears that they are basically used for color rather than to undermine the C tonality, especially since they come from the c-minor mode.

ex. 24-2

From measure 33 onward, Stravinksy experiments further with shifting tonalities. The use of D♭ major in the flute, against C major in the oboe, provides an interesting interplay between b♭ and b♮ in measure 37.

ex. 24-3

Thus far we have seen the linear use of pandiatonicism. The various lines define a tonality without the traditional force of harmonic function so necessary in the nineteenth century. However, Stravinsky occasionally uses pandiatonic harmony as well; especially in the block chords used for short transitional sections of transition. At measure 49 the homophonic transition introduces a sudden shift of scale which takes the listener by surprise.

ex. 24-4

The tonal center here seems to be c♯ as a result of the strength of the c♯ in the cello part. However, the scale that can be derived from this section is that of A major. Perhaps we should view this as an example of Phrygian mode, rather than as major or minor.

ex. 24-5

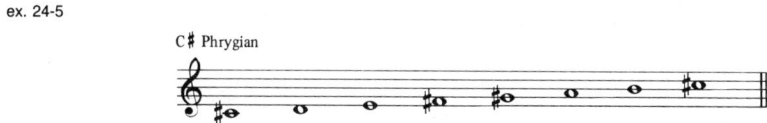

Certainly the overall tonal/chordal sound is closer to c♯ Phrygian than to A major. A final note on this passage: the third violin part and harp and second solo cello use f♮ rather than f♯, a borrowing from the minor side of the key which produces striking harmonic results.

The use of diatonic scales, in both the linear and harmonic dimensions, is fairly consistent in this and other neoclassic pieces by Stravinsky. The pandiatonic technique breathes new life into the centuries-old systems of major/minor tonality and the diatonic modes.

There are further changes in key center in the remainder of the piece, all of which should be noted by the student.

Another technique found in this piece, and a hallmark of Stravinsky's sound, is **ostinato.** An ostinato is a persistent repetition of a short bit of material, and is usually an accompanimental figure. Stravinsky's ostinatos are typically both short and irregular; in other words, they usually do not fit into the regular pattern of the meter. Compare:

ex. 24-6

In the irregular pattern, part of the musical interest lies in the syncopation that results from its conflict with the regular meter.

Beginning at measure 65, the accompaniment in the viola and second violin uses this form of ostinato. Stravinsky varies it further by adding sixteenth-note rests at different intervals. He thus produces both a sense of predictability (by the repetitive ostinato) and unpredictability (by the varying placement of the rest).

ex. 24-7

Stravinsky's interest in ostinato is matched by his fascination with unusual rhythms. The irregular placement of rhythmic accents, and the use of ***irregular metric schemes*** and ***fast-changing metric units*** are characteristic of Stravinsky's works and other music of the early twentieth century. Until this period most music retained a given meter for an extended period of time, generally for an entire movement. The early part of this century saw a movement away from such metrical regularity, a tendency to weaken strong pulse relationships within the meter, and a willingness to experiment with the pulse itself. Occasionally in this movement Stravinsky will shorten a measure, producing a slightly jarring effect.

ex. 24-8

Here the phrase has simply been shortened by one beat. Elsewhere several shifts may occur in a single phrase.

ex. 24-9

[musical score]

Note the extension of the first phrase by one sixteenth note, by the use of a $\frac{3}{16}$ measure. The next two-measure phrase is followed by a two-measure phrase that has been interrupted by the entry of the strings. Although quite subtle, the importance of this shifting phrase/metric structure is great.

Some of the music of Stravinsky explores the possibilities of **bitonal** and **bichordal** writing. (Although hinted at in this movement, there are no clear examples here.) As the terms imply, both techniques deal with the simultaneous use of two distinct elements: two different keys or two different chords used at the same time. In both cases, an important element is that of spacing. If too closely spaced, a polychord becomes a thick sonority, impossible to hear as a conflation of two or more entities.

ex. 24-10

The first example does not produce a clearly bichordal sound in the way that the second does. The same can be true of melodic lines.

STYLE CHARACTERISTICS: EARLY TO MIDDLE TWENTIETH CENTURY—TONAL COMPOSERS
based on Stravinsky's *Symphony in Three Movements*

melody	fairly short and repetitive, usually based on motivic patterns • ostinato patterns frequently employed • either conjunct or disjunct depending on the individual piece, but the basic concept is usually fairly conjunct • much use of pandiatonicism, modal and major/minor constructions
harmony	several types: 1) intervallically controlled and conceived; 2) extended tertian (usually adding sevenths and ninths); 3) pandiatonically/contrapuntally derived (resulting from the interaction of contrapuntal lines)
rhythm	three basic types: 1) very clear, Classical-type rhythms, extended through motivic manipulations; 2) irregular rhythmic groupings, with much syncopation; 3) mixture of metric schemes, producing irregular rhythms and phrase structures • rhythmic ostinato
texture	variable, depending on the piece • texture usually the result of multiple contrapuntal lines

Glossary

Bitonality   the juxtaposition of two distinct tonal areas, either melodically or harmonically.

Neoclassic   a term referring to various composers' music, ca. 1920 and following, which musically espoused the values of the Baroque and Classic periods. The important feature was clarity of phrase and formal design, rather than a return to Classic harmony.

Ostinato   persistent repetition of a short melodic and rhythmic pattern.

Pandiatonicism   the free use of the diatonic scale in a nonfunctional way. Usually, it implies the use of non-tertian harmony, without a strong tonal center.

Polychordal   the simultaneous use of two or more distinct chords.

Polytonality   the simultaneous use of two or more distinct tonal areas, either melodically (usually) or harmonically.

Suggested Exercises

1. Using any diatonic scale, write a two- or three-part piece utilizing pandiatonicism. Avoid functional harmonic motion. Use interesting and irregular phrase structure and strongly defined cadences.
2. Study other pieces by Stravinsky for harmonic and melodic content, as well as pandiatonic uses. Pieces displaying a strong use of pandiatonicism are the *Duo Concertant,* the *Octet,* and the *Sonata* for piano.

Before Reading Chapter 25

1. Listen to "Minor Seconds, Major Sevenths" from the *Mikrokosmos* by Béla Bartók (pages 230–32).

2. Trace the opening motive throughout the piece.
3. Look for cadences and phrase endings. Analyze the intervallic content of the harmonies, as well as their spacing.

BARTÓK

Minor Seconds, Major Sevenths (Mikrokosmos, No. 144)

Béla Bartók

"Minor Seconds, Major Sevenths," (*Mikrokosmos,* Vol. VI, No. 144)

    The use of texture as a separate parameter is important to a certain segment of twentieth-century music. Although textural variation is not exploited by all composers of this century, a few have been in the forefront of textural development. Certainly much of the orchestral music of Debussy and Stravinsky relies on textural effect as much as on harmonic, melodic, and contrapuntal technique.

    The use of **texture** in the works of Béla Bartók(1881–1945), in small piano works as in larger orchestral works, can produce a variety of effects depending on the intent of the piece. The present example gives us a carefully controlled sound-world, full of dense, chromatic textures that seem to produce a thick cloud of sound, at once ambiguous and clear, tightly controlled but free.

    As the title of the *Mikrokosmos* example suggests, the basic content of the piece, both melodic and harmonic, is derived from the minor second and its inversion, the major seventh. The first two measures present these intervals clearly.

ex. 25-1

Similar minor-second **clusters** (groups of notes in adjacent position, either half steps or whole steps) are evident throughout the piece. As can be seen in measure 2, other intervals come into play as well.

ex. 25-2

Although the cluster in the middle of this chord (g-$g\sharp$-a-$b\flat$) is entirely made up of half steps and the outer voices form a major seventh, the interval formed by the two lowest and two highest notes is a major third. This expansion from the first measure is significant because it allows Bartók the possibility of moving outside the strict minor second and major seventh usage.

In the first two measures, two other interesting features emerge. First, each hand is symmetrical with the other, imitating by the process of **melodic inversion.** The melodic intervals in the right hand move down, while those in the left hand move upward by the same intervals.

ex. 25-3

The second important feature appears when all of the pitches in the first two measures are arranged in ascending order.

ex. 25-4

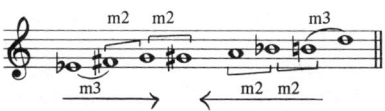

The scale thus produced is symmetrical, as the example shows. In addition, it is not constructed like any major, minor, or modal scale pattern. It is a **synthetic scale,** a scale devised by the composer. Another synthetic scale is the whole tone scale used by Debussy and others. Numerous synthetic scales have been used by twentieth-century composers; a few of the more important ones are given below.

ex. 25-5

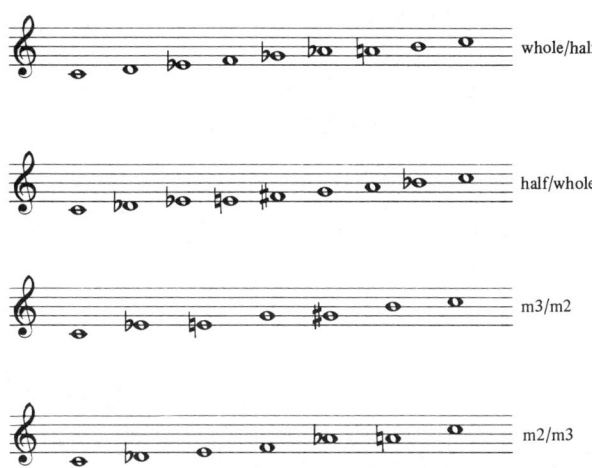

Each of these has been used by Bartók, as well as other composers. All these scales are **symmetrical** in construction, though this is not a necessary feature of new scales. The possibilities of devising scales are endless, and many others can be found throughout the twentieth-century repertoire.

This piece by Bartók shows a fascinating development of its scale as well as of the m2/M7 complex. Almost everything in the piece is understandable in terms of these two compositional principles.

The phrase structure is usually quite clear, as in the opening few measures. There are cadences in measures 2 and 4 (the latter extended into measure 5). Note the subtle development of the motivic rhythm ♪ ♩. in measure 3, and the condensing of the phrase in measures 5 and 6. Measure 7 is an important extension because of its later development.

There is a "modulation" in measure 8, where the left-hand cluster consists of *b-c-c♯* instead of *f♯–g–g♯* as at the beginning. We find that the entire scale has been transposed up a perfect fourth; this becomes clear in measure 12.

ex. 25-6

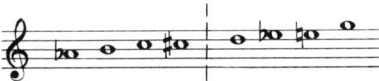

Much development and tonal expansion can be found in this section, but the basic scale continues to be used for the most part at this transpositional level.

Measures 18–21 serve as a transition by ***expanding the sonority*** from a minor second to two fourths a tritone apart, by means of half-step motion in each voice.

ex. 25-7

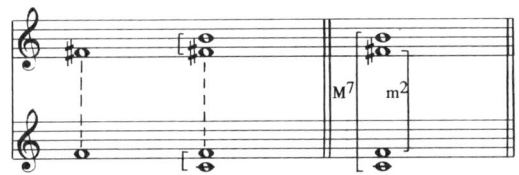

The tritone can be accounted for as part of the scalar formation.

ex. 25-8

The scale is divided in half by the tritone. Each **tetrachord,** or four-note segment, is bounded by a perfect fourth, and the distance between tetrachords is an augmented fourth.

The 32nd-note scales in measures 21–22 are merely transposed versions of the same scale.

ex. 25-9

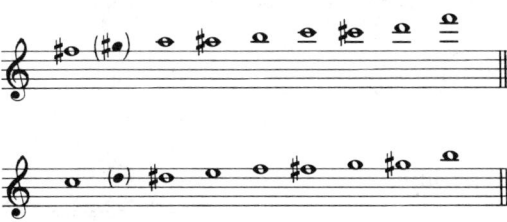

It is the scale we derived at the beginning of the piece, here presented at two levels a tritone apart. Thus, the scale finally appears here in scalar form for the first time.

The remainder of the piece can be seen as development of the material presented up to this point, each section following being similar to one that came before.

initial statement	developmental areas
m. 1____	37____40____61
m. 7____	35____39____53
m. 18____	43____48
m. 21____	52____63

STYLE CHARACTERISTICS: MID-TWENTIETH CENTURY
based on Bartók's *Mikrokosmos*

melody — usually motivic in construction, often fragmentary, expansion/contraction of phrase structure • (other pieces show a strong folk influence, using modal, major/minor, or synthetic scales)

harmony — emphasis on highly dissonant sonorities, using minor seconds and clusters as the basis for much of the overall harmony • usually employs one or two intervals as the basis for chord construction

rhythm — two basic types: 1) static, with weak pulse (slow movements); 2) driving, with a strong pulse (fast movements) • much use of irregular or shifting meters

texture	textural extremes: both very thick texture, with clusters or the like, and very thin textures, with wide space between parts
forms	various, mostly through-composed • (in other works, arch form—**A B C B A**—is frequently used both for individual movements and in multi-movement works)

Glossary

Cluster   a chordal sonority based on adjacent pitches. It may be diatonic, whole-tone, or chromatic.
Melodic inversion   replacement of each ascending melodic interval with the identical descending interval, and vice versa.
Symmetrical scale   a scale which has the same intervallic order both ascending and descending, the intervallic order in the second half of the scale being the exact retrograde of the first half.
Synthetic scale   any scale which is not major, minor, or modal.

Suggested Exercises

1. Discuss the possible tonal levels within the piece. Is there a tonal relationship between the beginning and ending of the piece? Relate the scale formations at the end with those of the chordal formations. What are the basic scale modulations that occur throughout the piece? Are certain pitch-levels more important than others?
2. With the following synthetic scale, write a piece in **ABA** form for piano. Structure the piece simply, with clear motivic ideas.

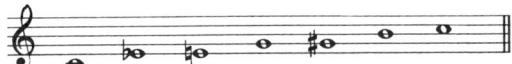

3. Analyze the following piece as thoroughly as possible.

Syncopation (Mikrokosmos, Book V, No. 33)   BARTÓK

Béla Bartók

© Copyright 1940 in U.S.A. by Hawkes & Son (London), Ltd. Renewed 1967. Reprinted by permission of Boosey & Hawkes, Inc.

Before Reading Chapter 26

1. Listen to the first of the *Three Piano Pieces,* Op. 11, by Arnold Schoenberg.
2. Analyze the phrase structure of the first piece (pages 241–43).
3. Consider the harmonic content and decide which harmonic intervals are most important.
4. Trace the material used in measures 1–5 throughout the piece.

I.

SCHOENBERG, Op. 11

26

Arnold Schoenberg

Three Piano Pieces, Op. 11, No. 1

    Until now, we have been dealing with music that somehow relates to the nineteenth century, either by gesture or in its use of a basic scale. Even the works of Stravinsky and Bartók, although sometimes highly chromatic, tend to establish a tonality by means of a scale, even if a synthetic scale. But other approaches were being used at the same time, with vastly different results.
    The early music of Arnold Schoenberg (1874–1951), prior to about 1908, was strongly in the mold of the nineteenth century. It borrowed heavily from Wagner, Brahms, and Mahler in its melodic, harmonic, and rhythmic ideas. However, he began to push the bounds of this highly chromatic tonal system to its very limit. The result was a fundamental change in the concept of harmony and dissonance as well as the use of **gestures.**
    A gesture, in this sense, is a small musical idea much like a motive, having a melodic or rhythmic identity, like a physical gesture that relates to the verbal expression of the speaker. In a broad sense, Schoenberg uses two kinds of gestures. In the first type, we can see the influence of the nineteenth century, producing a familiar, recognizable gesture such as the quasi-appoggiatura figure below.

Arnold Schoenberg

ex. 26-1

The downward motion suggests movement to a dissonant note on the first beat of each measure, be it an appoggiatura or a suspension. However, because the harmonic content is already dissonant, this is technically not true. Yet the gesture itself is so strongly stated that the idea of dissonance/resolution is still heard. Observe the strength of the "dissonance" and its "resolution" in the following.

ex. 26-2

a.

b.

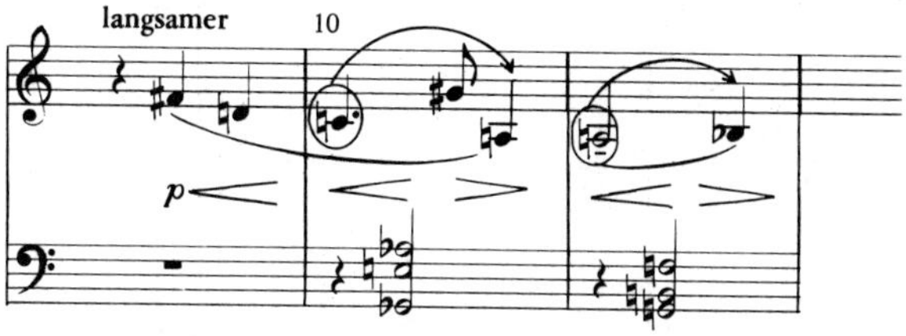

c.

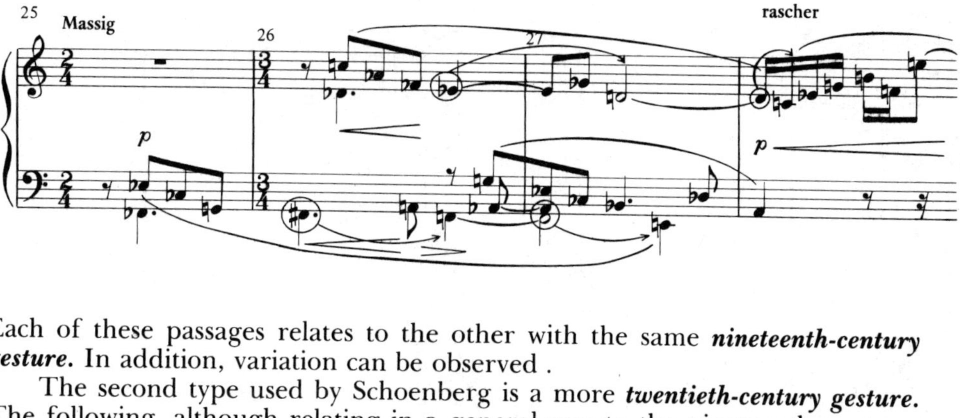

Each of these passages relates to the other with the same **nineteenth-century gesture.** In addition, variation can be observed.

The second type used by Schoenberg is a more **twentieth-century gesture.** The following, although relating in a general way to the nineteenth century, explores newer ideas rather than reiterating older concepts.

ex. 26-3

All three of these passages are related. The variation of the gesture is subtle but strong and can provide the basic format for the larger structuring of a work. This process can be seen throughout the movement.

    The chromatic expansion of the harmony has extended the richness of late-nineteenth-century harmony and at the same time almost totally abolished both the use of tonal centers and scales. There are two methods of aural organization displayed. One is by intervallic control of the sound and the other is by gestural control. The gesture tends to focus the listener's attention on a specific idea and allows us to follow the progression of that idea through the variations of it, even if they are somewhat removed intervallically or harmonically. The intervallic content is controlled in order to produce consistent relationships. The consistency of the intervallic use is important, so as not to present too much information too densely. The interval premise and/or gestural idea are changed, transposed, and sometimes inverted, creating a maze of musical material, but the mind still catalogues these changes and relates them to the original.

Note the intervals and gestures in the opening fourteen measures of this example. The melodic and harmonic material in measures 1–3 is extended in measures 4–8, ending with a cadential pattern that becomes an important element later in the movement.

ex. 26-4

This first section is followed immediately by a contrasting gesture in measure 12. It is extended in the next two measures.

With these two gestures established in the early part of the piece, we can trace the material through the remainder and watch the myriad of transformations that occur.

Motives from the opening measures are to be found in measures 17–33. For analytical purposes it may help to label as **a** the falling figure in measures 1–3, and to label as **b** the rising eighth-note figure in measures 4–5.

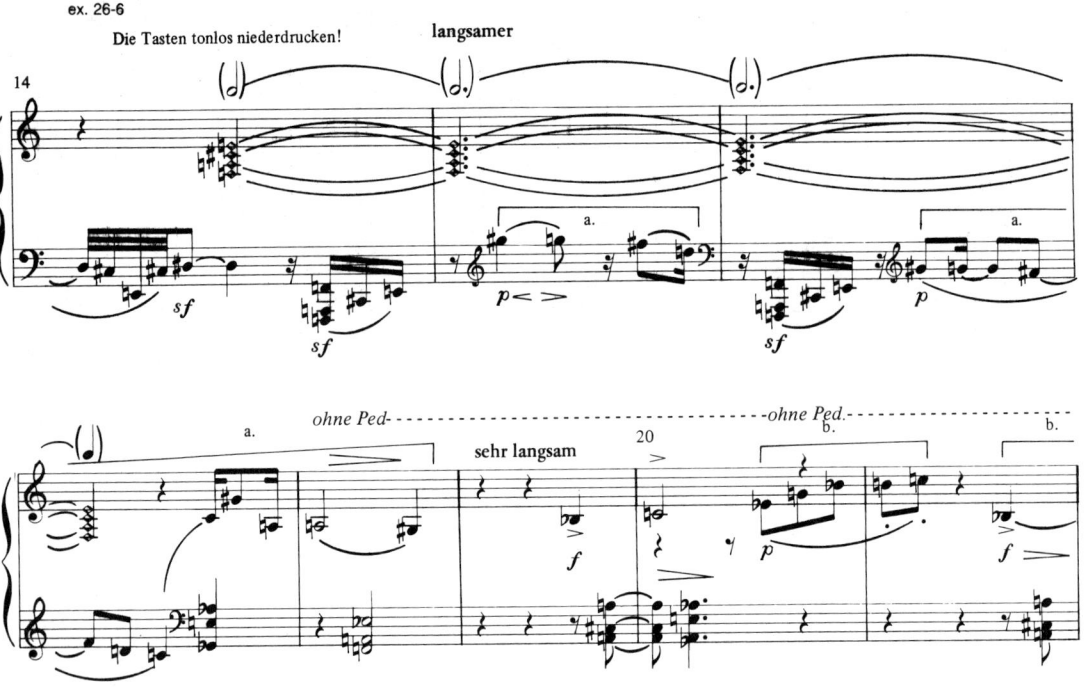

Note that the two ideas begin to be used closer together, their identities not lost but transformed.

Beginning in measure 34, there is a definite change in texture, while there remains a melodic relationship to the opening material.

ex. 26-7

The melodic extraction looks like this:

ex. 26-8

This melodic/rhythmic variation of **a** closes, like its original, with the introduction of another gesture. This can be seen as being very freely derived from measures 12–13.

ex. 26-9

From this point we proceed to another variation of the basic theme.

ex. 26-10

And to another:

ex. 26-11

This is closed with **b** as before.

ex. 26-12

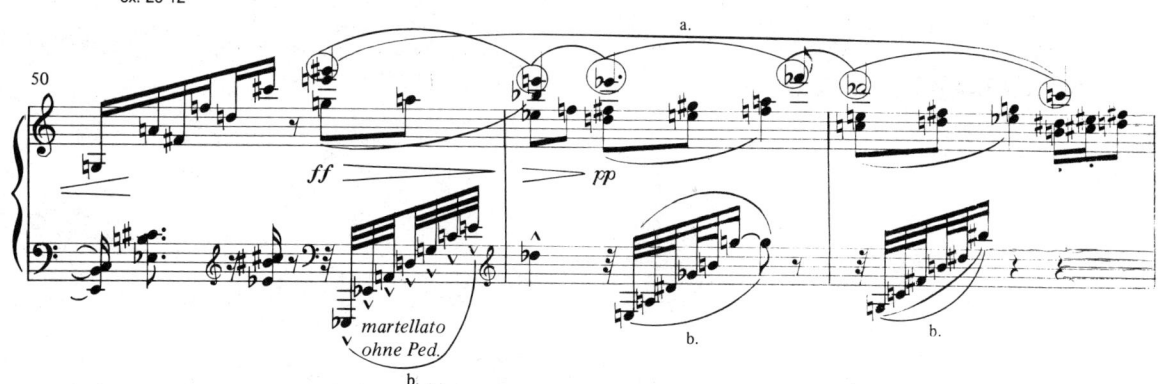

Not only is the theme still present in the upper voice, but the left-hand gesture is derived from the cadential left-hand material in measures 4–5.

The ending offers a final, simpler look at the opening material, giving a strong impression of recapitulation after the series of fantasy-like variations. The final cadence reiterates the falling half-step figure, recalling the first two measures.

ex. 26-13

Schoenberg usually avoids triadic figures and the resolution of tritone constructions, both melodic and harmonic. His preference is for chords based on fourths and tritones, often vertically alternating in appearance.

ex. 26-14

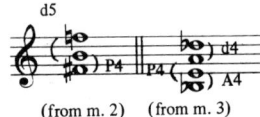

(from m. 2)   (from m. 3)

However, equally important sounds are the major seventh and minor ninth. It is difficult to decide which is more important, the fourth/tritone complex or the major seventh with an added tone. This latter kind of formation can be traced throughout the piece, in melodic as well as harmonic terms.

ex. 26-15

mit Dampfung (3. Pedal)- - - - - - - - - - - - - - - -

Another harmonic sound is used almost in opposition to the tritone/fourth. It is based on the third, but usually outlines an augmented triad with one addition. The augmented triad is perhaps the least-used third-based triad in previous centuries, possibly contributing to its appeal to early-twentieth-century composers.

ex. 26-16

The juxtaposition of the two intervallic bases for harmonic formulation is used as a structural basis, defining the sound of individual sections.

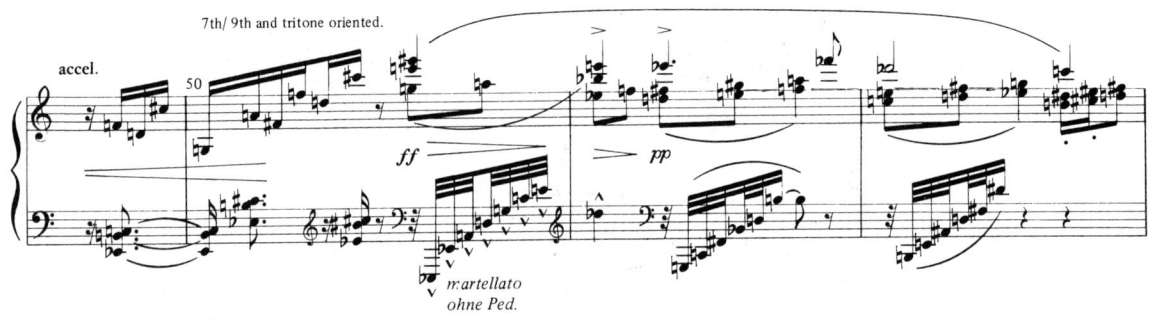

One additional concept that must be mentioned is melodic flow. The **melodic intervals** are extremely important in determining the musical direction. Perhaps the two most important melodic intervals are the third and the falling minor second. The latter produces a strong, almost functional pull, toward a given note.

ex. 26-18

Although this piece is not tonal in the same way that the Stravinsky and Bartók examples were, a strong sense of progression is produced through the development of gestures and consistent intervallic constructions.

STYLE CHARACTERISTICS: EARLY TWENTIETH CENTURY—ATONAL COMPOSERS
based on Schoenberg's *Three Piano Pieces,* **Op. 11**

melody   intervallically based (usually one or two intervals are of prime importance) • use of gestures as an organizing force; usually fairly short, fragmentary ideas

harmony   intervallically based • preference for fourth, tritone, and augmented triad; highly chromatic; avoidance of functional progressions

rhythm	two basic types: 1) smooth contrapuntal motion, without excessive syncopation or rhythmic displacement; 2) disjunct, syncopative, using smaller note values, and irregular rhythmic and metric patterns
texture	widely variable, depending on piece; preference for a fairly thick, contrapuntal texture

Glossary

Gesture   a relatively small musical idea, much like a motive, having a distinct melodic or rhythmic identity.

Intervallic harmony   the utilization of a small number of different intervals (usually two or three) for constructing harmonic sonorities.

Suggested Exercises

1. Using the following two gestures, write a very short piano piece in the style of Schoenberg.

ex. 26-19

2. Provide an analysis of the following piece from the *Six Little Piano Pieces,* from Op. 19, of Schoenberg. Consider the use of gesture, harmonic/melodic construction, and interval use.

SCHOENBERG
Op. 19, No. 4

© Belmont Publishers; used by permission.

Before Reading Chapter 27

1. Listen to *Three Songs,* Op. 25 by Anton Webern.
2. Bracket the phrase structure of the vocal line in the first song (pages 257–59).
3. Determine the most prominent intervals in the song.

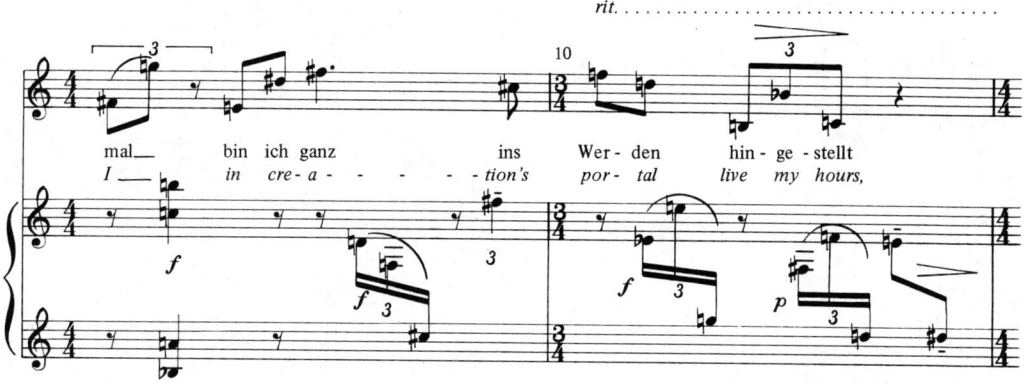

©Copyright 1956 by Universal Edition A.G. Wien, Used by permission.

27
Anton Webern

Three Songs, Op. 25

As a result of the highly chromatic writing of Schoenberg, as well as his most famous students, Anton Webern (1883–1945) and Alban Berg, there gradually arose a need for a greater organizational control of materials. The music of these three composers between 1908 and 1922 explored the full range of intervallic projection. Even so, Schoenberg especially found it increasingly difficult to organize his tonal materials in a meaningful and congruent manner. In 1921 he announced to his friend Josef Rufer that he had devised a method of musical organization based on the twelve chromatic pitches, a technique of ordering and controlling a series of pitches and intervals in a way that would produce a coherent structural basis for an entire piece. He called his technique "a method of composing with twelve tones," and it is now commonly referred to as the ***twelve-tone system*** of composition.

In its simplest form, the system deals with a series of the twelve notes, which generates and controls the musical material in the piece. In the "classical" procedure, all pitches are used in the prescribed order, no pitch being repeated until all the others have been heard. The row may be repeated as often as necessary. The original row of twelve pitches may also be employed (1) in reverse order, or **retrograde** form; (2) with inverted intervals, or **inversion** form, and (3) with the intervals inverted and in reverse order, or **retrograde-inversion** form.

If we now examine the Webern song, we can see that its original row and the derived forms of the row can be shown as follows:

ex. 27-1

Prime (Original) (P)

Retrograde (R)

Inversion (I)

Retrograde - Inversion (RI)

An important feature of this system is that the intervallic content of each row form is identical, even though different melodic shapes are generated. Only the order may change, and then only in a consistently retrograde way. Therefore, the consistency of the interval presentation is the highest possible.

Any piece may employ P, R, I, and RI orderings. In addition, each of these may begin on any of the twelve chromatic pitches. Therefore, if each ordering has twelve transpositions—twelve primes, twelve retrogrades, twelve inversions, and twelve retrograde-inversions—then the total number of possible rows based on any set is forty-eight. One way of listing these conveniently is in the form of a **matrix**.

In the matrix, the prime (P) is read from left to right; the retrograde (R) from right to left; the inversion (I) from top to bottom; and the retrograde-inversion (RI) from bottom to top. The number of each row, P-0, P-1, P-4, etc., indicates the number of half steps the row is above the original row, P-0.

ex. 27-2

An alternative type of matrix employs pitch names instead of notes on the staff.

	I-0	I-11	I-8	I-10	I-9	I-6	I-3	I-7	I-2	I-5	I-4	I-1	
P-0	F♯	F	D	E	E♭	C	A	C♯	G♯	B	B♭	G	R-0
P-1	G	F♯	D♯	F	E	C♯	A♯	D	A	C	B	G♯	R-1
P-4	B♭	A	F♯	G♯	G	E	C♯	F	C	E♭	D	B	R-4
P-2	A♭	G	E	F♯	F	D	B	D♯	A♯	C♯	C	A	R-2
P-3	A	A♭	F	G	F♯	D♯	C	E	B	D	D♭	B♭	R-3
P-6	C	B	G♯	A♯	A	F♯	D♯	G	D	F	E	C♯	R-6
P-9	E♭	D	B	C♯	C	A	F♯	B♭	F	A♭	G	E	R-9
P-5	B	B♭	G	A	A♭	F	D	F♯	C♯	E	E♭	C	R-5
P-10	E	E♭	C	D	D♭	B♭	G	B	F♯	A	A♭	F	R-10
P-7	C♯	C	A	B	B♭	G	E	G♯	D♯	F♯	F	D	R-7
P-8	D	D♭	B♭	C	B	G♯	F	A	E	G	F♯	D♯	R-8
P-11	F	E	C♯	D♯	D	B	G♯	C	G	B♭	A	F♯	R-11
	RI-0	RI-11	RI-8	RI-10	RI-9	RI-6	RI-3	RI-7	RI-2	RI-5	RI-4	RI-1	

The matrix is an essential reference tool, both for composer and theorist, for locating pitch material within the piece.

Webern, who had adopted Schoenberg's system by 1925, makes strict use of the technique in the present song.

ex. 27-3

In this passage, the row is kept in strict order. Two forms of the row are used, the prime and the retrograde-inversion. The row can be seen to control not only the melodic aspect of the piece (in both piano and voice) but also the harmony. In this song, the presentations of the row in the piano are usually separate from those of the voice. Even in this piece, however, the row is divided between the piano and the voice at one point, in measure five.

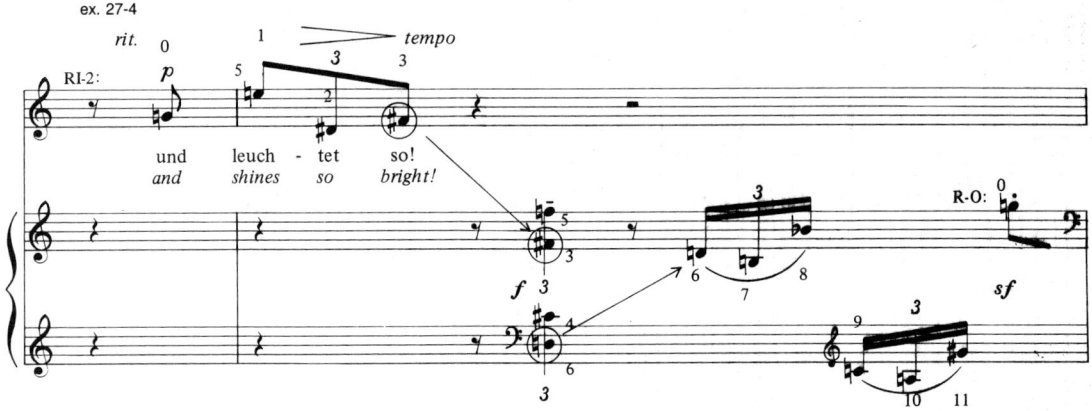

ex. 27-4

For the rest of the song, the row content of the parts remains separate.

ex. 27-5

The extreme simplicity of Webern's row usage here should be noted. Although all four basic orderings are used, they occur at only two pitch levels.

ex. 27-6

No other row form appears. Thus, in this case Webern has deliberately limited his resources rather than try to explore all of the forty-eight possibilities.

Notice that the original and inverted forms used here both have the same last note, G. This fact is exploited in several places to effect a melding of the rows, such as in measure 2, and a smooth transition from one row form to another.

ex. 27-7

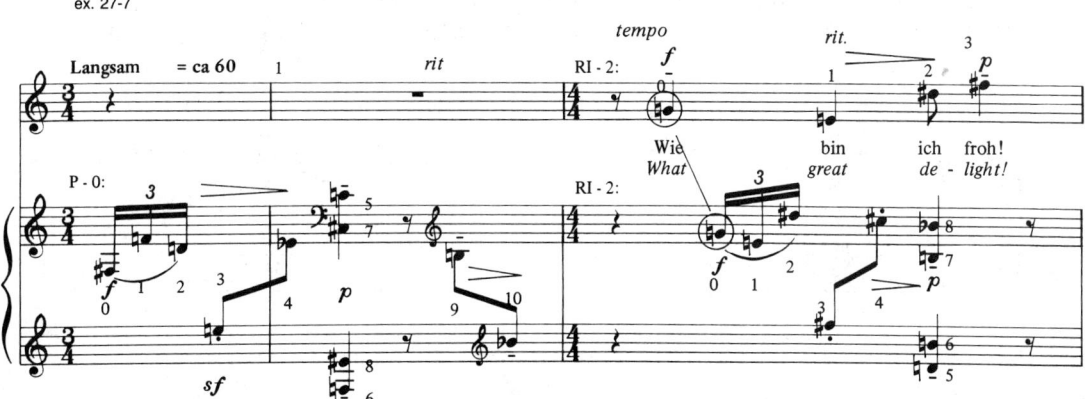

The accounting for all pitches in terms of row forms is not the only possible way of analyzing a twelve-tone piece. As in any other music, there are melodic and rhythmic motives as well as larger constructive principles at work. Identification of the row forms is necessary but should never be the only and final goal of analysis.

Phrases in Webern's music are usually carefully constructed and finely shaped. As a general rule, the end of a phrase is designated by a *ritardando* and the beginning of the next phrase by an *a tempo* marking. The larger phrases can be constructed by the logical combination of these sub-phrase groups. The first vocal phrase comprises measures 2–5; the second, measures 6–8; the third, measures 8–10; and the last, measure 11. Note that their lengths are progressively shorter: in number of measures, 4–3–2–1. The entire piece is framed by a one-measure piano introduction and close. The original row appears at the beginning and the retrograde at the end—in other words, the song ends exactly where it began. In fact, on closer examination we may observe that all of the rows are retrograded, creating a large palindrome.

```
           P-0   RI-2   R-0   I-2   RI-2   P-0   I-2   R-0
measure    1     2-5    6-8 ——————  9-11 ————  ———— 11-12
```

There are three rhythmic motives used in the piano.

ex. 27-8

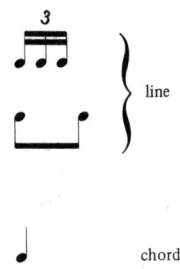

Because the intervallic construction of the row emphasizes m2/m3 configurations, the triplet figure is invariably some kind of variation of the m2 (or m9, M7, etc.) and m3 (or M6). The interval created by the eighth-note figure is variable.

ex. 27-9

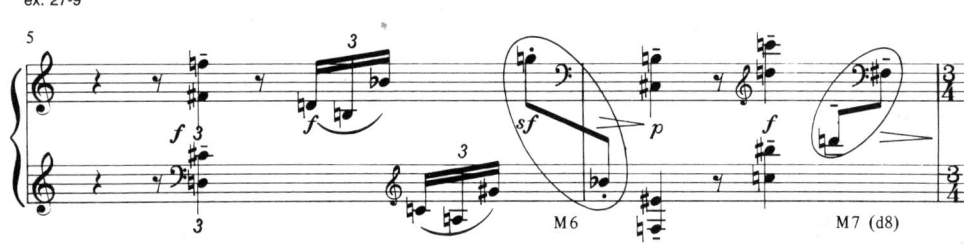

The quarter-note chord is usually, though not always, arranged as two M7s (or m9s) at varying intervals from another.

ex. 27-10

These motivic ideas in the piano are shifted rhythmically through the use of rests and by changing their order, producing an effect of both unity and variety.

STYLE CHARACTERISTICS: MID-TWENTIETH CENTURY—TWELVE-TONE COMPOSERS
based on Webern's *Three Songs*, Op. 25

melody	extremely fragmentary, motivic, in terms of both pitch and rhythm • short and clear-cut phrases • predilection for angular, disjunct melodic motion, with much use of intervals of the seventh and ninth
harmony	intervallically based • twelve-tone derived • not based on tertian concepts at all • contrapuntal lines generally more important than harmonic sound
rhythm	fragmentary, motivic
texture	sparse • very thin, widely spaced chords • contrapuntal textures rarely consisting of more than two voices
techniques	twelve-tone • use of rhythmic retrogrades and other experiments • canon, retrograde canon

Glossary

Matrix   a chart which contains all of the 48 possible forms of a given twelve-tone row.
Row forms
  Prime (original)   an ordering of the twelve notes of the chromatic scale
  Retrograde   the original series presented in reverse order.
  Inversion   all intervals of the series presented in strict inversion.
  Retrograde-inversion   the inverted row presented backwards.
Twelve-tone system   a system of pitch organization by which a composition is based on one arrangement of the twelve pitches of the chromatic scale. This serial arrangement, or *row*, may be used at any transposition, in retrograde form, inverted form, or retrograde-inversion form.

Suggested Exercises

With the given row (from Webern's *Concerto*, Op. 24), compose a short, strict twelve-tone piece for voice and piano in the style of Webern. Construct three or four motives before beginning the piece. Organize your row usage to avoid excessive repetition or complexity. Try to use each of the four basic orderings of the row somewhere in the piece. Label each note in the piece, and be prepared to discuss your motivic use.

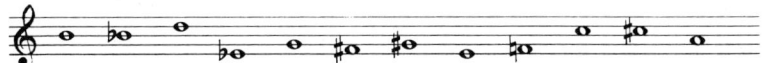

Before Reading Chapter 28

1. Listen to the *Quartet for the End of Time* by Olivier Messiaen.
2. Note the rhythmic repetition in the piano and cello throughout the first movement (*Liturgie de cristal*, pages 268–74).
3. Note the repetition of pitch material in the cello line in the first movement. Analyze the cello's significant intervals.
4. Analyze the intervals used in the clarinet and violin parts.

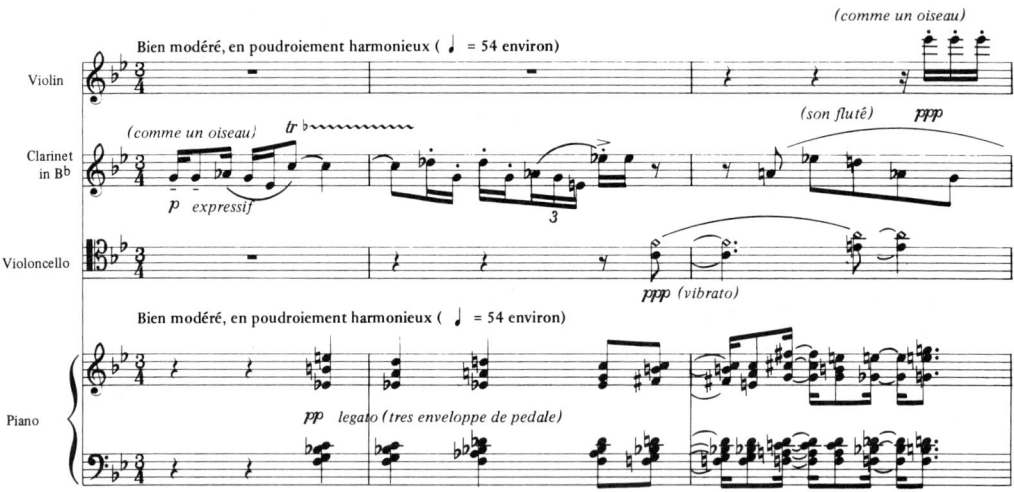

Copyright 1942 Durand S.A. Used by permission of the publisher, Theodore Presser Company sole representative U.S.A.

269

28

Olivier Messiaen

Quatuor pour la fin du temps (*Quartet for the End of Time*), first movement: *Liturgie de cristal*

    Many composers in the twentieth century have been fascinated by compositional techniques and procedures from other centuries. Older techniques may provide an organizational basis for the composer, a way of presenting and ordering his ideas.

    The works of Olivier Messiaen (born 1908) show a variety of influences. His strong interest in the Catholic liturgy has resulted in his quoting of chant and use of modal references; a knowledge of early music has given him a battery of compositional procedures; his long-held interest in transcribing birdsong adds an element both natural and fantastic to his melodic writing; and interest in Indian music has added rhythmic subtlety from another culture.

    The *Quartet for the End of Time* was written while Messiaen was in a Nazi prison camp in the early 1940s, and was dedicated to the three fellow prisoners with whom he performed the work. It is a powerful eight-movement work that spans a wide emotional range and explores a great many musical procedures, some of which are developed by Messiaen, some borrowed from previous centuries, and others developed earlier in the twentieth century.

    In the first movement the texture is composed of two musical strata. The violin and clarinet carry a repetitive line that ebbs and flows, gradually growing toward a dynamic and rhythmic climax. The piano and cello, on the other hand, are almost completely static, contributing only a constant background.

In his introduction to the score, Messiaen briefly discusses the foundation of the piano part. It is based on a rhythmic pattern which is repeated with no variation throughout the movement.

ex. 28-1

The metric placement of the pattern changes constantly; its initial presentation is:

ex. 28-2

In addition to its rhythmic repetition, the piano part is also limited in its use of chords. A progression containing 29 chords is repeated, like the rhythmic pattern, throughout the movement.

ex. 28-3

Because there are 17 rhythmic values and 29 chords, there occurs a constant and kaleidoscopic shifting in the relationship of the two patterns.

Messiaen's technique here is none other than the fourteenth-century principle of **isorhythm:** the strict repetition of a pitch pattern (***color***) and a rhythmic pattern (***talea***) throughout the piece. Messiaen undoubtedly knew the music of that century and consciously used this principle in constructing the movement.

If we look closely, we can see that the cello line contains a similar repetitive pattern. The repeated rhythm, or talea, of the cello is:

ex. 28-4

and the repeated pitch pattern, or color, is:

ex. 28-5

Since the patterns comprise five pitches and fifteen note-values respectively, every third repetition of the pitch patterns employs the same note-values.

Look closely at the cello's rhythmic pattern, and note its underlying principle of organization.

ex. 28-6

The second half of each pattern is the reverse of the first half; in other words, each pattern is a retrograde of itself. Messiaen calls this kind of rhythmic pattern **non-retrogradeable rhythm.** The term means simply that since the pattern is the same when performed backwards as when performed forwards, it cannot produce a distinctive retrograde pattern. Much of Messiaen's music experiments with this kind of rhythmic construction.

The isorhythmic basis of the cello and piano parts is maintained without change throughout the movement. They create a background that is static, yet constantly undergoing subtle changes because of the irregular construction of each isorhythmic pattern. Messiaen refers to this accompaniment as a kind of celestial harmony, the ever-present stasis of the universe.

Overlaid on top of this static element we find more activity of a repetitive kind, in the form of repetition and expansion of motivic ideas. The character of the motivic fragments is derived from natural sound—the songs of birds. Messiaen has long been fascinated by birdsong, and has catalogued the songs of hundreds of species. This avocation has influenced his music on numerous occasions, both freely as in this movement (note the marking, *comme un oiseau,* like a bird) and in direct imitation of a specific bird (with exact pitches and rhythms copied from the birds' actual song) as in other works.

In this movement we have a general representation of two birds, one in the violin and the other in the clarinet. Each has its own character, established by rhythmic and pitch motives. The clarinet is marked by grace notes, fast notes (increasingly exploited through the movement) and trills. A cadential figure consisting of a fast triplet followed by two repeated sixteenth notes is also used, with great effectiveness.

ex. 28-7

The violin plays a strongly contrapuntal role throughout the movement, responding and reacting to the clarinet's initiative. The motivic ideas of the violin do not change as dramatically as the clarinet's. The frequency of response does increase, though. The violin's three main motives are:

ex. 28-8

Their repetition is not formalized in any specified order, but there is a general increase in the density and frequency of motivic use throughout the movement. The climax in the violin coincides with that in the clarinet.

ex. 28-9

Each instrument seems to employ pitch in its own fashion. The violin line emphasizes the following pitches:

ex. 28-10

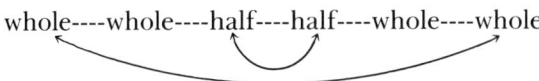

Notice that this scale is intervallically **symmetrical,** and thus is intervallically identical in its retrograde form.

ex. 28-11

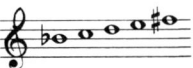

The cello line comprises only five notes:

ex. 28-12

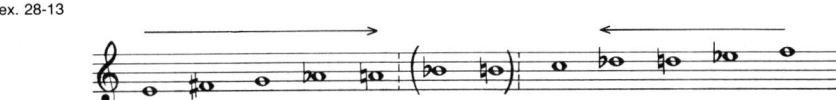

These produce a whole-tone scale lacking only a g♯. Like the violin scale, the whole-tone scale is symmetrical in construction, as well as being totally consistent intervallically.

The clarinet line is the most complicated, encompassing more pitches than any of the others. Its basic scale seems to be:

ex. 28-13

The sound at the beginning in the clarinet is clear:

ex. 28-14

In addition, the notes c and $a\natural$[1] become important later on, particularly in the trills. $D\flat$ and g become important for repeated notes, and the cadential figure $a\flat-g-e-e\flat$ is used throughout.

Possibly as important as the specific scales and intervals employed is the fact that certain pitches appear only in certain registers with rare exceptions. Observe:

ex. 28-15

This use of notes in specified octaves is not rigid in this piece—as the exceptions testify—but this principle is applied more consistently in later pieces, both by Messiaen and by other composers. For some composers, it serves as an extension of twelve-tone procedure and as such becomes important in certain serial music.

An important passage, analytically, occurs near the end.

ex. 28-16

On the surface this passage seems to end in a simple scalar run; when viewed closer it can be seen to contain several scales used in this and other pieces by Messiaen, including the a) wholetone, b) whole/half- (or half/whole-) tone, and c) whole/half/half- (or half/half/whole-) tone scales. All of these are to be found in other movements of this piece, to a greater or lesser extent.

The most important interval of this piece is unmistakably the tritone. The **melodic content** of every part is permeated with the tritone, from the whole-tone references of the cello to the subtle implications of the clarinet. The tritone is clearly exposed in the violin part.

---

[1]Remember this is a B♭ clarinet, so all written pitches will sound a M2 lower.

ex. 28-17

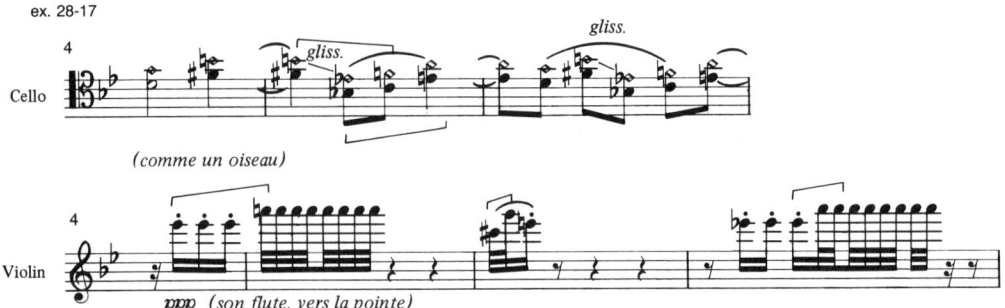

The interval is more than evident elsewhere as well.

ex. 28-18

There are other important intervals, some of which combine to produce the tritone, including interlocking major thirds and other composite intervals.

The sound of a piece may be tied to the specific intervallic and scalar use; the projection of the piece may be related to the various compositional techniques used throughout. However, the reason a piece works as a musical unit is more visceral, more direct than any of the above. The musical concept, the basic projection of thought from one individual to another, supersedes all of the theoretical material we can muster.

The worth of the *Quartet for the End of Time,* and this movement in particular, lies in the ability of the composer to present clear ideas in a convincing format with a clear understanding as to content, reason, purpose and direction. The logic and overall presentation is clear, as is the philosophical premise. Messiaen, like other composers before him, combined his musical techniques and concepts to help him produce a coherent musical statement of import.

STYLE CHARACTERISTICS: MID-TWENTIETH CENTURY
based on Messiaen's *Quartet for the End of Time*

melody   various types: modal, based on chant; melody based on synthetic scales, often symmetrical; major/minor; imitations and exact transcriptions of birdsong melodies; often strongly repetitive, both in pitch and rhythm

rhythm   motivic, with certain small rhythmic units used for specific purposes (cadences, etc.) • non-retrogradable rhythm • stratified rhythm • isorhythm • birdsong influence • Indian influence

harmony   two distinct types: 1) based on synthetic scale formations; 2) based on tertian formations, but usually with multiple added tones

Glossary

Isorhythm   a constructional principle in which one or more voices uses a repeated melodic pattern (color) and a repeated rhythmic pattern (talea). These patterns may or may not coincide; the melodic pattern may be longer than the rhythmic pattern, thereby overlapping it. Originally a fourteenth/fifteenth-century principle, this has also been used in the twentieth century.

Non-retrogradeable rhythm   symmetrical rhythm; a rhythmic pattern that is identical when performed forwards or backwards, the second half being an exact retrograde of the first half.

Ostinato   persistent repetition of a short melodic and rhythmic pattern.

Suggested Exercises

1. Using the whole/half scale, compose a piece for clarinet and violin. Consider using a two-part form (**A B**). Develop distinct motives for each section.
2. Complete an analysis of another movement of the *Quartet for the End of Time*.
3. With the following rhythmic patterns (from *Quartet for the End of Time*, movement VI) as the basis, write a single-line piece using the whole-tone and whole/half/half-tone scales as the generating sources.

4. Using two different synthetic scales, write a piece for violin and cello which employs an isorhythmic scheme. Use patterns of different lengths for the two instruments. Use non-retrogradeable rhythm as the basis for your talea pattern. Be careful of the harmonic intervals created.

Before Reading Chapter 29

1. Listen to the *Dies Irae* by Krzysztof Penderecki (first movement, pages 286–304).
2. Study the new symbols at the beginning of the score, and review standard terminology employed in the work (*sul ponticello, col legno*, etc.).
3. Listen for sectional divisions within the piece.

Explanation of Symbols

- raised by ¼ tone
- raised by ¾ tone
- lowered by ¼ tone
- lowered by ¾ tone
- highest note of the instrument
- lowest note of the instrument
- molto vibrato
- very slow vibrato with ¼ tone frequency difference
- very rapid non-rhythmicized tremolo
- repeat the notated group of notes as rapidly as possible
- jarring sounds
- play between bridge and tailpiece (on 2 strings)
- play arpeggio on 4 strings behind the bridge
- play on tailpiece
- play on bridge
- several irregular bow strokes
- s.t.   sul tasto
- b.ch. hum
- P.G.   grand pause

I. Lamentatio

The sorrows of death compassed me . . . [Psalm 116]

Bodies of children
From crematories
Will fly
High above history.
Bodies of boys,
Bodies of girls
In crowns of thorns
Will flock together.

Bodies of men
From field-graveyards
Will march to conquer.
Will be free. [Broniewski Ciala *(Bodies)]*

The utmost hunger and the limits of strength
Even Christ did not follow such a path of doom
He never knew that racking discord
Between a human soul and an inhuman world [Aragon Auschwitz*]*

Bodies from camps,
From murdered cities,
Bodies with halters,
Bodies with wounds,
Bodies of doom,
Bodies of wrong
Will come in hosts,
Will never rest. [Broniewski Ciala *(Bodies)]*

In huge crates
Dry hair-tufts billow
Of strangled people,
And a small braid,
A pigtail with a ribbon,
Pulled in a class-room
By naughty boys. [Różewicz Warkoczyk *(A Pigtail)]*

Translation of Instrument Names

Coro	chorus
fl	flute
fg	bassoon
cfg	contra-bassoon
sxf brt	baritone saxophone
cr	horn
tr	trumpet
tn	trombone
pti	cymbals
gng	gong
cmp	chimes
cp	chimes
gr c	bass drum
tmt	tam tam
tp	timpani
arm	organ
pf	piano
vc	cello
vb	double bass

DIES IRAE

ORATORIUM
OB MEMORIAM
IN PERNICIEI CASTRIS IN OŚWIĘCIM NECATORUM
INEXSTINGUIBILEM REDDENDAM

I LAMENTATIO
CIRCUMDEDERUNT ME FUNES MORTIS..... (PSALMUS 114)

KRZYSZTOF PENDERECKI
1967

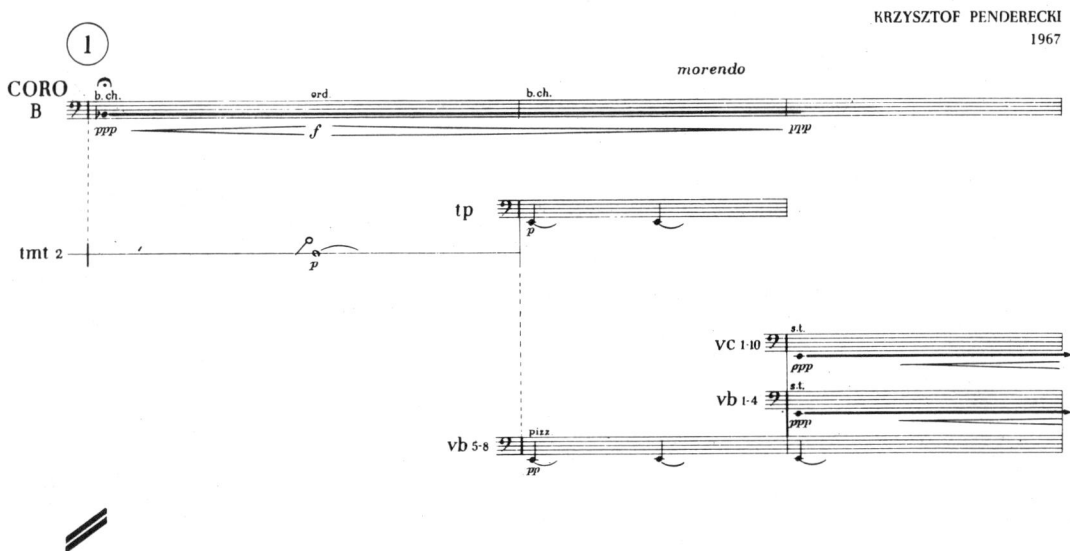

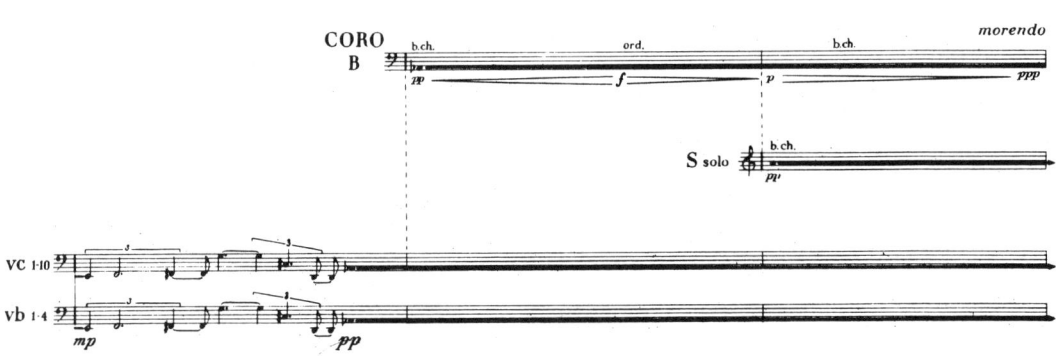

Copyright 1967 by Polskie Wydawnictwo Muzyczne, Kraków, Poland, for: Poland, Albania, Bulgaria, Czechoslovakia, German Democratic Republic, Hungary, Rumania, Union of Soviet Socialist Republics, Chinese People's Republic, Cuba, North Corea, North Viet-Nam.
© 1967 by Moeck Verlag, Celle, for the rest of the world.

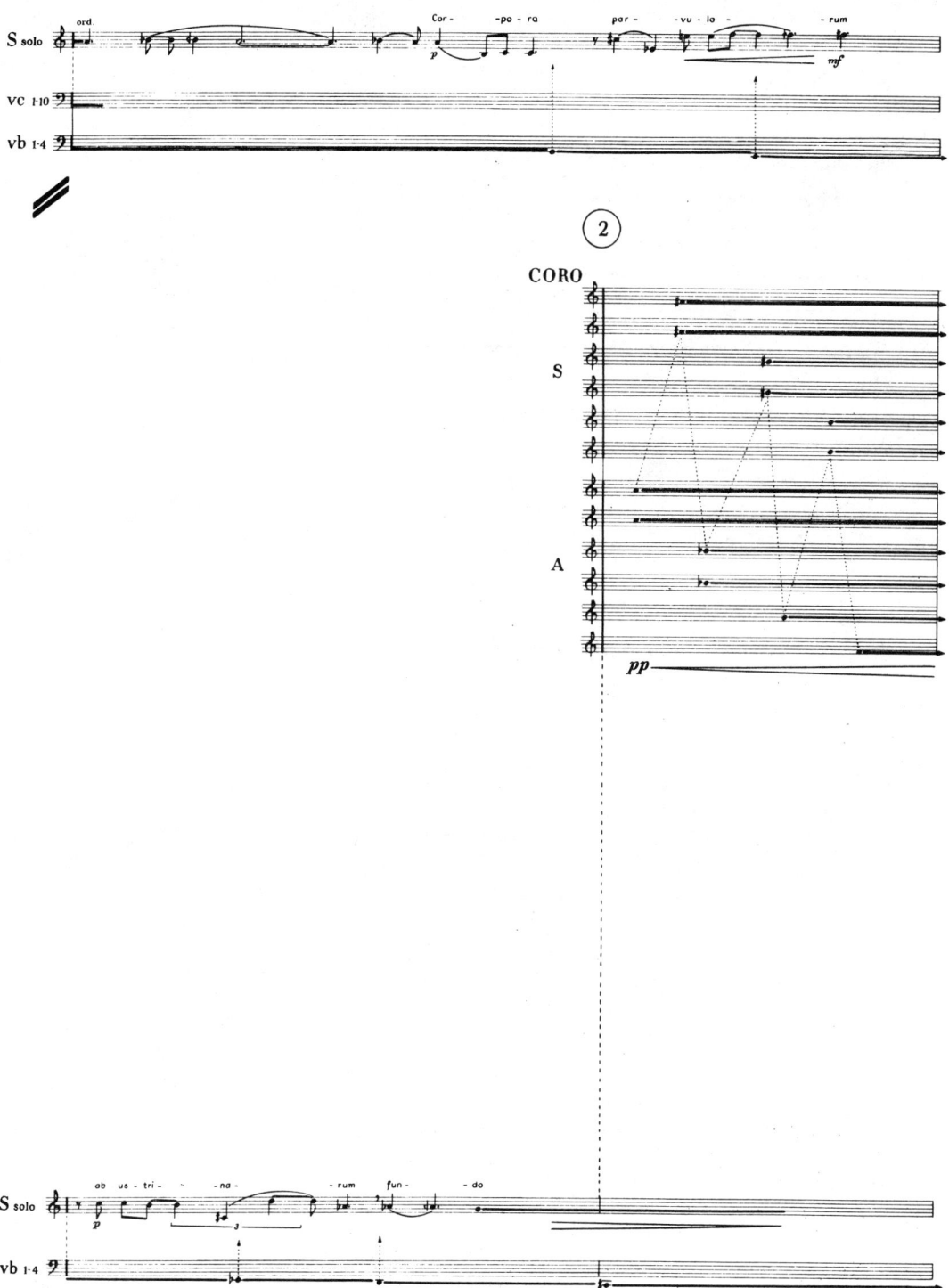

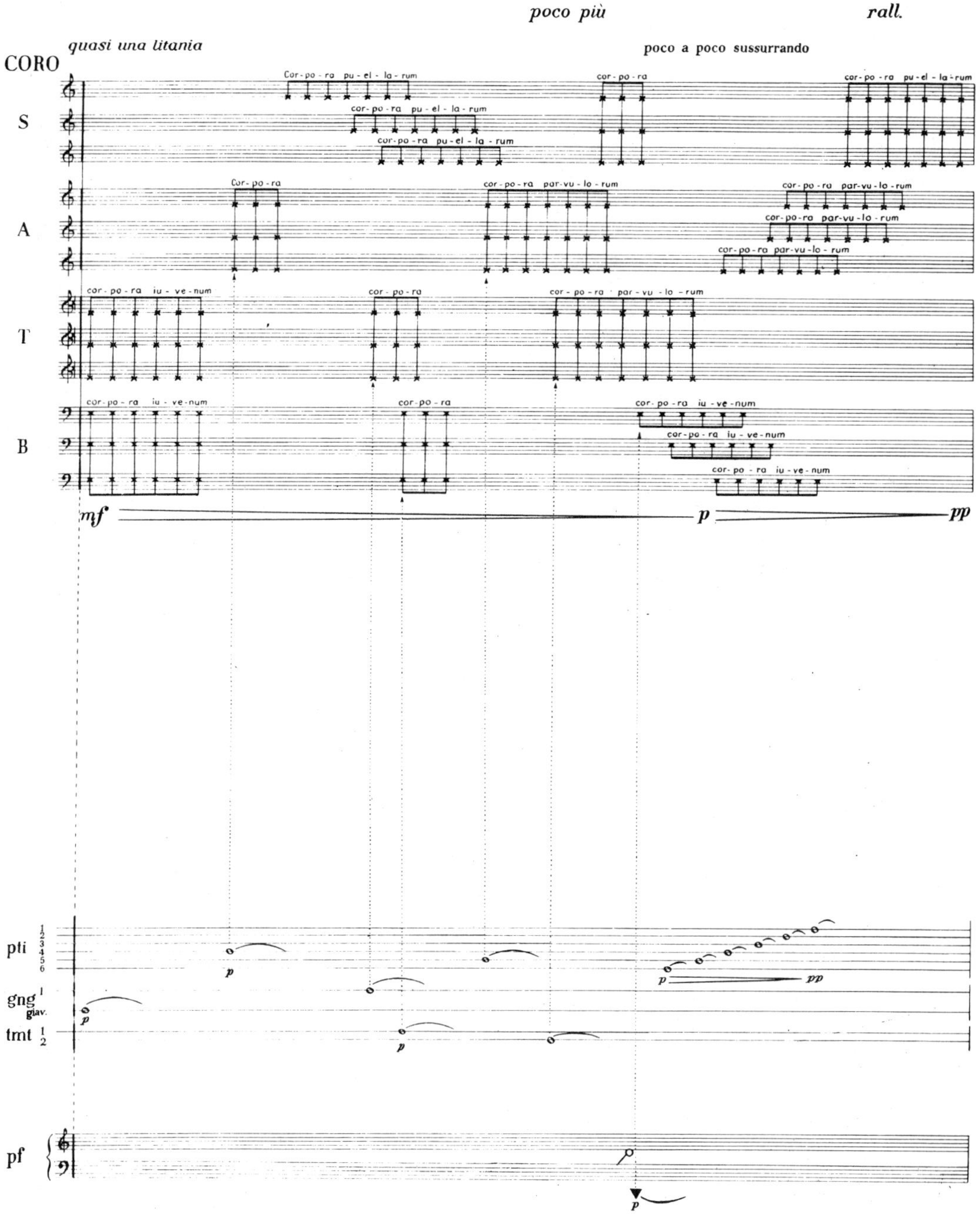
poco più
rall.
quasi una litania
poco a poco sussurrando
CORO
S
A
T
B
cor-po-ra pu-el-la-rum
cor-po-ra
cor-po-ra par-vu-lo-rum
cor-po-ra iu-ve-num
mf
p
pp
pti
gng glav.
tmt
pf

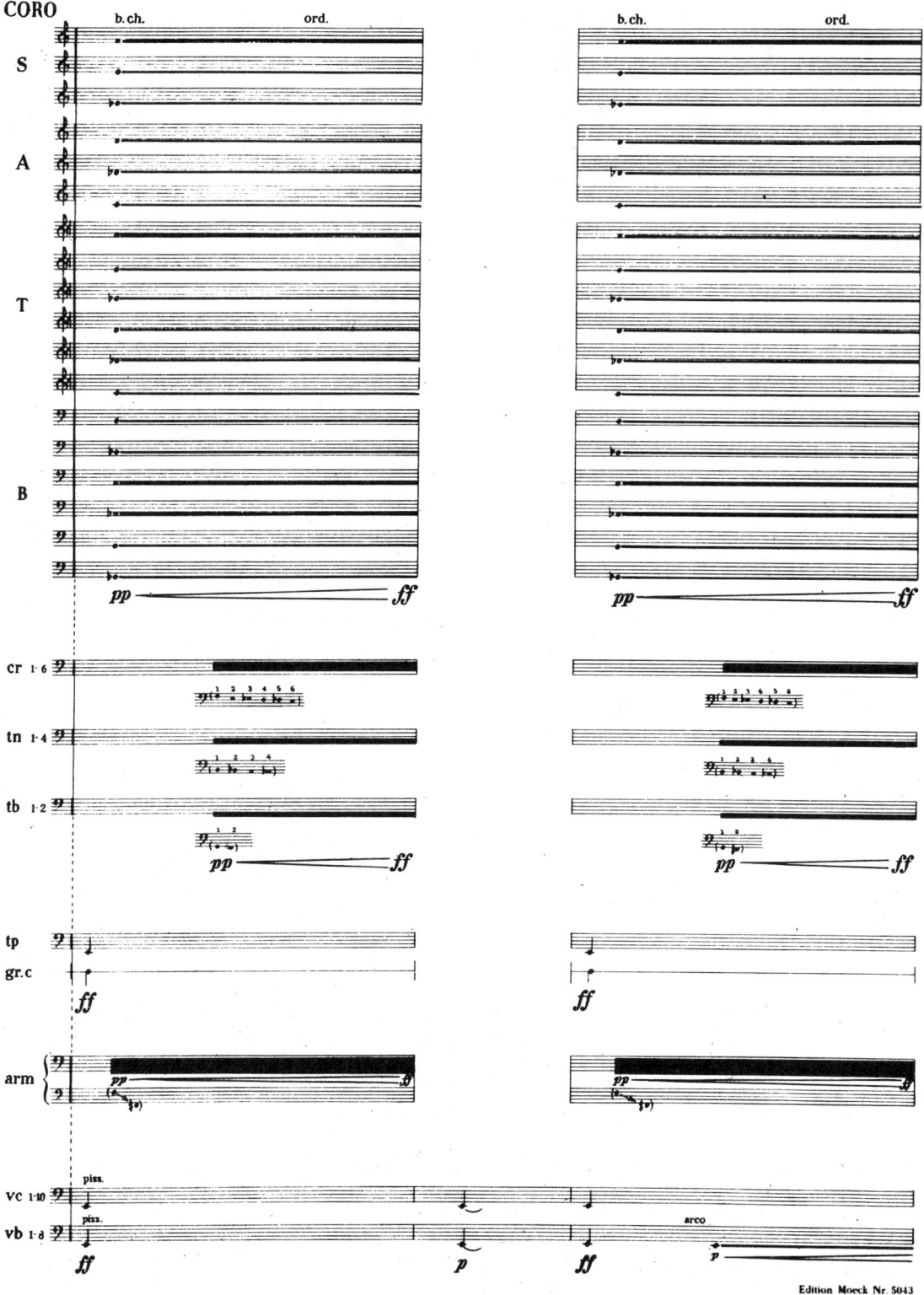

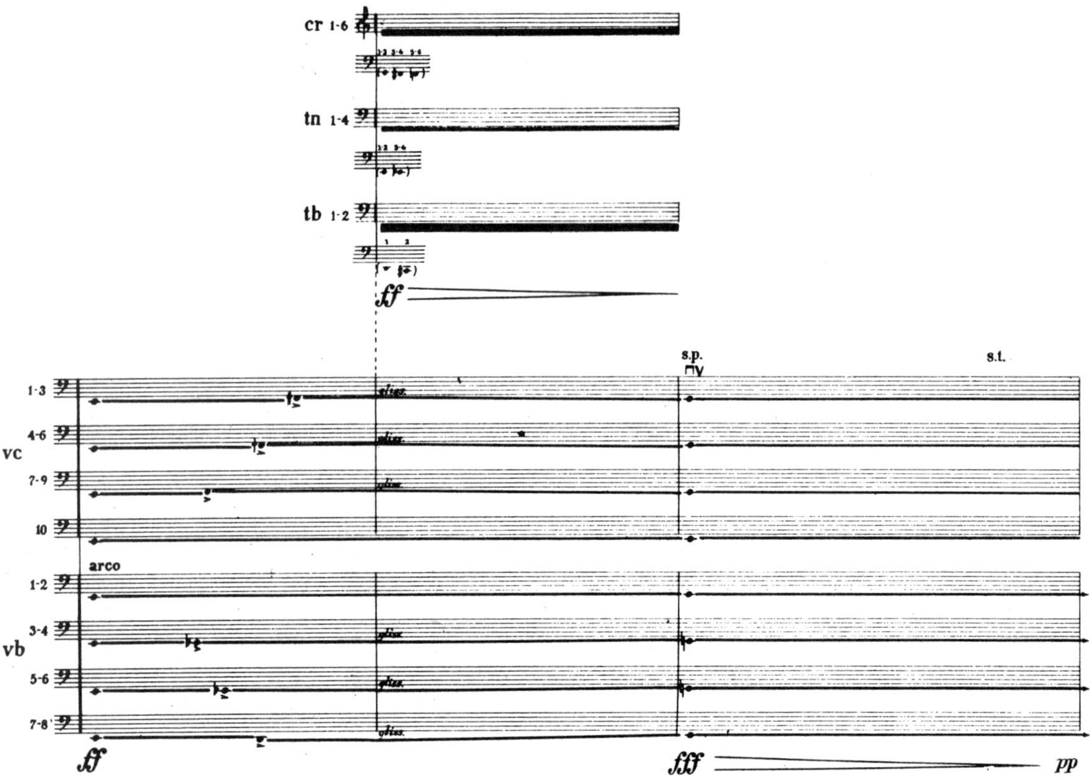
cr 1-6
tn 1-4
tb 1-2
ff
s.p.
s.t.
1-3
4-6
vc
7-9
10
arco
1-2
3-4
vb
5-6
7-8
gliss.
ff
fff
pp

5
tp
gr.c
vb 1-8
p
mp
fff
mf
ff
f

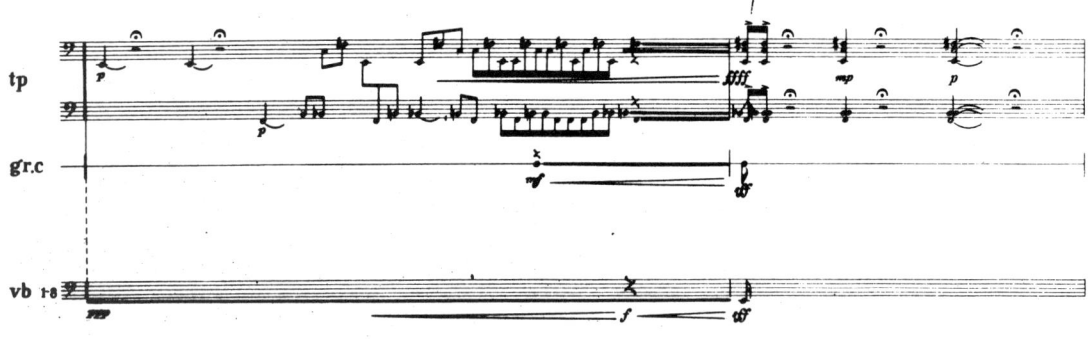

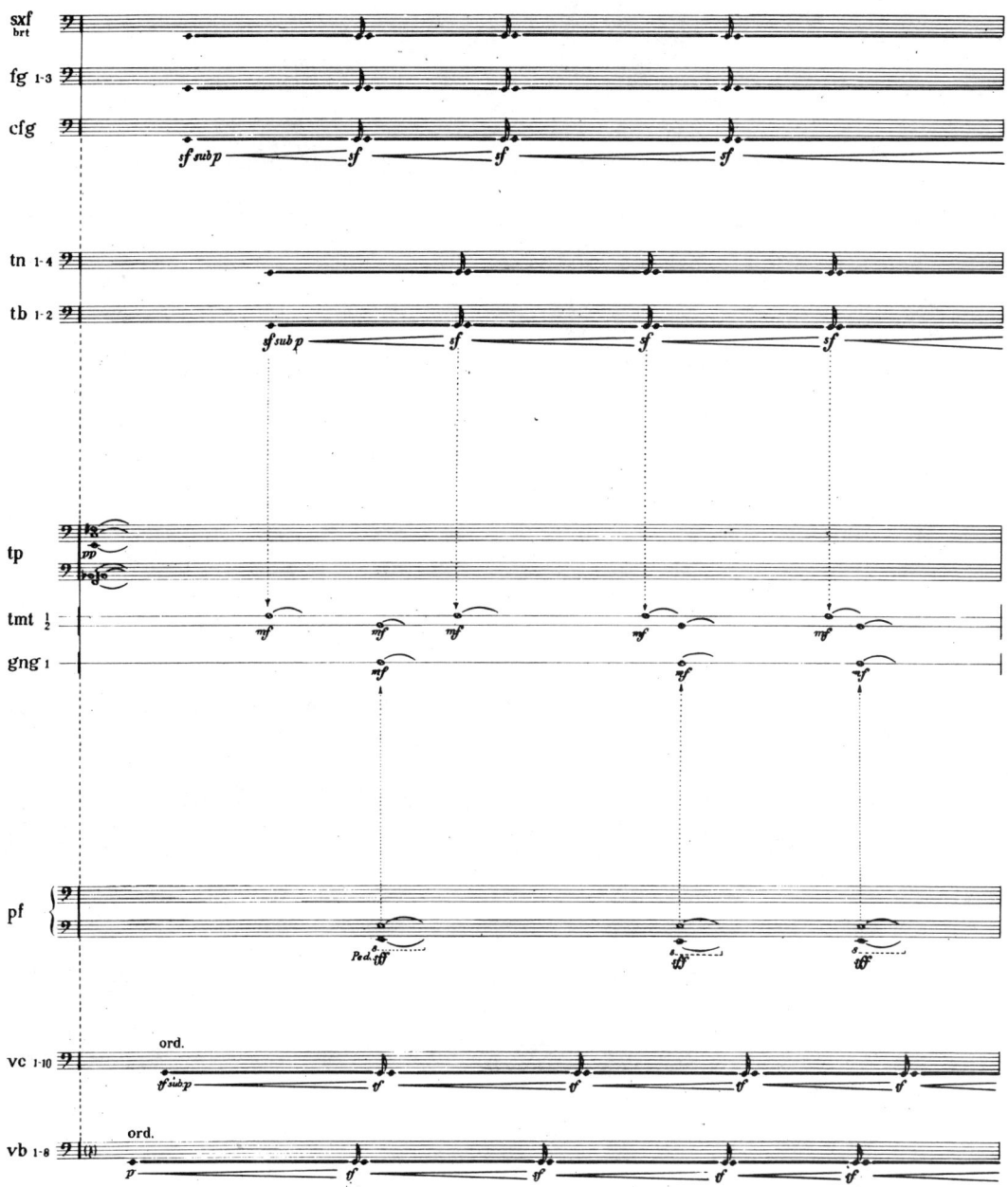

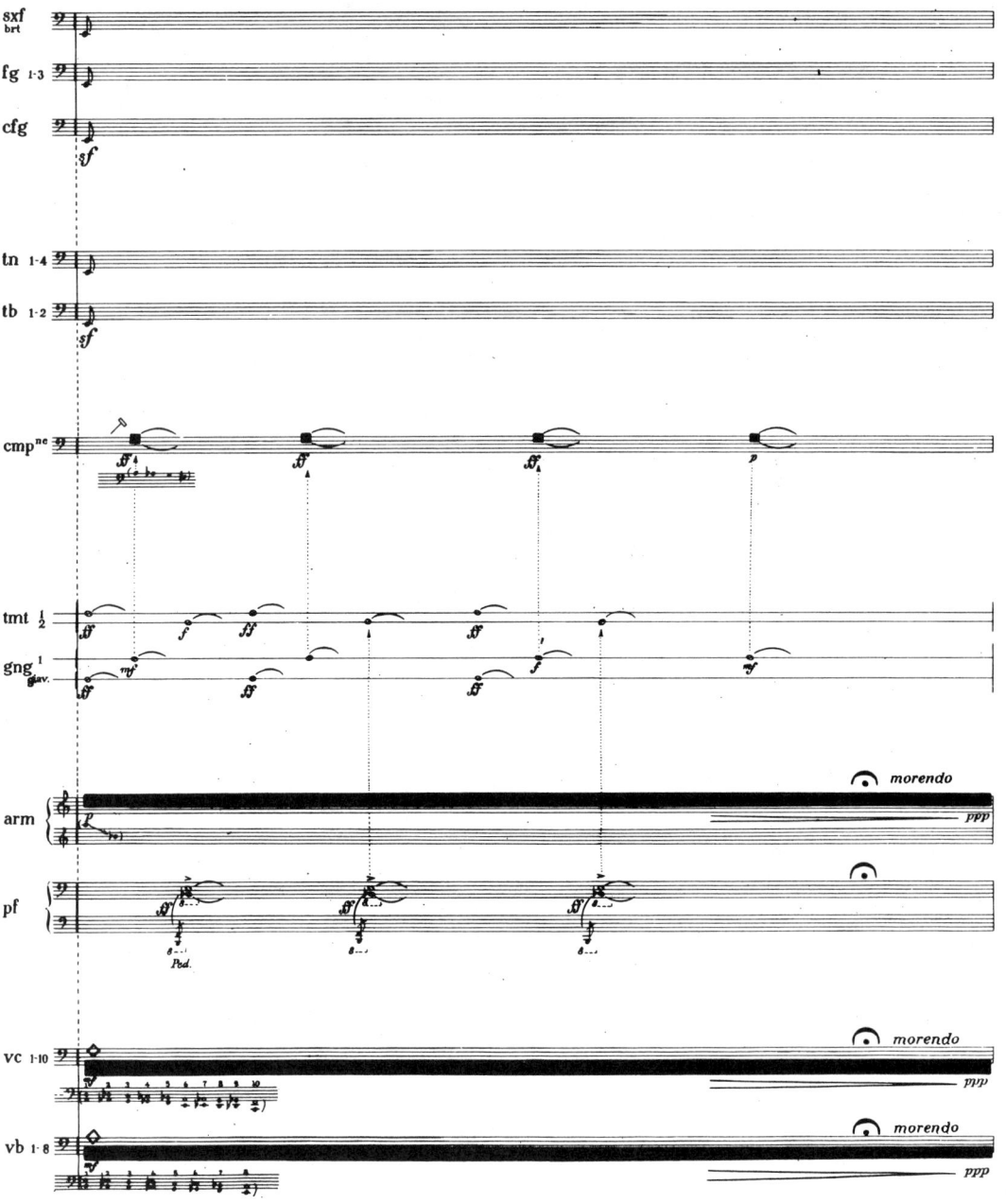

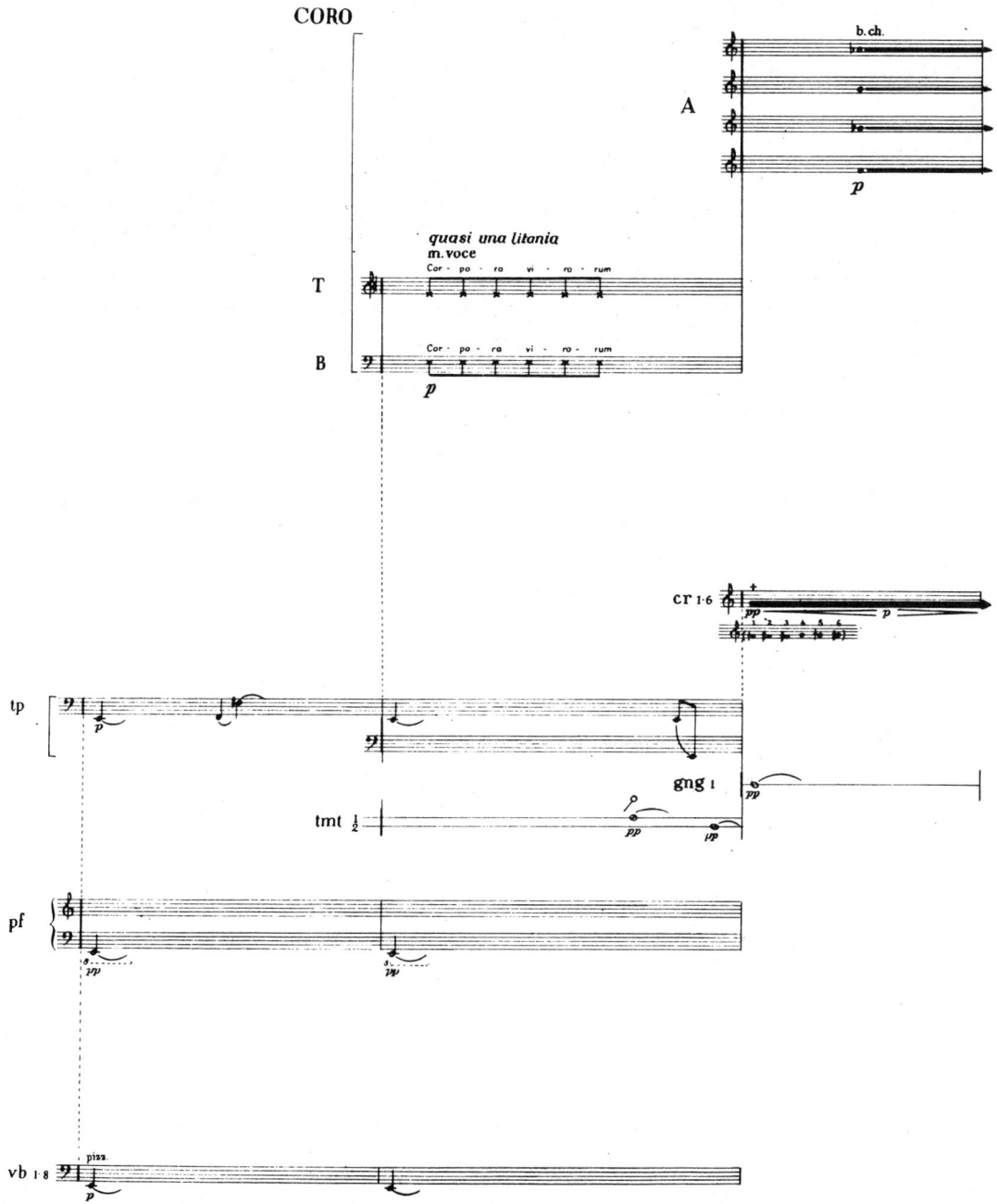

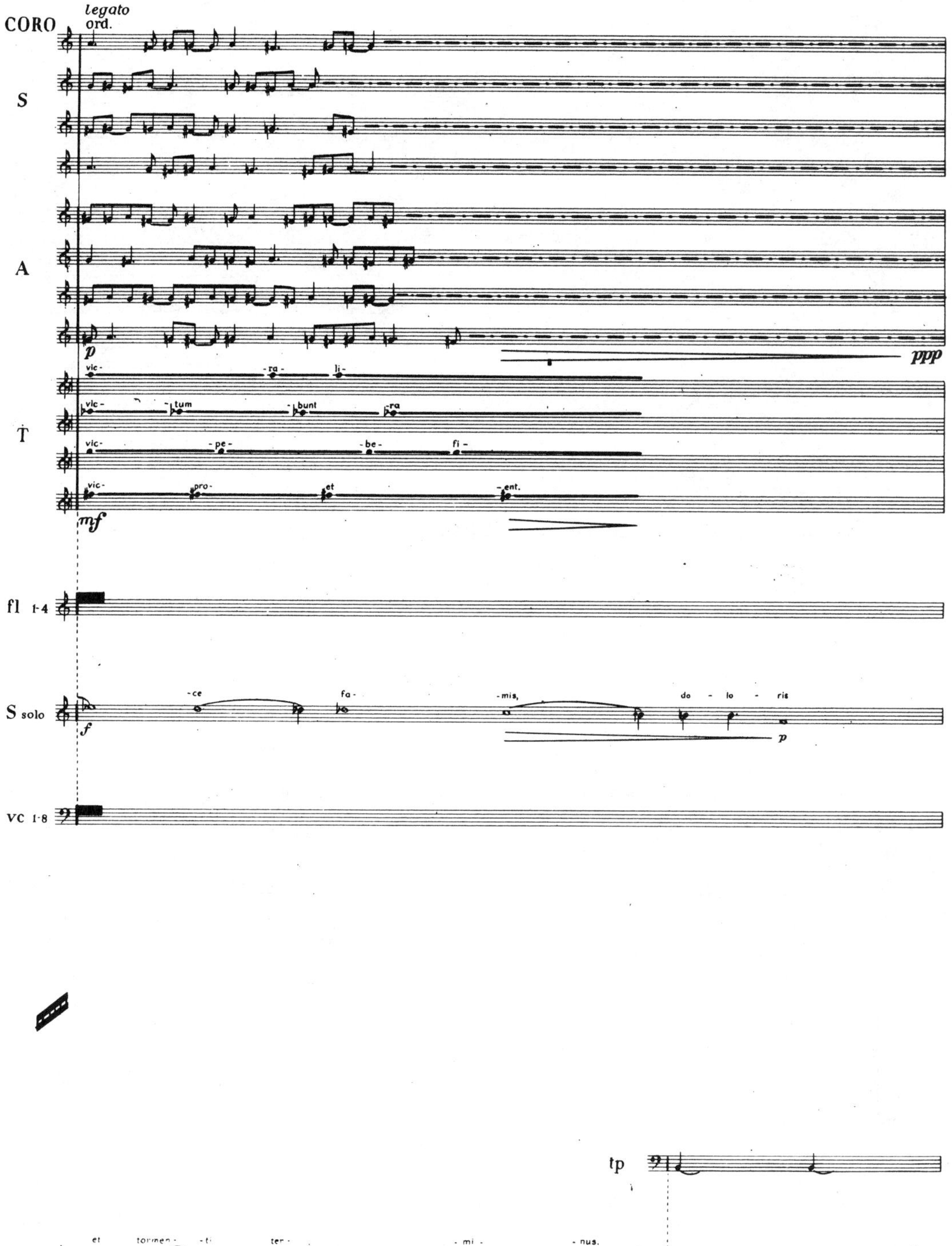
CORO
legato
ord.
S
A
T
p
ppp
vic- -ra- li-
vic- -tum -bunt -ra
vic- -pe- -be- fi-
vic- pro- et -ent.
mf
fl 1-4
S solo
-ce fa- -mis, do - lo - ris
f
p
vc 1-8
tp
S solo
et tormen- -ti ter- -mi- -nus.
mf
p
pp

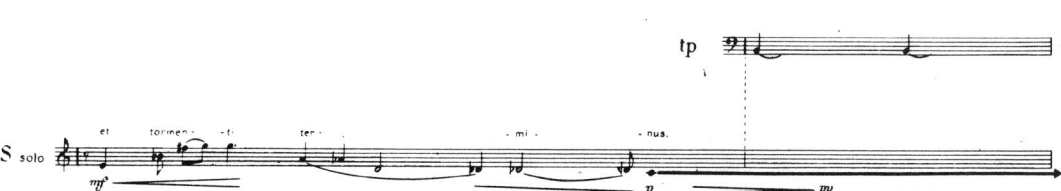

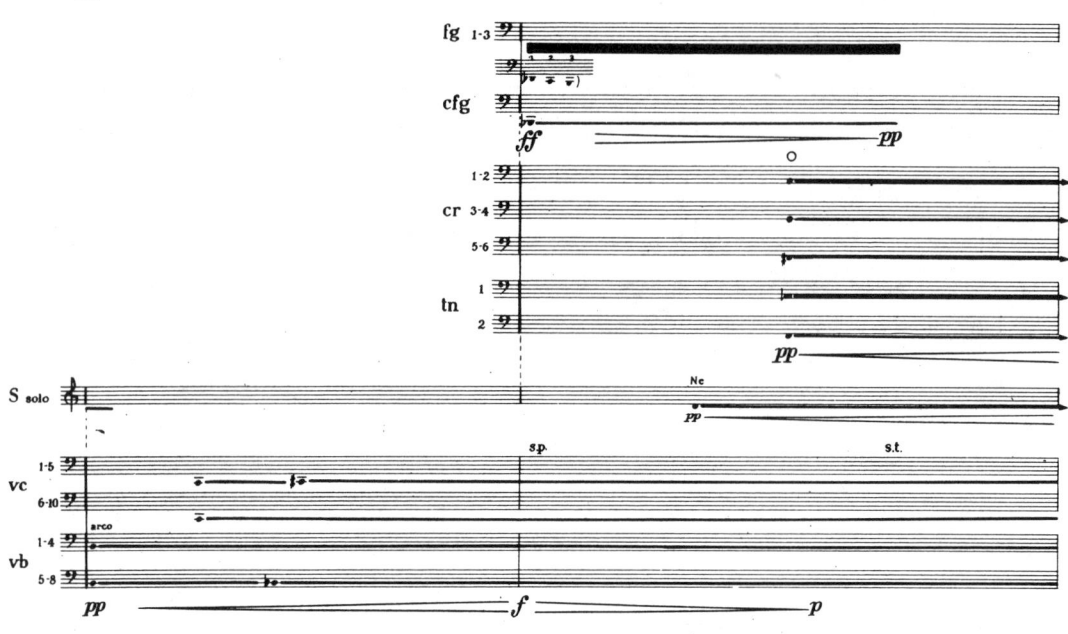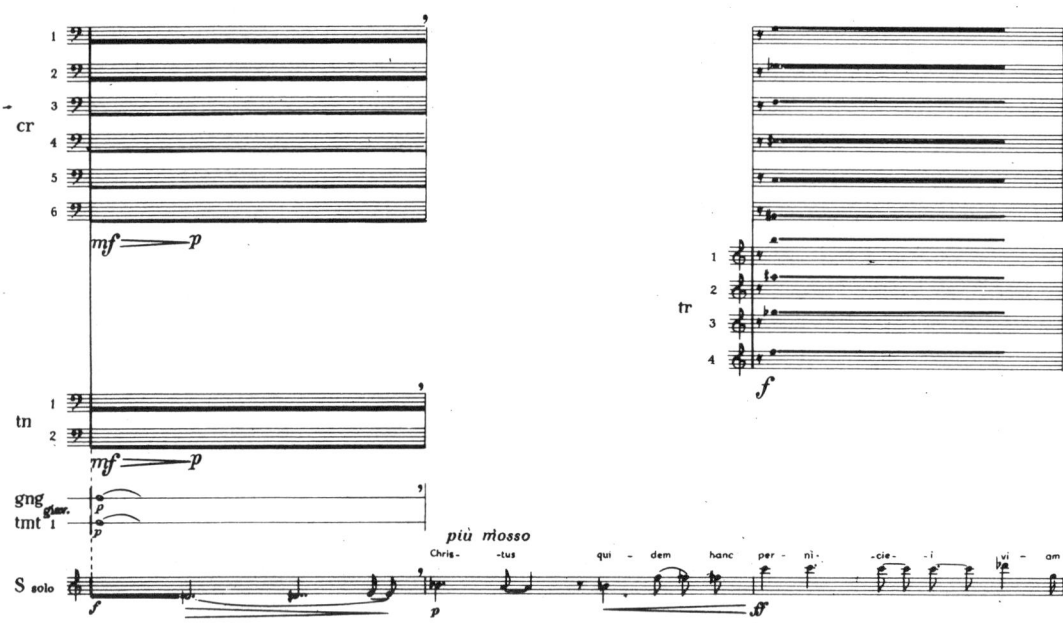

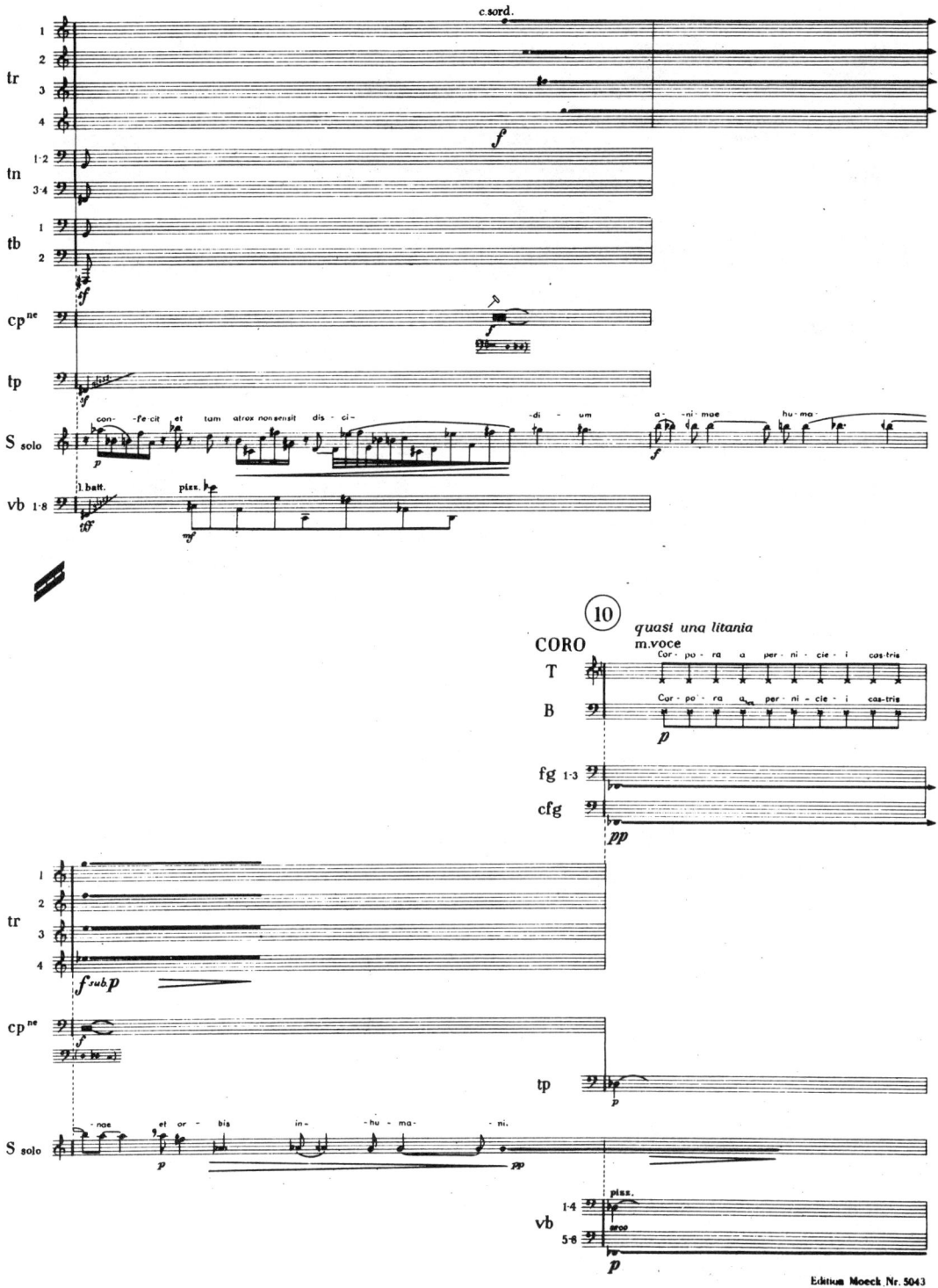

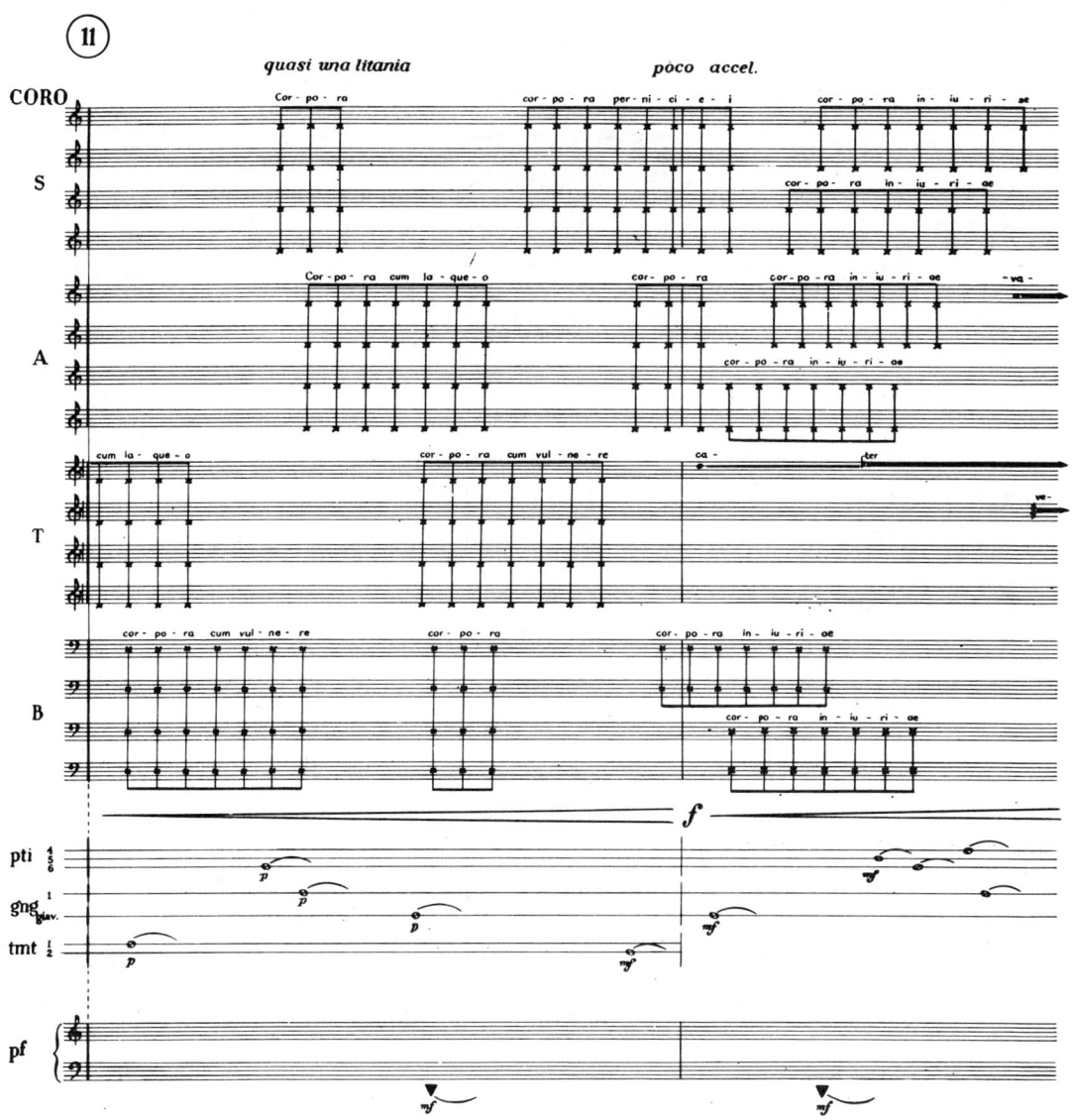

29

Krzysztof Penderecki

Dies Irae, "Lamentatio" (first movement)

In the late 1950s and early 1960s many aspects of music were reexamined. The use of pitches, rhythms, notation, melody, and harmony were all given new impetus by the subsequent developments and changes. The Polish composer Krzysztof Penderecki (born 1933) has been an important innovator in recent years. In particular, his use of clusters, his development of new notation, and his exploitation of new sounds from traditional instruments have proven significant for contemporary composition.

The *Dies Irae* explores all of these new areas, demonstrating why many of the pieces Penderecki wrote in the 1960s became so important and influential. The rhythmic notation is a combination of traditional and non-metric **proportional notation.** The horizontal spatial relationships on the page indicate the relative time placements of each event. Usually Penderecki provides a time indication for each page when dealing with proportional notation, to indicate specifically that the length of the page coincides with the amount of time indicated. In the present example, Penderecki does not provide specific timings, but allows the conductor great freedom in determining the length of each passage.

Measures, or at least bar lines, are retained in this piece, but the use of standard note forms to indicate durational values is rare. In most cases, the length of a note is shown by the length of the line extending after it. Lines and dotted lines are also employed to indicate duration of tone clusters and repetition of melodic patterns. For example:

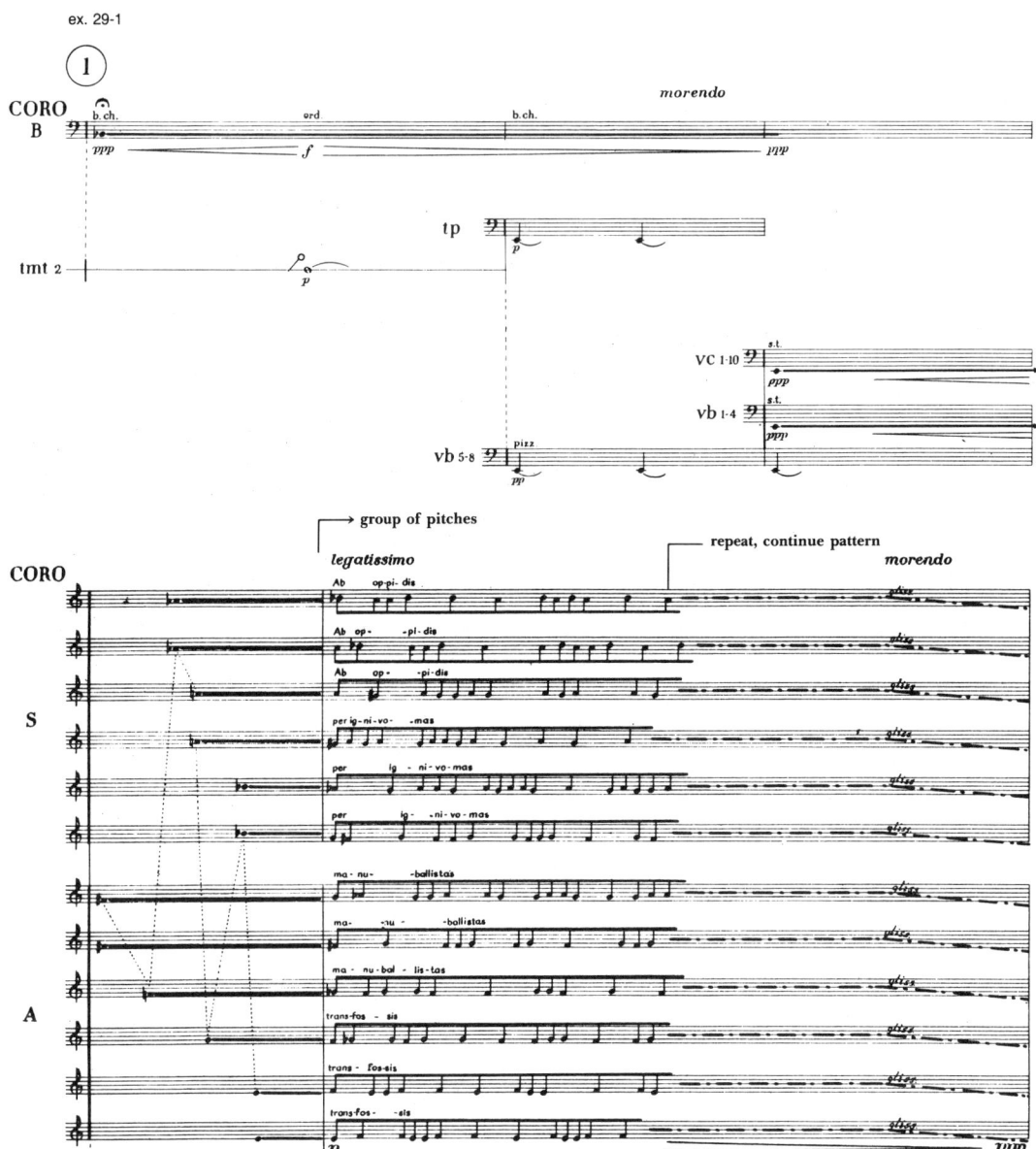

ex. 29-1

This score often gives only a representation of the sound, with pitches indicated below. The following shows a section of score and its equivalent.

ex. 29-2

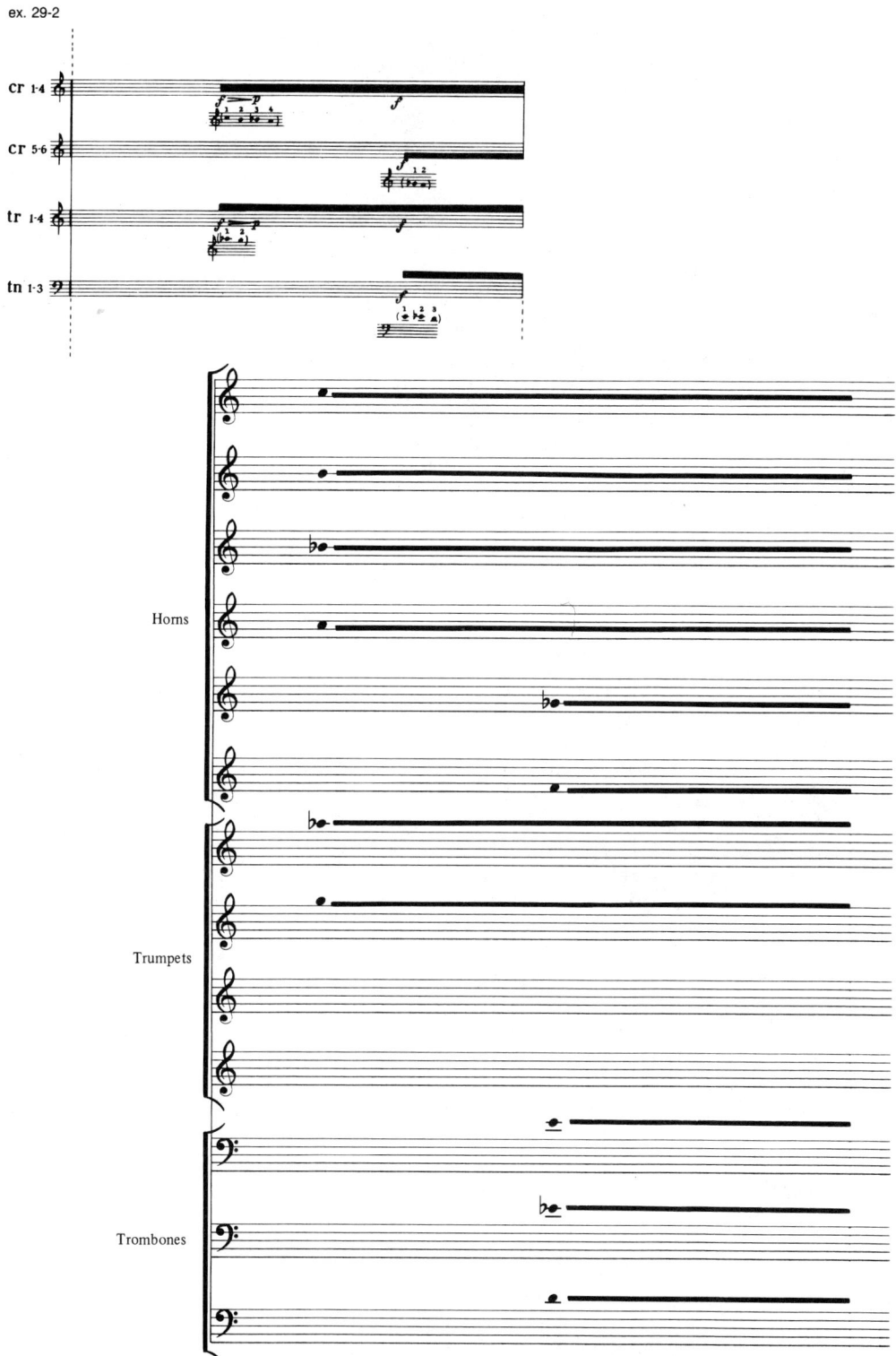

It is obvious that the composer preferred his final version as the more compact of the two, and because it is also easier to read.

The characteristic sound of the "Lamentatio" is primarily produced by the *cluster.* Clusters can be formed with diatonic pitches, whole tones, half tones or quarter tones:

ex. 29-3

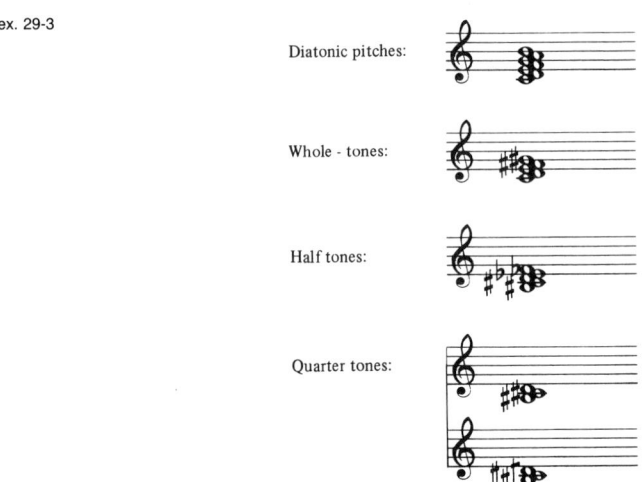

Though each is constructed by the grouping of adjacent pitches, each has a different sonority. Of course, Penderecki was not the first to use the cluster; as we have seen, Bartók used it early in his career, as did many other composers in the early part of this century, especially Henry Cowell and Charles Ives. Penderecki, however, has made this sound a primary part of his harmonic language.

Several new instrumental techniques in this piece require new symbols to indicate the method of performance. A full list is given in the beginning of the score. Using these symbols, Penderecki exploits the extremely wide range of sound production of which stringed instruments are capable. In this movement, however, the exploration of new textures is of primary importance; the new instrumental techniques are more fully explored in the other movements of the *Dies Irae.*

The musical content of the piece is radically different from the music of the past. Penderecki's approach to sound involves large clusters rather than traditional melody, harmony, and counterpoint. Penderecki gradually builds up a sound and then spatially moves it. One of the major developmental techniques in the piece is this *moving* cluster.

However, even though the sound and the notation represent a radical departure from the past, there still remain many links to traditional musical concepts. There are several melodic ideas and shapes; a kind of harmonic progression is created; groups of pitches and chords form phrases with appropriate cadences, phrases that can be grouped together to form sections; dramatic climaxes are created by means of musical motion to and from points of tension and repose.

The opening "motive" is a **gesture** typical of Penderecki. It consists of only one pitch, but produces a musical flow through the use of dynamics that makes us hear it in the same way that we hear other melodic ideas.

ex. 29-4

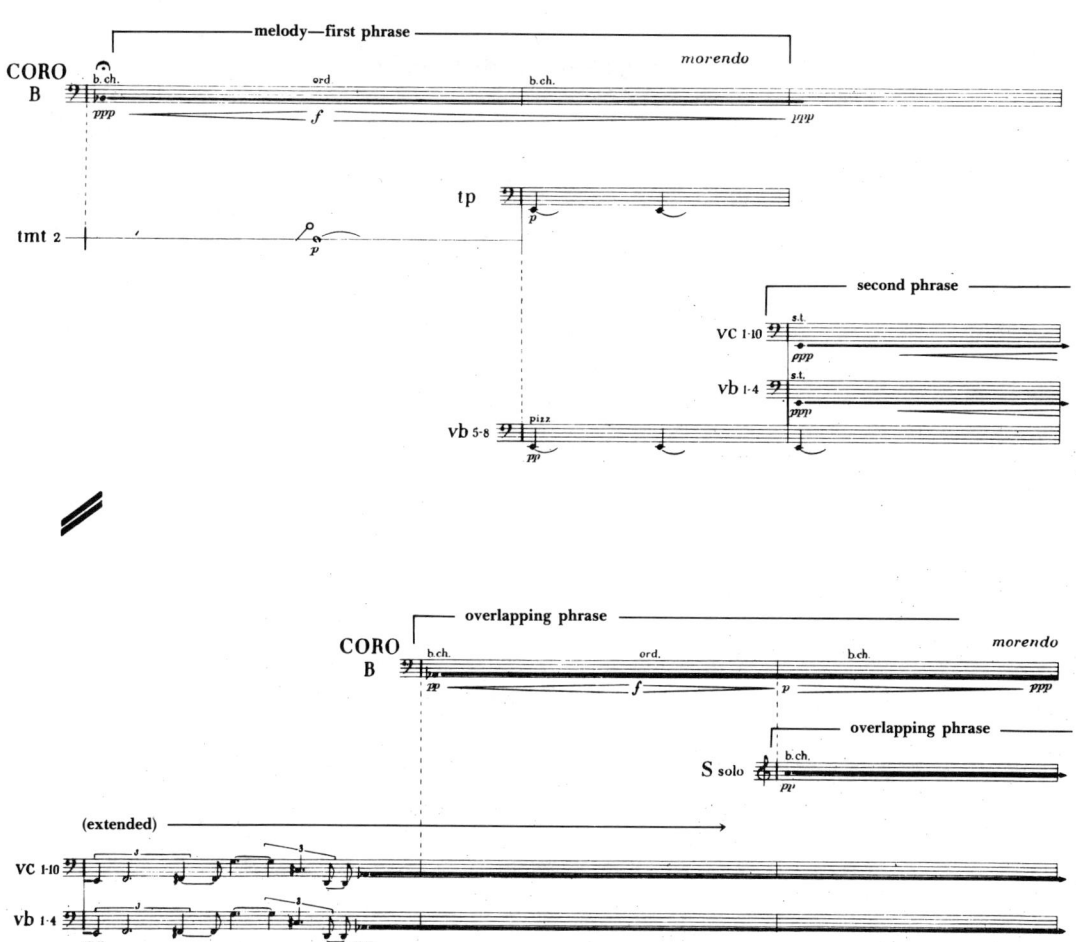

The example shows not only the first idea, but the extension of it as well, with overlapping phrases beginning with the second choral entry and soprano entry.

Sometimes Penderecki uses a chord or cluster in the same manner as a melodic line.

ex. 29-5

Although this cluster is stationary, Penderecki also calls for clusters created by nonstationary instrumental parts.

ex. 29-6

There are some cases when the overlapping text lines create a "contrapuntal" texture.

ex. 29-7

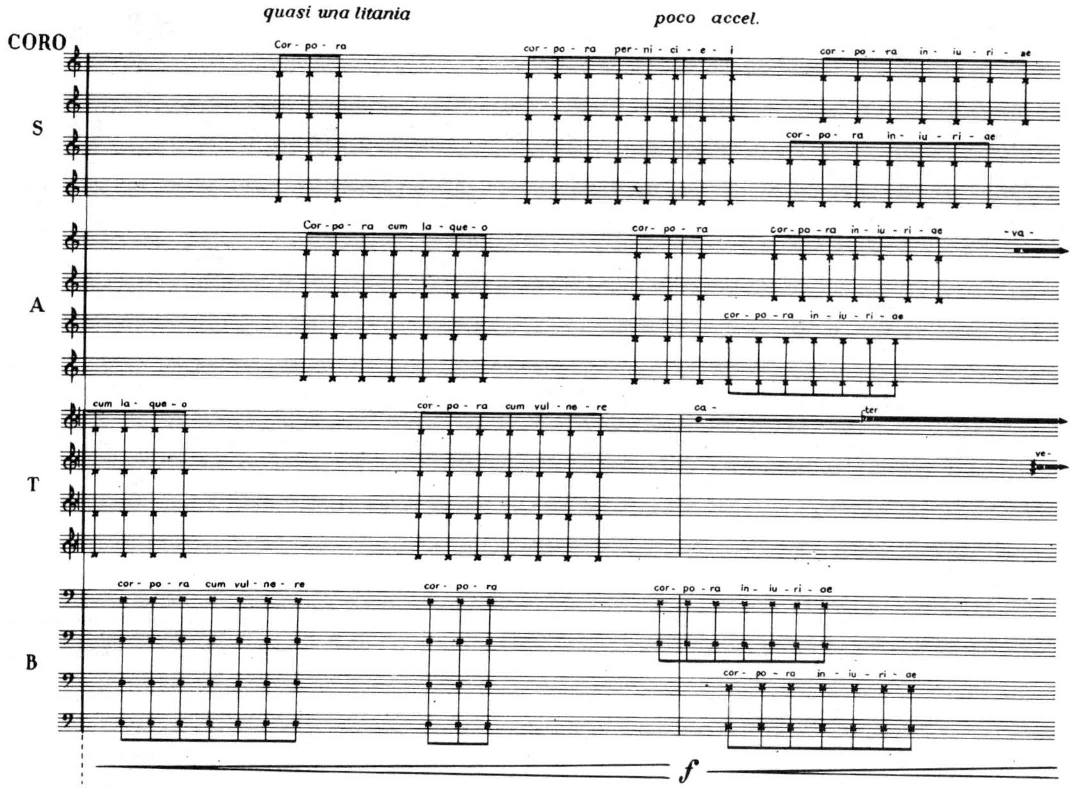

quasi una litania
poco accel.
CORO
S
A
T
B
Cor - po - ra
cor - po - ra per - ni - ci - e - i
cor - po - ra in - iu - ri - ae
Cor - po - ra cum la - que - o
cum la - que - o
cor - po - ra cum vul - ne - re
ca -
ter
ve -
va -
f

The sections of the piece can be discerned from the ***grouping of phrases.*** Several phrases, usually overlapped, are grouped together followed by a strong cadence on a chord which ends the section.

ex. 29-8

end of phrase
morendo
CORO
B
b.ch.
ord.
ppp
f
tp
tmt 2
beginning of new phrase
s.t.
vc 1-10
vb 1-4
vb 5-8
pizz
pp

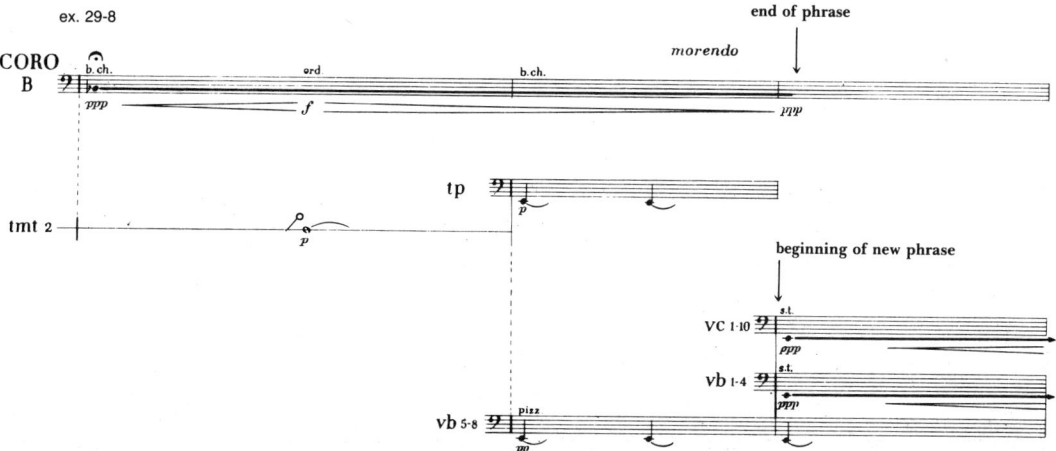

CORO
B
b.ch.
ord.
b.ch.
morendo
pp
f
p
ppp
beginning of new phrase
S solo
b.ch.
pp
end of phrase
(extension)
vc 1-10
vb 1-4
mp
pp
end of phrase
beginning of new phrase
S solo
ord.
Cor- -po - ra
par- -vu - lo - -rum
p
mf
vc 1-10
vb 1-4
beginning of new phrase
CORO
S
A
pp
end of phrase
S solo
ab us - tri - -na - -rum fun- -do
p
vb 1-4

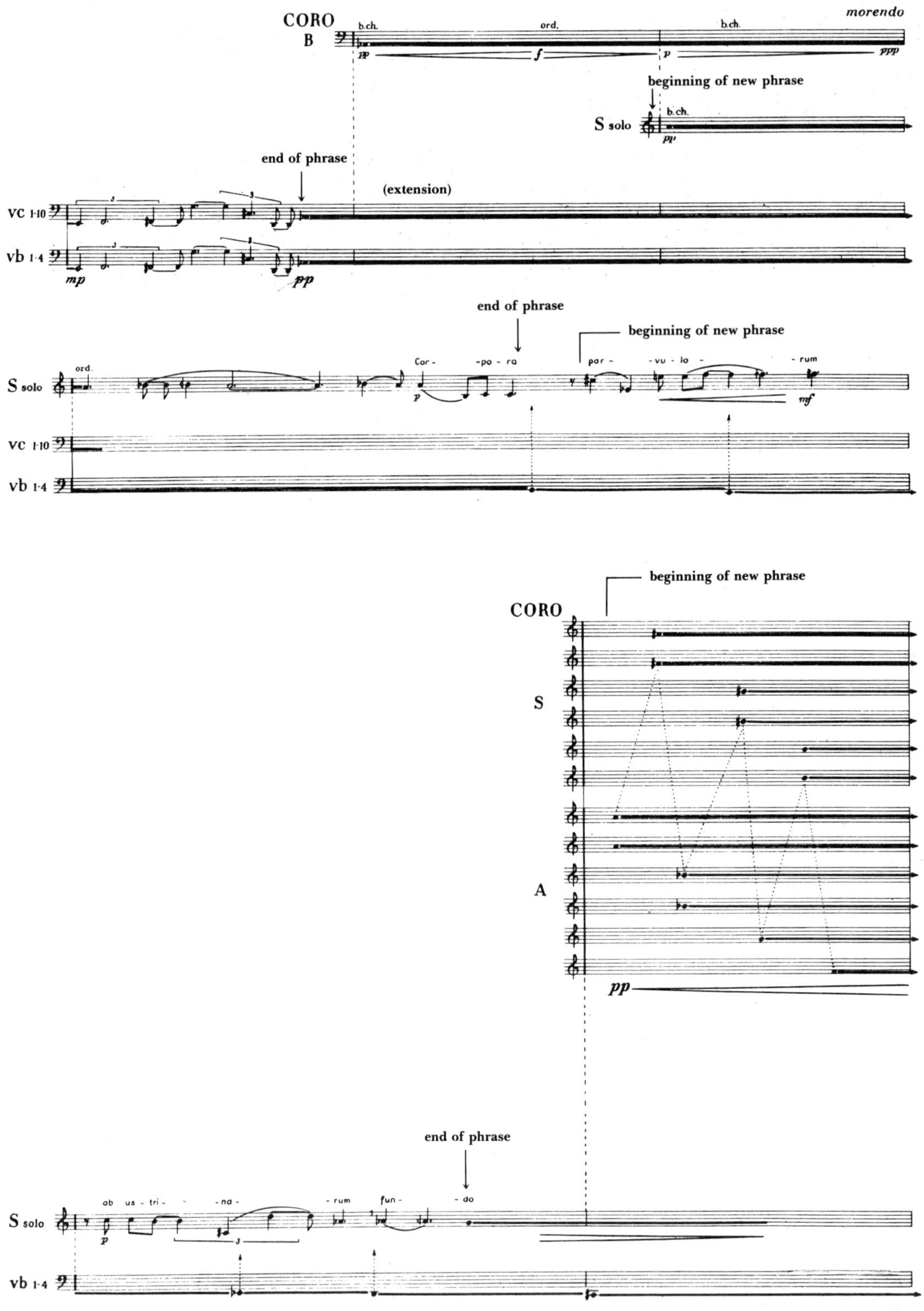

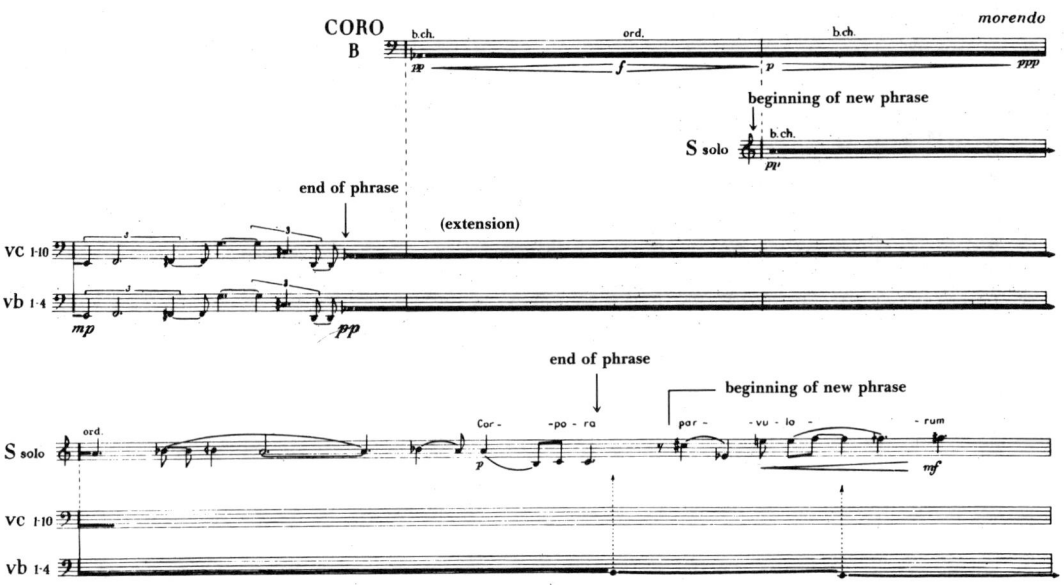

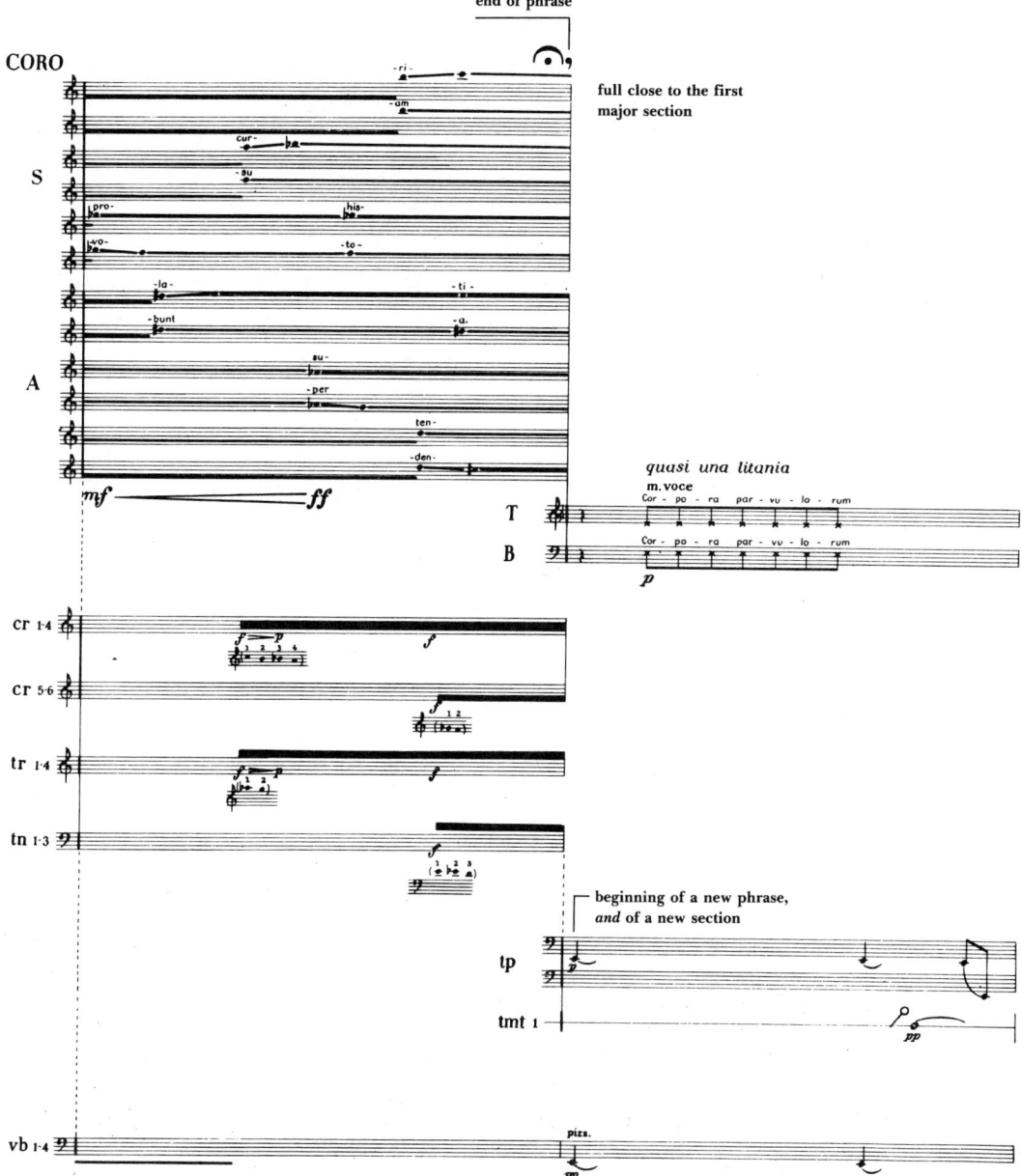

The musical ideas used here are the single-note motive, the soprano's melodic phrase, and the chordal ending.

Following this section, two musical ideas play a large role in the rest of the musical action in the piece: the single timpani pitch and the spoken chorus part (usually on the word "corpora").

ex. 29-9

This is then extended (at ④) by the moving chord, the repeated timpani note, and the chordal cadence, and further extended (before ⑤) by a combination of the timpani pitch (*e*), the single-note motive from the beginning, and another chordal cadence.

The timpani material at ⑤ produces a further extension, as does the material at ⑥.

ex. 29-10

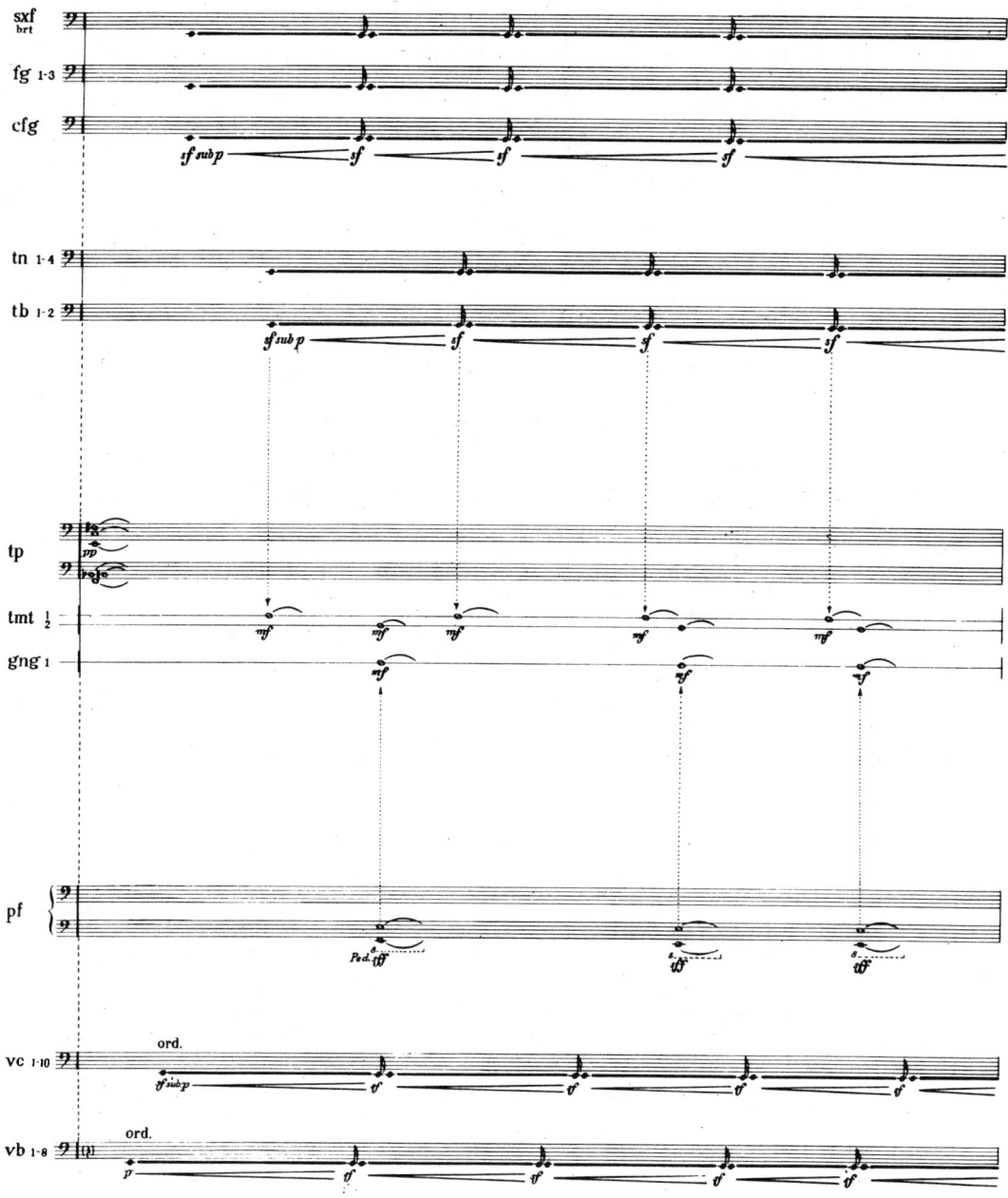

All of the material in the piece is derived from these basic ideas. They are extended and developed, overlapped and juxtaposed in an effort to create unity and an overall sense of structural design and motion through the piece.

The **harmonic material** is primarily based on the half-step (occasionally, quarter-tone) clusters. When a single line is used it, too, emphasizes the half step. There are expansions of this as well.

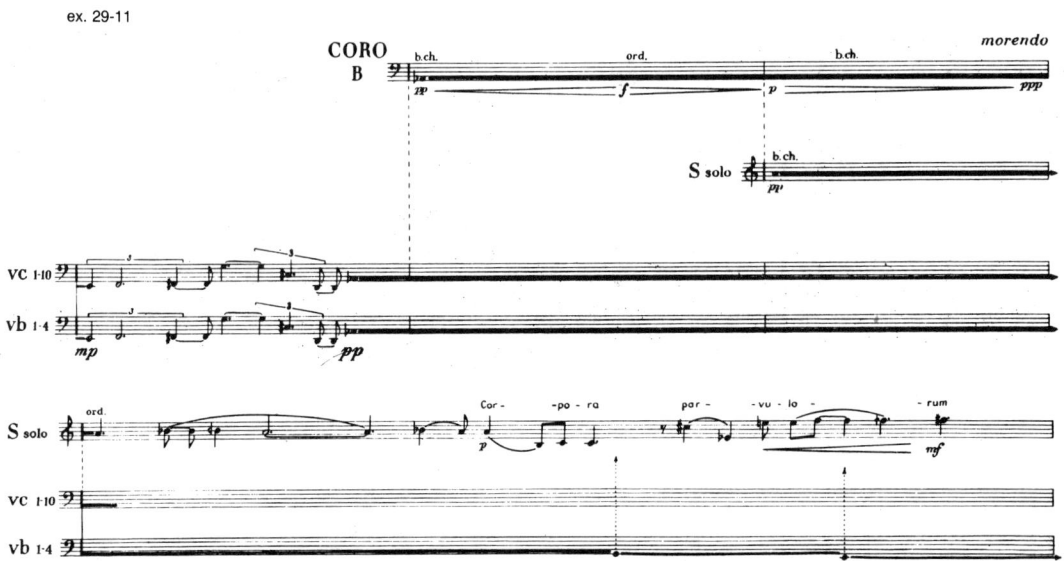

ex. 29-11

The half step is heard prominently here, often registrally expanded to a major seventh or minor ninth (augmented octave). In addition, there is a strong use of the tritone. The quarter tone is used only occasionally here, but is nonetheless an important component of the style, being used both melodically and (especially when the full string section is employed) as the basis for harmonic clusters.

The overall design of the movement reflects the phrasing, the flow of gestural ideas, and the expression of an overall dramatic plan. The first dramatic climax occurs at ⑥, and this quickly dies away. Likewise, there is a steady flow of motion toward a climax at ⑫. This, too, gradually fades to the end of the movement. The general shape, then is:

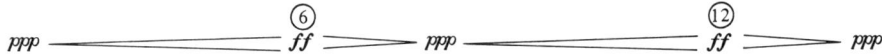

This kind of **wedge shape** is used by many composers in the twentieth century. It is a product of dynamics or the building-up of texture or, in some cases, both.

STYLE CHARACTERISTICS: MID-TWENTIETH CENTURY—EXPERIMENTAL COMPOSERS
based on Penderecki's *Dies Irae*

melody	true melody rare except in solo vocal writing • clusters used in the same way that single lines are used, moving them up and down and in various shapes
harmony	based on clusters built from whole tones, half steps, quarter tones, and combinations of these intervals • moving clusters
rhythm	basic destruction of the pulse in many cases • frequently static • predominance of proportional notation, indicating time spans by means of visual space
texture	usually extremely thick • clusters of half and quarter tones predominate • all ranges utilized, from the highest to the lowest sound obtainable from the instruments

Glossary

Cluster   a chordal sonority based on adjacent pitches. It may be of whole tones, half tones, quarter tones or diatonic.

Proportional notation   a new notational system based on the premise that duration is indicated by space on the page. For instance, lengths of notes are usually indicated by the length of the line after the notehead.

Wedge-shape   the use of texture, dynamics, melody or a combination of forces to produce a dramatic shape of increasing or decreasing size: $<$ or $>$.

Suggested Exercises

1. Write a piece for four instruments from the same instrumental family (woodwinds, brass, or strings) using clusters of major and minor seconds. Structure the piece in an A B B' A' design, with each section using a different interval basis. Use proportional notation. The piece should last three minutes.
2. Provide a complete analysis of the phrase structure of the "Lamentatio."

Before Reading Chapter 30

1. Listen to *Madrigals,* Book IV, by George Crumb.
2. Analyze all of the melodic intervals in the voice part on the first page of "¿Por qué nací entre espejos?"
3. Analyze all of the intervals in the second section (between the second and third double bars).

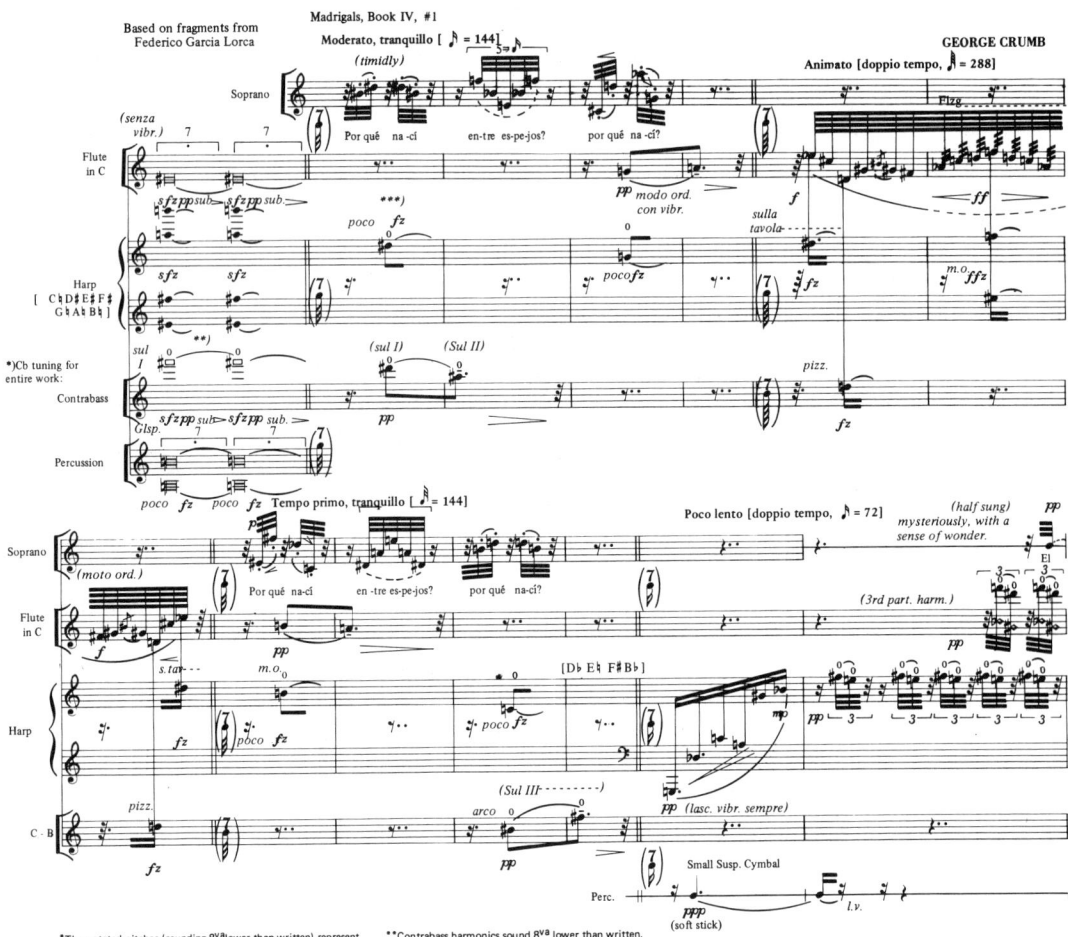

George Crumb

30

(*Madrigals,* Book IV, No. 1) "¿Por qué nací entre espejos?"

      Various styles, techniques, and compositional aesthetics have been explored throughout the twentieth century, and such exploration continues today. Many different kinds of composers are writing at present. However, as in any period, there are always certain composers with an arresting and distinctive style who capture a wide audience. George Crumb (born 1929) is such a composer.

      The initial impact of a work by Crumb resides in its extremely intricate, carefully controlled sound. The dramatic moments are few, and these are often unexpected interjections rather than dramatic climaxes produced by sustained crescendos. Common instruments are often made to produce unusual sounds, adding additional flavor to Crumb's distinctive sonorities.

      As in the works of any composer, a body of identifiable musical ideas is presented and developed within a piece by Crumb. With Crumb, the prominent musical moment is the **gesture.** In certain cases this may function as a motive, but usually the entire complex of sound, sometimes even considering the disposition of all the instruments, must be taken into account.

      The first section of the present work (up to the second double bar) contains some clearly identifiable gestures.

ex. 30-1

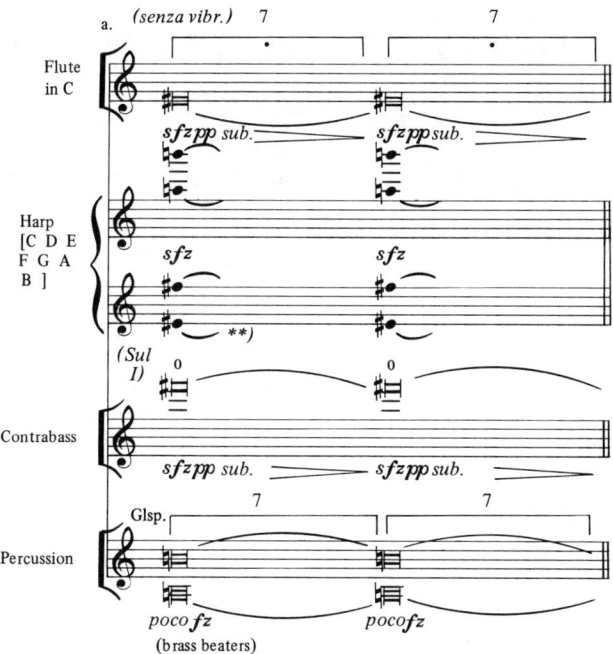

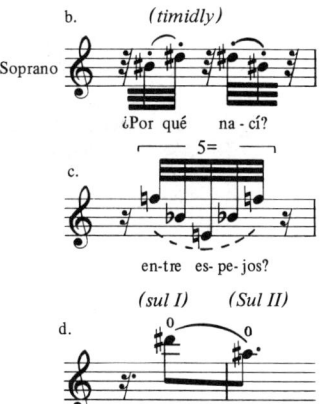

Two extensions of the first idea can be seen in the sixth bar. Both the linear presentation of the chord and the *sfz* idea are used.

ex. 30-2

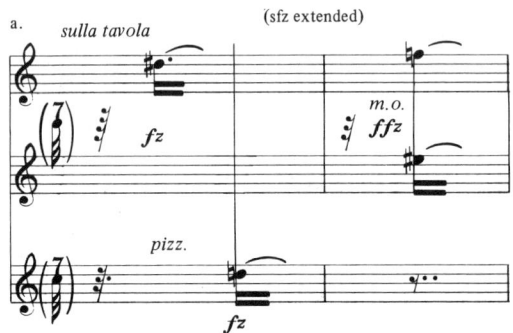

The sections are delineated by the double bars. The second section relates to the introductory two chords by means of the harmonic references as well as the *sfz* gesture. These brief, wistful ideas are quietly intertwined. Their relation to both the introduction and the first section indicates that this could be considered a development; however, it should perhaps be regarded as an extension.

The third section looks very much like the opening section, using the same gestures in almost the same order.

The next section (from the fourth to the fifth double bar) is as long as the opening three sections combined, and contains development of the material previously presented.

ex. 30-3

This section presents a contrast to the opening three sections.

It is followed by a basic repetition of the first three sections. Therefore, the large form appears as:

$$\text{a–b–a—c—a–b–a}$$
$$\text{A} \quad \text{B} \quad \text{A}$$

This large sectional design seems to correlate with the small-scale musical design. Consider the b section.

ex. 30-4

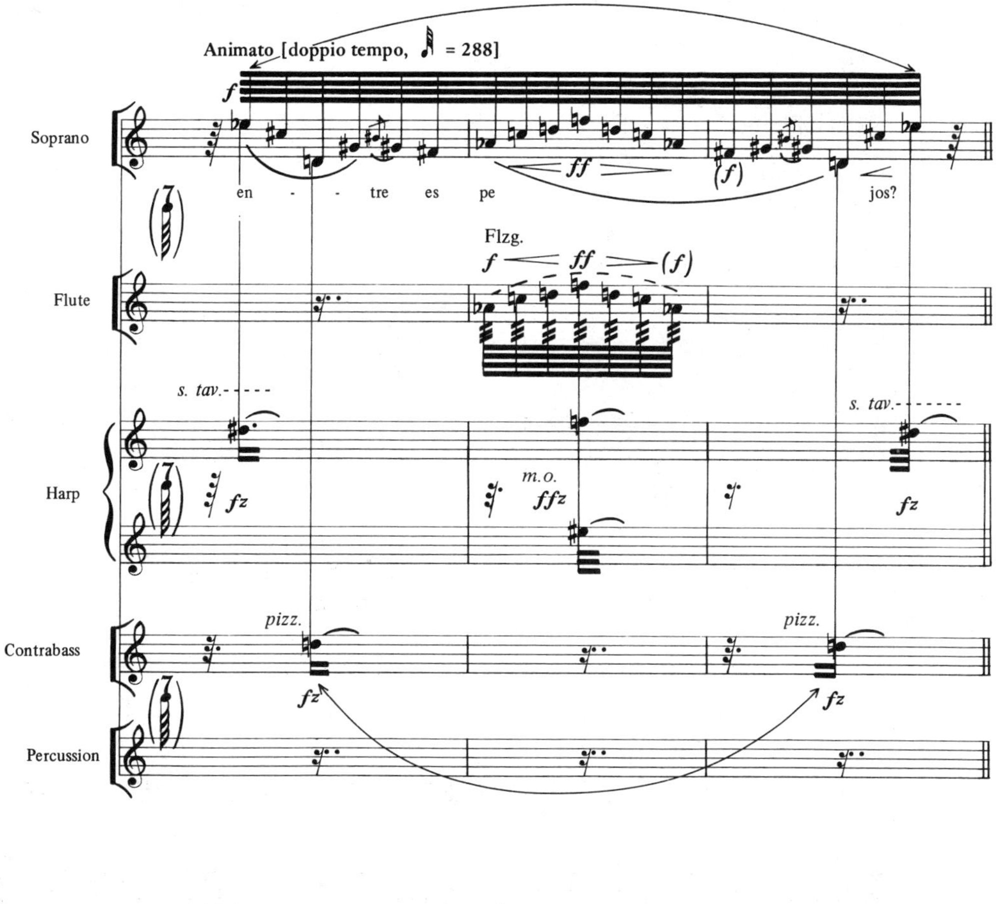

Its *symmetrical nature* is striking. In fact, this passage is exactly the same when read backward as when read forward; it is a mirror image of itself, a strict retrograde. This one fact may unlock others in our attempt to analyze the structure of this piece.

Compare the first and last sections of the piece:

ex. 30-5

The voice part in the beginning is transferred to the instruments (flute, then violin, then double bass) in the final section, while the instrumental part in the beginning is transferred to the voice. And, perhaps most crucial, the entire section is presented in retrograde at the end. Notice also that the *sfz* chords at the beginning of the piece reappear at the end, forming a kind of frame around the whole movement.

Could this **retrograde motion** be the fundamental premise of the piece? Compare the second and penultimate sections:

ex. 30-6

Similarly, compare the third section and the third from the end:

In each case the original material is almost exactly mirrored in the later section. The **C** section also follows this idea:

ex. 30-8

The notes at the beginning and end of this section are not exactly the same, but all the gestures and intervals are identical in reverse order. The exception to this entire retrograde premise is the voice in this section, which is rhythmically free. (Note that it also does not employ pitched sound.)

Not only are the large sections mirrored, but so are the small ones.

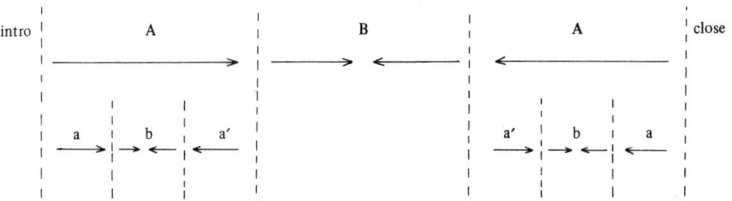

The relationship between **a** and **a′** is that the intervals are the same but in reversed order. The pitches, however, are different.

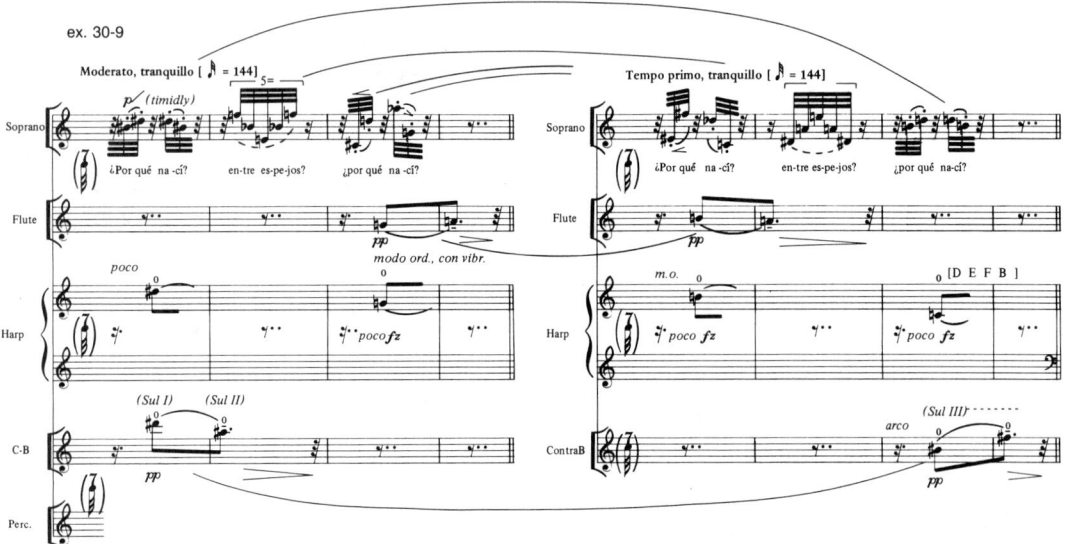

The whole piece, then, is basically a retrograde version of itself. The reason must lie in the phrase "Why was I born surrounded by mirrors?" The text's most prominent image apparently suggested to the composer the compositional premise of the piece. Not only does each phrase and small section have retrogradeable elements, but even the use of the text at the beginning and the choice of 7 as the basic metric unit are permeated with retrograde implications. The first chord is even two mirrored ninths, separated by a third.

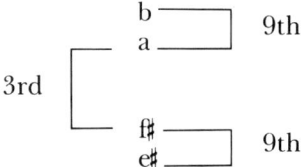

The pitch material is much more varied. In contrast to the rather rigid technique of retrograde, the vocal intervals used at the beginning contain great variety of sounds.

ex. 30-10

From this arrangement almost any relationship can be drawn upon for development.

It is important to see which pitches are emphasized within the piece. There are two basic ways of emphasizing a pitch, by accent or duration.

ex. 30-11

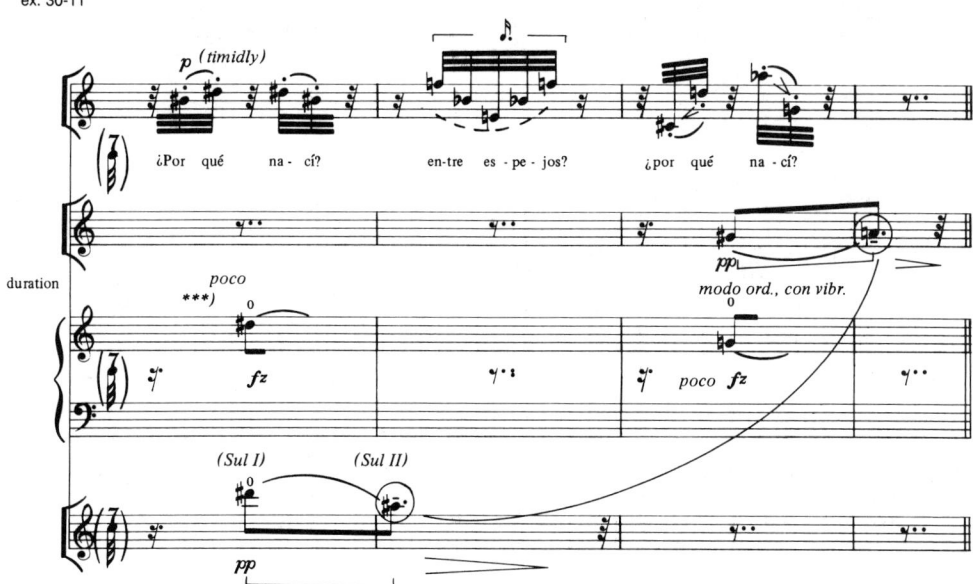

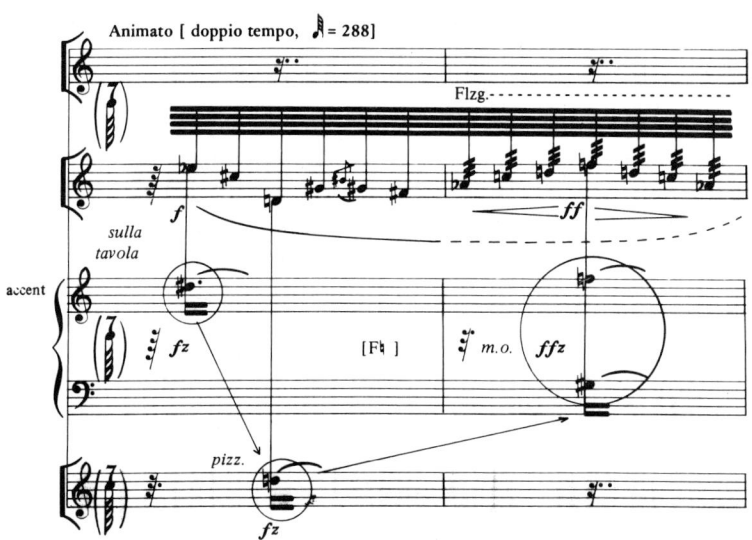

Tonal references are produced by highlighting one pitch from a more florid line. In this way Crumb can imply tonal motion, and resolution tendencies such as the hint at Phrygian cadential motion in the first example (a♯–a). The shaping of a line can highlight certain intervals, as in the case of the flute line in the second section.

ex. 30-12

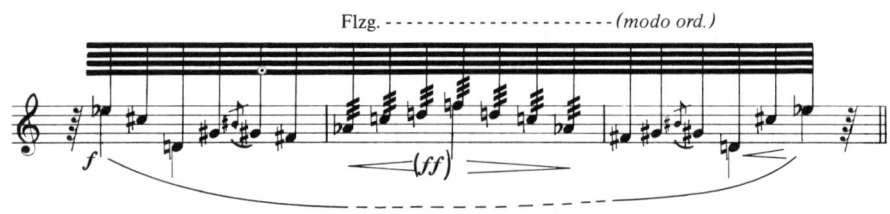

The tritone is heard prominently throughout this section and through the whole piece.

Techniques, intellectual schemes, charts and diagrams and matrices ultimately do not produce a piece of music. They may influence, direct, and consolidate a composer's ideas, but the final arbiter is the ear. George Crumb is no different from preceding composers in this regard. The characteristic sound of the tritone pervades the piece, even though it is sometimes difficult to extract.

STYLE CHARACTERISTICS: MIDDLE TO LATE TWENTIETH CENTURY—EXPERIMENTAL COMPOSERS
based on Crumb's "¿Por qué nací entre espejos?" *Madrigals,* Book IV

- **melody**   fragmentary, based on gestures and motives
- **harmony**   intervallically based • predilection for open, thin texture and harmony • emphasis on tritone and sevenths • a basic intervallic sound established and exploited throughout a given piece
- **rhythm**   short, fragmentary rhythmic motives • precisely notated (little or no use of proportional notation) • subtle juxtapositions of irregular groupings • constantly shifting metric divisions
- **texture**   sparse, thin • chordally based, rather than employing rigorous counterpoint

Glossary

Retrograde motion   reverse motion.
Symmetrical   the presentation of an idea that is the same forwards as backwards.

Suggested Exercises

Study the use of pitch throughout this movement. Compare the faster pitches to the longer ones, and determine the overall intervallic sound heard and any tonal centers that might be heard. In addition, discover the different approach to pitch in the first three sections (after the beginning two chords) and the longer middle section (*poco lento*). What conclusions can be drawn?

Many "mirrors" may be found when dealing with music in its historical context. Ideas of technique and organization keep recurring. The use of borrowed musical material has resurfaced throughout history, only to be discovered again in this century. Rhythmic and textural complexity have increased and diminished and increased again. Techniques of canon, imitation, isorhythm, retrograde, inversion, expansion/contraction, augmentation/diminution, all have moved in and out of favor, depending on the tastes and sensibilities of the time.

Perhaps the only aspect of music in which a more or less progressive change has occurred is in its harmony. Gradual but constant changes subtly alter the harmonic sound from one generation to the next through the centuries; it seems only natural for progressive harmonic development to continue.

The melodic and harmonic content of a piece, more than other constructional elements are thus wedded to their time. The dialect of a time is intact, with its peculiar shadings: its cadence use, harmonic flow, dissonance use, and so on. It is these areas that we must understand and master in order to know the composer's thought processes. If this is possible, then we may be able to realize the most important aspect of music, or of any art, and that is to be able to directly communicate with another soul. Only by responding to the composer's clues may we master his works, wherein reside all of his mind and soul.

Index

Added tone harmony, 201, 202
Alberti bass, 4, **13,** 116
Altered dominant, 69, 70
Appoggiatura
    18th century usage, 12 **13**
    19th century usage, 117, 118 **124,** 148, 152
Arpeggiated pedal, **202**
Augmented dominant, 69
Augmented sixth chord, 22, 157, 158

Bach, Johann Sebastian (1685–1750), 3
Baroque binary form, 5, 10
Bartók, Béla (1881–1945), 229, 233
Bass clarinet (transposition), 166
Bass pedals, 116
Beethoven, Ludwig van (1770–1827), 28, 33, 34, 37, 39, 58, 59, 60, 62, 65, 68, 69, 70, 71, 78, 114
Bichordal, 228
Bimodality, 115, **124,** 149, 177
Binary form, 33, **37,** 81
Birdsong (use by Messiaen), 277

Bitonality, 228, 229 (definition)
Brahms, Johannes (1833–1897), 171, 176

Cadences 5, 6
Cadence (Schoenberg), 247
Cadential extension, 34, **37**
Chaconne, 78
Chambonnieres, Jacques Champion (c. 1601–1672), 33
Change of mode, 35
Chopin, Frederic (1810–1849), 107, 114, 116, 122, 123, 124
Chordal mutation, **70,** 78, 80, 81, 121, **124,** 156, 177, 182
Chromatic expansion, 246
Chromatic inflection, 20, 21, 22, 24, 25, 27
Chromatic modulation, 62, **70,** 148
Chromatic passing tone, 148, 152
Chromatic step progression, 178
Circular transition, 24, **28**
Classical harmony, 4, 13
Classic period, 3, 4, 13, 20

Closing theme (in sonata-allegro form), 8, **13**
Cluster, 234, 236, **238**, 305, 306, 308, 309, 310, 316, **317**
Coda (codetta), 34, 59, 68, **70**
Codetta (in sonata-allegro form), 8, **70**
Color, 277
Contraction (of phrase lengths), 59, 61
Couperin, Louis (c. 1626–1661) 33
Crumb, George (b. 1929), 317, 320, 330

Debussy, Claude (1862–1918), 185, 191, 192, 197, 199, 201, 202, 203
Deceptive cadence, 68
    as used by Wagner, 149
Der Doppelgänger, 72–75, 76
Development (in sonata-allegro form), 8, 10, 13, 59
Development section, 22, 23, 25, 27, 62, 63
Diatonic clusters, 308
Diatonic planing, 195
Dies Irae (Penderecki), 284, 286–304, 305, 317
Diminished seventh chord, 121
Dissonance
    Chopin, 117
    Classic and Pre-Classic, 13
    Wagner, 148, 149, 152
Dominant ninth chord, 26, **28**, 64, **70**

English horn (transposition), 166
Enharmonicism, 116, 117, 157, 180
Enharmonic modulation, 35, **37**, 119
Escape tone, 118
Expansion (of phrase length), 59
Exposition (in sonata-allegro form), 8, 10, 13, 59

First theme (in sonata-allegro form), 8, 13
Forms
    Classic and Pre-Classic, 13
    Classic, 27
    Early nineteenth century, 37, 70, 81
    Mid-twentieth century, 238
French sixth, 79, 80, 157, 158
Functional harmony, 191

German sixth, 80
Gesture, 244, 245, 246, 247, 248, 250, **256**, 309, 316, 320, 322, 327

Half-tone clusters, 308
Handel, George Frideric (1685–1759), 3
Harmonic acceleration, 61
Harmonic content
    Brahms, 176ff
    Penderecki, 316
    Schoenberg, 252, 253
Harmonic usage (Classic), 24
Harmonic rhythm, 64, 152
Harmony
    Classic and Pre-Classic, 4, 13, 27

Harmony (Cont.)
    Early nineteenth century, 37, 70, 81
    Mid-nineteenth century, 124
    Late nineteenth century, 167, 183
    Early twentieth century, 202, 229, 255
    Mid-twentieth century, 237, 267, 283, 317, 330
Haydn, Franz Joseph (1732–1809), 1, 5, 10, 12, 13, 22, 114
Hemiola, 182

Instrumentation, 100, 101
Instruments (of the orchestra), 100, 101
Interchangeability of mode, 114, 115
Intermezzo in AM, op. 118, no. 2 (Brahms), 171–76, 182
Intermezzo, op. 76, no. 7, 183–85
Intervallic harmony, 193, 196, **256**
Intervallic use
    Messiaen, 282
    Schoenberg, 247, 252, 253, 254, **256**
    Webern, 266
Inversion (melodic), 234, **238**
Inversion (of a row), 261, **268**
Irregular meter, 227
Isorhythm, 277, **283**
Italian sixth, 67

Key relationships (Classic period), 8

La cathédrale engloutie (Debussy), 185–90, 191, 192, 202
Lietmotiv, 159, 167 (definition)
Linear chromaticism (Wagner), 156, 178
Liturgie de cristal (Messiaen), 268–74
Longing motive (Wagner), 159
Lorca, Federico Garcia, 318
Love potion motive (Wagner), 159
Lower neighbor, 118

Madrigals (Crumb), 317, 318–19, 320, 330
Matrix, 261, 262, 263, **268**
Melodic inversion, 234, **238**
Melody
    Classic and Pre-Classic, 13
    Classic, 27
    Early nineteenth century, 37, 70, 81
    Mid-nineteenth century, 123
    Late nineteenth century, 166, 183
    Early twentieth century, 202, 229, 255
    Mid-twentieth century, 237, 267, 283, 317, 330
Mendelssohn, Felix (1809–1847), 85, 100
Messiaen, Olivier (b. 1908), 268, 275, 276, 277, 281, 282, 283
Metric shifts, 180
Mikrokosmos (Bartók), 233
Minor Seconds, Major Sevenths (Bartók), 229–32, 233
Minuet-trio, 10, 11, 12, **13**, 27
Mirror (retrograde), 324, 327

Modal use (Stravinsky), 225
Mode (use in Debussy), 200, 201
Modulation, 8
Motivic material (Classic period), 9, 13
　in Beethoven, 59, 60
Mozart, Wolfgang Amadeus (1756–1791), 15, 20, 22, 24, 27, 114

Neapolitan sixth, 68, 81
Neoclassic, 220, **229**
Nineteenth century gesture, 245
Ninth chord, 26
Nocturne in D♭ (Chopin), 107–13, 114, 119, 121, 122, 123
Nonfunctional chromaticism, 156
Nonfunctional diminished seventh chord, 121
Non-retrogradeable rhythm, 227, **283**
Notation (new), 305

Orchestra (instruments of), 100, 101
Orchestration, of strings, 102, 103
　of entire orchestra, 105, 106, 107
　of timpani/brass, 106, 107
　in Wagner, 160
　of winds, 104, 105
Ostinato, 226, 227, **229, 283**
Overtone series, 101

Palindrome, 266
Pandiatonic, 221, 224, 225
Pandiatonicism, 221, 224, 225, **229**
Parallel chords, 121
Passacaglia, 78
Passing chords, 121
Passing dissonance, 118
Passing tone (chromatic), 148, 152
Pathétique Sonata (Beethoven), 33
Pedal, 26, 62, 78, **82**, 120, 178, 179, 197, **202**
　arpeggiated, **202**
　bass, 116
　inner, **124**
Penderecki, Krzysztof (b. 1933), 284, 305, 309, 310, 317
Pentatonic planing, 195
Pentatonic scale, 201, **202**
Phrase grouping (in Penderecki), 311ff
Phrase use (Stravinsky), 227
Piano Sonata in cm, op. 13 (Pathétique) (Beethoven), 28–32, 33, 37
Piano Sonata in CM op. 53 (Waldstein) (Beethoven), 39–57, 58
Picardy third, 81
Pivot chord, 62
Planing, 121, **124,** 195, **202**
　diatonic, 195, **202**
　pentatonic, 195, **202**
　real, 195, **202**
Polychordal, **229**

Polytonality, **229**
Prelude to Tristan and Isolde (Wagner), 127–46, 147
Prime (of a row), 261, **268**
Programmatic intent, 199, 200
Proportional notation, 305, 317

Quarter-tone clusters, 308
Quartet for the End of Time (Messiaen), 268–74, 275, 282, 283

Rameau, 33
Real planing, 195
Recapitulation (in sonata-allegro form), 8, 10, 13, 23, 27, 59, 66, 67, 68
Retardation, 12, 13
Retransition, 23, **28**
Retrograde-inversion (of a row), 261, **268**
Retrograde (of a row), 261, **268,** 324, 325, 327, **330**
Rhythm, Classic and Pre-Classic, 13, 27
　Early nineteenth century, 37, 70, 81
　Mid-nineteenth century, 122, 124
　Late nineteenth century, 180, 183
　Early twentieth century, 202, 229, 256
　Mid-twentieth century, 237, 256, 267, 283, 317, 330
Rhythmic practice (Classic period), 4, 13
Rhythmic use (Webern), 266
Rondeau, 33, **37**
Rondo
　large, 33, 34, **37**
　small, 33, 34, **37**
Row, 260, 264, 265, 266, **268**
Rubato, 123
Rufer, Josef, 260

Schoenberg, Arnold (1874–1951), 240, 244, 245, 252, 255, 256, 260, 263
Schubert, Franz (1797–1828), 76, 81, 82
Second theme (in sonata-allegro form), 8, 13, 22, 23
Sequence (melodic, harmonic), 63, 120
Shifting meter, 180
Sonata allegro, 5, 8, 10, **13,** 20, 22, 24, 25, 27, 33, 37, 59, 66, **70**
Sonata rondo, 33, 34
Stravinsky, Igor (1882–1971), 205, 220, 222, 226, 227, 228, 229
Strophic, 81, **82**
Style characteristics
　Pre-Classic, 13
　Classic period, 27
　Early nineteenth century, 37, 81
　Mid-nineteenth century, 123
　Late nineteenth century, 166
　Early twentieth century, 229, 255
　Mid-twentieth century, 237, 267, 283, 317, 330
Substitute dominant, 79, 81, **82**
Sudden modulation, 6
Sudden shifts, 6, **14,** 27
Symmetrical, **330**

Symmetrical presentation, 324
Symmetrical scale, 235, **238,** 280
Symphony No. 5 ("Reformation") (Mendelssohn), 85–99, 100
Symphony in Three Movements (Stravinsky), 205–19, 220, 221, 229
Synthetic scale, 235, **238**

Talea, 277
Techniques (mid-twentieth century), 267
Ternary form, 33, **37,** 81
Tertian harmony (non-functional), 193, 194, **202**
Tetrachord, 237
Texture
    Pre-Classic, 3, 13
    Classic, 27
    Early nineteenth century, 81
    Mid-nineteenth century, 124
    Late nineteenth century, 167, 180
    Early twentieth century, 202, 229
    Mid-twentieth century, 233, 238, 256, 267, 317, 330
Third relation, 26, 27, 65, 67, **70,** 149
Three Piano Pieces, op. 11 (Schoenberg), 240–43, 244
Three Songs, op. 25 (Webern), 257–59, 260, 267

Through-composed, 76, 81, **82**
Tonality (discussion of), 191
Transition, 22, 24, 28, 35, 59, 60
Transposition (of instruments), 101, 102, 166
Triadic harmony (non-functional), 193, 194
Tristan and Isolde, Prelude (Wagner), 127–46, 147
Twelve-tone row, 260
Twelve-tone system, 260, **268,** 281
Twentieth century gesture, 245

V_9 chord, 64, **70**
V_{13} chord, 121

Wagner, Richard (1813–1883), 126, 148
Webern, Anton (1883–1945), 257, 260, 263, 266, 267
Wedge shape, 316, **317**
Whole-half-half scale, 281
Whole-half scale, 281
Whole-tone clusters, 308
Whole-tone scale, 201, **202**
    in Messiaen, 280, 281

Ys Cathedral, 199